SACRED ECSTATICS
The Recipe for Setting Your Soul on Fire

The Keeneys

Copyright © 2019 The Keeneys
All rights reserved.
ISBN-13: 978-0-9973762-5-8

CONTENTS

Part One: Introduction to Sacred Ecstatics   1

   1 The Pinnacle Experience of Sacred Ecstasy   3

      Outsiders and Outcasts
      The Sacred Vibration and Rope to God
      Testimony
      Sacred Ecstatics: The Recipe for Setting Your Soul on Fire
      Going to the Crossroads

   2 The Spiritual Thermometer   43

      First and Second Creation
      The Temperature Range of Spiritual Experience
      Adjusting the Spiritual Temperature with Music
      Spiritually Cooked Dreaming
      Taking the Spiritual Temperature of the Helping Professions
      Hot Shamanism, Cold Shamanism
      Beware Constructing a Simple Good/Bad Dualism Between Hot and Cold
      The Spiritual Thermometer is the Rope to God
      Setting Sacred Words on Fire

Part Two: The Recipe for Setting Your Soul on Fire   85

   3 Building the Big Room   87

      Moving from Small Glass to Vast Sea
      Skillful Talk

  Take My Hand
  Spiritual Masonry: Laying the Right
   Cornerstone
  The Rope to God is a Song: Your Link Between
   Earthly Ground and Heavenly Sky
  Forever Expanding Sacred Ground

4 Getting Spiritually Cooked   123

  Striking the Match
  Keep it Sweet
  A Joy Better Felt Than Told
  The Arrival of Song
  Healing and the Higher Energetics of Sacred
   Ecstatics
  Rhythm Overthrows Word
  Getting Spiritually Cooked: A Contemporary
   Testimony
  The Dancer Who Received a Nail
  Sacred Ecstatics: Welcome to the Mystery Show
  Bowing Before Mystery

5 Reentering the Everyday   183

  Cooling Down for Reentry
  Remaining Inside the Big Room
  Mystical Prescriptions
  Shining Your Light

Part Three: The Sacred Ecstatics Life   217

 6 Visiting the Spiritual Classrooms   219

  Taking the Spiritual Temperature of Visionary
   Experience

*The Dissolution of Boundaries and the Blending
    of Forms*
Mystical Water
Laying and Following Spiritual Tracks
Preparing for Mystical Travel

7   The Four Changing Directions   269

The Spiritual Metabolic Cycle
The Spiritually Cooked Life
Making the Vertical Rope Primary
*Bringing the Dynamics of Sacred Ecstatics
    Down to Earth*
Don't Forget Your C.M.C.
The Ongoing Turning of the Ecstatic Wheel

Epilogue   315

References   318

Part One

Introduction to Sacred Ecstatics

1

THE PINNACLE EXPERIENCE OF SACRED ECSTASY

Sacred Ecstatics welcomes the soul igniting ecstasy that renders you unable to resist shouting, singing, and dancing with joy. Rather than seek inner peace, a calm mind, and a relaxed body, you are asked to do the opposite: light an inner fire, awaken higher emotion, and make soulful commotion. Anything less leaves you unsatisfied and on a continuous search for something that is unquestionably felt missing in your life — the sacred ecstasy of being near the divine. Over time, most spiritual ways devolve into accentuating mind-full belief and palliative relief at the cost of losing direct, bliss-full encounters with ineffable mystery. To find your way to supreme happiness and deep fulfillment you must learn how to set your soul on fire.

We call for the return of sacred ecstasy, the extraordinary experience that gives birth to the fully awakened mystic, shaman, healer, and spiritual teacher. This overwhelming and life-changing personal encounter with the numinous is a super-charged sensate immersion from head to toe, installing something mysterious within that circulates the greatest bliss. Surpassing all understanding and explanation, such inspired ecstasy touches the roots of your being and leads to an instant rebirth of identity, purpose, and everyday presence in the world. Those who experience it regard this as the definitive moment of their lives — it is what initiates and makes you ready for the most incredible life possible, one filled with mystery and vibrant elation.

In his book *Cosmic Consciousness*, Richard Maurice Bucke offers the testimony of a woman simply identified as C.M.C., born in 1844, who received this kind of pinnacle spiritual experience:

> The sense of lightness and expansion kept increasing . . . the atmosphere seemed to quiver and vibrate around and within me . . . and more strange than all, there came to me a sense of some serene, magnetic presence—grand and all pervading . . . And still the splendor increased. Presently, what seemed to be a swift, oncoming tidal wave of splendor and glory ineffable came down upon me, and I felt myself being enveloped, swallowed up.
>
> I felt myself going, losing myself . . . Now came a period of rapture, so intense that the universe stood still, as if amazed at the unutterable majesty of the spectacle! Only one in all the infinite universe! The All-loving . . . I was on the great highway, the upward road . . . with deathless hope in the heart and songs of love and trust on the lips. I understood now, the old eternal truths, yet fresh and new and sweet as the dawn . . . *Every longing of the heart was satisfied,* every question answered, the "pent-up, aching rivers" had reached the ocean—I loved infinitely and was infinitely loved! The universal tide flowed in upon me in waves of joy and gladness, pouring down on me as in torrents of fragrant balm.
>
> The infinite love and tenderness seemed to really stream down me like holy oil healing all my hurts and bruises . . . There is nothing in the universe to compare with it—such joyous repose and sweet unconcern—

saying to us, with tenderest love: All is well, always has been, and will always be. The "subjective light" (it seems to me) is magnetic or electric—some force is liberated in the brain and nervous system—some explosion takes place—the fire that burned in the breast is now a mounting flame . . . In my experience the "subjective light" was not something *seen*—a sensation as distinct from an emotion—it was emotion itself—ecstasy. It was the gladness and rapture of love, so intensified that it became an ocean of living, palpitating light, the brightest of which outshone the brightness of the sun. Its glow, warmth and tenderness fill the universe. That infinite ocean was the eternal love, the soul of nature and all of one endless smile. (Bucke 1969, 326-28)

Direct encounters with infinite mystery have been called entering the "Kingdom of God" or "Kingdom of Heaven" by Jesus, "meeting Gabriel" by Mohammed, "achieving nirvana" by Buddhists, attaining "moksha" by Hindus, "receiving God's ostrich egg" by the Ju/'hoan Bushmen, and experiencing "cosmic consciousness," by Bucke, among other names from diverse traditions. Not all of these experiences involve the kind of full-blown emotional ecstasy reported above by C.M.C. but are instead described as an awakened state of mind or consciousness. Without diminishing the extraordinary nature of any powerful awakening experience, it is time to acknowledge that the past and present over-emphasis on the mind's consciousness has resulted in practices that try to suppress, disqualify, or annihilate ecstatic emotion rather than intensify it. We choose a different compass setting whose "true north" is not just expanded consciousness—it is *sacred ecstatic experience* that emphasizes heightened emotion and its exhilarating embodied expression. We seek the "one endless smile" worn in C. M. C.'s ecstasy.

Peak experiences of ecstatic emotion are powerful enough to launch religious movements. While people first gather to stay near the original inspiration, they paradoxically later become distanced from it as a new emphasis on maintaining a social community or institution overshadows the life-changing experience these forms first meant to advance. This process finally results in the disappearance and even forbiddance of mystically ignited, emotionally charged, and bodily involved ecstasy. It doesn't take long for the aggrandizement of ideological texts, linguistic reductions, abstract seductions, and persuasive interpretations to choke ecstatic emotion and body motion. Nearly every spiritual tradition follows this tragic trajectory in some form.

For example, early shamanism, concerned with what Mircea Eliade called "archaic techniques of ecstasy," historically drifted away from wild and spontaneous outbreaks of ecstasy as it became domesticated and regulated with routines that were restrained, predictable, and conveniently taught. In the beginning, shamans were chosen and made by the gods, often through intense trials and ordeals that precipitated incredible ecstatic experience. As Eliade quotes N. V. Pripuzov, "one destined to shamanship begins by being frenzied" (1964, 16). Only later did shamans become arbitrarily selected through familial inheritance or—in cultures where shamanic traditions have been lost, forgotten, or were never present—by workshop training. As this shift in authority devolved from spirit to institution, the originating experience all but disappeared. Whereas early shamans trembled, shook, shouted, and improvised, the wild and frenzied embodiment of ecstasy was later abandoned in favor of a toned-down, domesticated ceremonial routine. Tragically, ways of the earliest technicians of ecstasy were forgotten and future generations became guardians *against* the evocation of formative ecstatic experience. Even the definition of ecstasy has been rung dry of every drop of spirited emotion the term formerly indicated, redefined by less emotionally inclined scholars as an observable, measurable shamanic state that looks more like a cataleptic trance than a shaking dance (Keeney & Keeney, 2019a). The smiling delight of C.M.C.'s bliss-soaked ecstasy has been recast as a frozen stupor with hypnotic daze and joyless gaze.

The same exorcism of heightened emotion and moving bodies took place in other spiritual traditions. The status of a leader, teacher, or healer was then conferred by group election rather than direct mystical transformation via ecstatic excitation. Again, the life-changing pinnacle experience of founding practitioners was later traded for social membership and institutionally prescribed titles and roles. When sacred ecstasy is no longer valued, songs are sung with less soul as rocking prayers and dancing down the aisles fade away. Shamans retire their fire to practice a habituated routine, healers only offer the balm that calms, teachers disqualify emotional experience and prioritize memorized answers, and mystics exalt transformed consciousness rather than heart-altering ecstasy.

Of course no spiritual institution or tradition admits that the originating spiritual experience has gone absent. To the contrary, institutional leaders insist that spirituality is more authentic when social control and educational training are appropriately administered. When hearts are no longer made ready to be moved by a higher mystery, few even notice that domesticated shamans no longer shake with ecstasy. Here spirited dance gives way to sitting trance where daydreamed fantasy rather than awakened emotional ecstasy prevails. Similarly, no importance is given to prophets, preachers, or spiritual teachers who return from the wilderness to share trembling songs and dancing prayers. In the same way, healers default to routinely administering repetitive techniques, protocols, and models rather than being deeply moved to create unique treatments for each person. When initiation by direct experience of sacred ecstasy is devalued or ignored, only the diploma that hangs on the office wall defines who is legitimized to care for spiritual concerns.

It is vitally important to acknowledge how spiritual ways too often and too quickly become emotion-less, motion-less, sense-less, heart-less, body-less, soul-less, spirit-less, mystery-less, and divine-less as they devolve from ecstatic embodiment to the abstract discourse of talking heads and the routines of ritual guardians. Accounts of how initiatory spiritual experience is diminished or rendered extinct by social institutions are well documented.[1] Though it is important to be reminded about the tendency toward ecstatic decay, our primary aim goes further. We wish first and foremost to bring back the sacred ecstatic experiences that ignite the most transformative inspiration, set your soul on fire, and spiritually alter your whole being and surroundings rather than only your consciousness. Our position is to stand upon the vastest ground and surrender to the broadest, deepest, highest, and holiest source of all mystery, making way for the heart-opening spiritual fire that only comes through experiential intimacy with the sacred. This is the way of ecstatic spiritual transformation, what we call Sacred Ecstatics.

---

[1] Max Weber, a founder of the field of sociology, was one of the first scholars to discuss the transition from charismatic authority (authority solely granted by charismatic experience) to institutionalized authority, where a social community, rather than sanctification from the divine, grants ordination (1963). Weber cites as examples the appointment of the dalai lamas and popes, carried out by an institutionally approved group who make the final selection. When a social group determines whether appropriate charismatic gifts reside in the selected leader, it elevates social decision over divine anointment, even conflating the important difference between the two (Weber, 2015). Sociologist of religion Peter Berger extends Weber's work and points out that "a freely flowing spirit" is a potential revolutionary force against all institutions, including the religious institution that tries to house it. Hence, an institution establishes a "spirit of order" that serves to protect and maintain a social institution from the chaos that the "free spirit" might inspire, doing so at the cost of "calcifying" the latter (2004, 127).

Kalahari Bushman *n/om-kxaosi* (healers and shamans) of southern Africa teach that being "cooked by God" is the most important experience and outcome in any person's lifetime. While they rarely discuss the meaning of their Sky God, *!Xun!a'an*, and do not give much importance to what anyone intellectually believes or doesn't believe about the nature of a supreme deity, they regard the felt presence of God as vitally important. Without a highly charged emotional connection to the ultimate source of it all, what they call a "rope to God," you will trick yourself into thinking that you can solely rely upon your own mentally construed advice and all its conceptual devices. This inevitably gets you lost and assures that you will never get spiritually cooked. For the Bushmen, receiving this rope is best fulfilled through a journey to the sky village where you have a personal meeting with God or an ancestor who is close to God. At this place of mystery you are given a spiritual rope that will forever connect you to the original source and force of all healing, mystical experience, and spiritual renewal. This mind-blowing, heart opening experience ignites an inner fire and leaves you with a direct hookup to the numinous.

The primacy of sacred ecstatic experience must be invited back to all ways of being in relationship to spiritual matters. We call for the ecstatic anointment of mystics, shamans, healers, ceremonialists, and spiritual teachers via fire-born spiritual rebirth. We should follow the experiences that ignited the great spiritual originators rather than the precepts of their subsequent institutions. No matter which religion may have later followed, in the beginning was an encounter with the same sacred fire.

Perhaps we could benefit from another outbreak of the medieval dancing mania, the Saint Vitus Dance, maybe this time called the vital dance of sacred ecstasy. It may be a corrective antidote that wakes us up from the lethargic spell of soulless shamans, profit-making prophets, non-moving teachers, uninspired ministers, and far-too-subtle energy healers. Let's announce the arrival of the exciting mystery that sets your soul on fire and gets you spiritually cooked—dancing in the street with ecstatic feet and spiritual heat, doing so to return ecstatic emotion to all forms of spiritual practice including healing, visioning, praying, singing, drumming, dancing, and working the spirit.[2]

False prophets and teachers can be difficult to recognize because they employ all the terms and concepts popular among the masses. It is the absence of ecstatic emotion and body commotion, not the content of their speech and text, which marks them as distant from that of which they speak and is a clear indication that they have not been spiritually cooked. Speaking words like "spiritual awakening," "energy," "ecstasy," "light," "love," "soul," and "spirit" does not assure their presence in the one making the pronouncement. If these words are spoken in a manner that does not exemplify, enact, and embody their intended truth, they end up conveying the opposite. For example, hearing a spiritual teacher talk about "joy" in a non-joyful way communicates and evokes the absence of joy. We like to quote Zora Neale Hurston who said it this way: "If you haven't got it, you can't show it. If you have got it, you can't hide it" (2010, 192).[3] If you congruently and authentically speak of spirituality, your expression will be on fire with the spirit.

All spiritual work and expression are in need of being shaken, awakened, cooked, and transformed by the fire and fervor of sacred ecstasy. When any spiritual way comes back to life, it returns to its ecstatic roots. Whatever is claimed to be spiritual but

---

[2] We often use the traditional phrase from the African diaspora, "working the spirit" to indicate all ways of ecstatic praise, celebration, and worship.

[3] This was later changed to this more popularized version known today: "Those who don't got it, can't show it. And those who got it, can't hide it." While it is unclear who authored this version, there is no doubt as to its genesis with Hurston.

does not evoke ecstatic emotion is desperately in need of a revival. Healers and the healing professions require emergency treatment with the shaking medicine that can cure their phobia of creative improvisation and spirited expression. Shamans are in critical need of being emotionally brought back to ecstatic life by the spiritual electricity that can jolt them free from movement paralysis, while spiritual teachers urgently require a supercharged dose of holy light that can re-illuminate their path and restore mystical sight.

Do not only talk about the sacred fire or look at it from afar while emotionally detached. Jump inside to feel the higher burn that can turn your life around. What Moses saw at Horeb was a "bush burned with fire and the bush was not consumed" (Exodus 3:2). You must be thrown into that burning bush and let your soul catch fire. Don't worry—this fire won't harm, consume, or destroy you; it is there to joyfully fill you with ecstatic emotion and its creative dynamism. Once you are spiritually cooked, you will find it impossible to remain calm and still when the divine is near:

> I used to wonder what made people shout, but now I don't. There is a joy on the inside, and it wells up so strong that we can't keep still. It is fire in the bones. Any time that fire touches a man, he will jump. (Johnson 1969, 74)

Consider the ecstatic transformative experience of Charles G. Finney, the great revivalist preacher of the nineteenth century:

> Without any expectation of it, without ever having the thought in my mind that there was any such thing for me, without any recollection that I had ever heard the thing mentioned by any person in the world, the Holy Spirit descended upon me in a manner that seemed to go through me—body and soul. I could feel the

impression, like a wave of electricity, going through and through me. Indeed it seemed to come in waves and waves of liquid love; for I could not express it in any other way. It seemed like the very breath of God. I can recollect distinctly that it seemed to fan me, like immense wings.

No words can express the wonderful love that was shed abroad in my heart. I wept aloud with joy and love; and I do not know but I should say, I literally bellowed out the unutterable gushing of my heart. These waves came over me, and over me, one after the other, until I recollect I cried out, "I shall die if these waves continue to pass over me." I said, "Lord, I cannot bear any more;" yet I had no fear of death. (Bucke 1969, 288)

Compare the fire, electricity, and waves of emotion C.M.C. and Charles G. Finney experienced with the account Paramahansa Yogananda gave of the "smoldering joy" that accompanied his experience of samadhi:

All objects within my panoramic gaze trembled and vibrated . . . until all melted into a luminescent sea; even as sugar crystals, thrown into a glass of water, dissolve after being shaken . . . An oceanic joy broke upon calm endless shores of my soul. The Spirit of God, I realized, is exhaustless Bliss; His body is countless tissues of light. A swelling glory within me began to envelop towns, continents, the earth, solar and stellar systems, tenuous nebulae, and floating universes . . . The divine dispersion of rays poured from an Eternal Source, blazing into galaxies, transfigured with ineffable auras. Again and again I saw the creative

> beams condense into constellations, then resolve into sheets of transparent flame. By rhythmic reversion, sextillion worlds passed into diaphanous luster; fire became firmament . . . Irradiating splendor issued from my nucleus to every part of the universal structure. Blissful *amrita*, the nectar of immortality, pulsed through me with a quicksilverlike fluidity. The creative voice of God I heard resounding as *Aum*, the vibration of the Cosmic Motor . . . (Yogananda 2015, 94)

Each of these testimonies emphasizes an experience of intense emotion along with a surrounding light, vibration, and electricity that also dwells and swells within. It should be disconcerting that experiential descriptions of this kind of extraordinary bliss are often missing or are quickly marginalized in so many spiritual teachings in favor of emphasizing ideological interpretation and/or scientific reductionism. There arguably has been a push in recent times to remove religious experience from religion and extract the spirit from spirituality. Religious scholar June McDaniel (2018) concludes in her important book, *Lost Ecstasy: Its Decline and Transformation in Religion*, that religious ecstasy "has been suppressed in both the academic study of religion, and in much of the modern practice of religion" by those who trivialize and pathologize ecstatic mystical experiences as "a symptom of ignorance, fanaticism, and superstition" or as "a symptom of psychiatric ailments, brain misfirings, epilepsy, and even calcium deficiency"(59).

In spite of the many attempts to quash it, sacred ecstasy has still awakened, healed, renewed, nurtured, highly excited, and totally remade diverse seekers throughout history and all over the world. Its transforming love is here to stay and cannot be kept at bay by those too fearful of religious emotion and embarrassed by embodied devotion. Let's ignore their demeaning talk and boldly seek the big-hearted fire that is stronger than lower naming and shaming. If you long to be spiritually cooked by sacred ecstasy then remember you're in good immortal company, surrounded in all directions by the soft, sweet, yet powerfully wise healers, soul singers, smiling shamans, *seiki* dancers, musical mystics, God trackers, *n/om* doctors, holy spirit ambassadors, and sacred vibration capacitors who pray with the same spiritual steam and longing dream of St. Augustine: "May the live coal of Your Love grow hot within my spirit and break forth into a perfect fire; may it burn incessantly on the altar of my heart; may it glow in my innermost being; may it blaze in hidden recesses of my soul."

Outsiders and Outcasts

William James, in his classic book, *The Varieties of Religious Experience* (1958), argued that ecstatic emotion is central to religious transformation. Thought or contemplation alone cannot deeply and lastingly transform a life. James cites Leo Tolstoy's personal discovery that "reasoning intellect by itself" is meaningless and that people are in need of the "irrational sentiment or faith that brings in the infinite" (153). Lack of spiritual fulfillment, Tolstoy concluded, arises in the lifestyle of "the upper, intellectual, artistic classes . . . the life of conventionality, artificiality, and personal ambition" (153). A voice within him spoke: "to acknowledge God and to live are one and the same thing. God is what life is" (154). After that moment, a light entered Tolstoy and the "energy of life" came back, saving him from attempting suicide. He subsequently chose to embrace "the life of peasants" whose personal and heartfelt relationship to God, rather than lofty explanation and exaltation of material wealth, made them more capable of experiencing the infinite.

Ibn al-'Arabi, often called "the Great Shaykh" by Sufis, similarly found a peasant whose "love of God" surpassed the more educated and privileged teachers. One of his important teachers was Fatima bint Ibn al-Muthanna, a holy woman who lived in Seville between the 12th and 13th centuries. She lived in poverty and was "head over heels in love with God," something that brought contempt and even a beating from the local muezzin, the leader of prayer at the nearby mosque (Pagani 2018, para. 2). Ibn al-'Arabi met her when she was ninety-five years old and immediately became her student. He was ashamed to directly look at her because "she had the fresh beauty of a 14-year-old girl in the fullness of her grace. She had a spiritual state with God" (para. 4). Fatima often said to him: "I am surprised by those who say they love God but are joyless" (para 6.) She especially delighted in playing the tambourine to express her joy for God. Ibn al-'Arabi took care of her until her death and she mentioned he was her favorite student, describing him thus: "I have never seen anyone like him: when he comes to me, he comes with his whole self, without leaving any part of him outside. And when he leaves, he leaves with his whole self, without leaving any part of himself behind" (para. 5).

Sacred Ecstatics especially honors the guides who embody divinely inspired joy rather than the textually bound teachers who lack the sacred emotion needed to set one's spiritual life in motion. In Judaism, this wondrous splendor (Zohar) is sought with a readiness to be lit by a burning love (*nitlahavout*) that brings the mystery and consummation of divine union (*devekut*). Here we find establishment challengers like Rabbi Nachman from Breslov (1772-1810) who early on taught the importance of music, dance, and foolishness as the means of inducing higher joy. For Hindus, the lesser-known ecstatics of Bengal point to the fervor and bliss that makes use of the physical senses rather than sublimates them in the search for divine contact (McDaniel 1989). Similarly, many Christian ecstatic reports are found among enslaved Africans and other outsider evangelists of old who were unexpectedly struck and anointed by a volt of divine lightning instead of elected by a social vote.

Traditions that host a relationship to sacred ecstasy, including world religions such as Christianity, Judaism, Islam, and Hinduism, repeatedly regress into minimizing or arresting heightened emotional experience. It then becomes necessary to journey to the countryside or remote regions to locate an outcast master teacher, a spiritually prodigious peasant guru, or an unknown ecstatic maestro who still embodies sacred ecstatic know-how. In the Kalahari, absent of libraries, ashrams, and monasteries, there historically have been more living somatic temples of ecstasy than among those who maintain the institutionalized religions of Italy, Greece, India, and China. The emotionally ecstatic song-and-dance mystics of every religion are usually placed out of sight and their teachings silenced to please the power players and scholastic bookworms. The lesser-known ecstatic wisdom guides have historically held the real nose of discernment and the practical know-how for accessing the splendor, joy, love, light, higher affect, extreme excitement, energetic vibration, and oceanic waves of emotion that true seekers are longing for.

Even when this kind of colossal ecstatic experience and radical teaching are welcomed back to an old or new spiritual tradition, practical questions arise regarding how to best host its return. Should rigid rules shape ecstatic expression to be more predictable and socially acceptable? Should it be allowed to be more improvisational, or is it best to concoct some mix of restriction and freedom? In historical retrospect we find ecstatic spiritual traditions going back and forth between social control and anarchy. When regimented constraint overtakes improvisational freedom, ecstatic experience begins to vacate ceremonial space, only leaving room for requirements that serve maintaining the institution or traditional forms. Yet when recognizable forms and social structures are wholly rejected, a situation can become ungrounded and end up lost in disorganized muddle with insufficient deference to the leadership of wisdom elders. At the same time, a purposefully balanced "middle way" may result in expression that is too diluted and compromised to host any ecstatic fire. There is no simple set of precepts that can be applied to all contexts that host sacred ecstasy. You need a cooked, situational ethics inspired by the movement up and down and all around the whole range of ecstatic expression, led by a higher and wiser source rather than self-governed (and often naïve) efforts to shape and control it.

We join with the oldest ways of setting your soul on fire, whether found on the Kalahari dance ground, the seiki benches of old Japan, in the praise houses of the Caribbean, or in the early sanctified and holiness black churches of the United States, among other places. These great enduring ecstatic wisdom traditions, especially that of the Kalahari Bushmen, provide a legacy of how to hold ecstatic experience, nurture it, and be in an evolving relationship with its ongoing, changing nature. As members and authorized teachers of several of these traditions, we set forth well-established guidelines for how to get spiritually cooked in ways that uphold its spiritual impact and enhance your continued reentry into its renewing fire.

Our work is unique in that we desire to introduce people from any and all religious or spiritual traditions to sacred ecstatic experience. We embrace a broad mystical orientation to ecstatic transformation that celebrates and honors all those who have been spiritually cooked along with their testimonies and teaching. Our focus on the primacy of ecstatic experience means that we give the least concern to descriptions of spiritual belief, whether people follow a particular religion, or say they are "spiritual but not religious." The dearth of ecstatic spiritual know-how in modern times means that most religious and spiritual-but-not-religious people are more the same than different—both lack familiarity with the heat of sacred ecstasy. We welcome you to go past worrying about labels and instead reach for the ecstatic jumper cables that can re-start your spiritual engine, making you ready for a truly remarkable journey that sets your soul on fire.

The Sacred Vibration and Rope to God

If you have a close encounter with the utmost mystery you will spontaneously tremble, quake, and shake with ecstasy. How could there possibly be any other response? Such a full-blown spiritual experience instantly overwhelms your mind, pierces your heart, and electrifies your whole body. All spiritually cooked ecstatics would recognize the experience described by Teresa of Avila:

> I saw in his hand a long spear of gold, and at the iron's point there seemed to be a little fire. He appeared to me to be thrusting it at times into my heart . . . and to leave me all on fire with a great love of God.
> The pain was so great, that it made me moan; and yet so surpassing was the sweetness of this excessive pain, that I could not wish to be rid of it. The soul is satisfied now with nothing less than God. (Teresa of Avila 2006, 226)

In the aftermath of such an experience you find that it has permanently left a sacred vibration inside of you. Teresa of Avila trembled and shook so much that she was later named (and mocked) in the nineteenth century as the "patron saint of hysterics" (Underhill 1911, 58). The Bushman n/om-kxaosi would more respectfully and enthusiastically acclaim that she had "been cooked" and "received an arrow, nail, thorn, or spear from God." The sacred vibration is the mark of someone spiritually cooked.

When a red-hot sacred arrow or spear crosses the somatic border and takes up residence, it brings the pulse of ecstatic life that resonates with the divine. Compare Teresa of Avila's heart spearing with this comment by a Kalahari Bushman doctor:

> Whether shot by a bow or thrown by a hand, an imagined sharp object shoots out of God's heart and pierces the healer, bringing a love [from God] . . . You can only understand our healing and teaching through receiving nails and arrows . . . which are all derived from God's love. (Keeney and Keeney 2015, 37)

Those who have experienced this powerful penetrating contact with the numinous, no matter where in the world it took place, regardless of the name chosen to describe it, and independent of the cultural tradition to which they belong, share this common bond—they all find themselves with a newly acquired sacred vibration inside their bodies. Without question, this is the most physically felt outcome of being spiritually cooked. It indicates that you were touched, pierced, and instilled with a mysterious, life-giving, action-inspiring, creative force. The sacred vibration settles within you and remains afterward, ready to spring into vibratory action whenever reawakened.

The sacred vibration is delivered through a "rope to God"—your felt connection with the ultimate source of mystery. In the strongest and hottest sacred ecstasy you may actually feel, hear, or see a thread, string, or cord hanging from the sky. Other ecstatic cultures variously call this numinous rope a hollow bone, empty tube, sacred pipe, spiritual channel, or main line to the divine. Receiving this rope and being instilled with its vibrational current are inseparable. As a divine conduit it delivers what feels like spiritual electricity surging throughout the body. Its dynamic force has been called many names including seiki, n/om, universal life force, and holy spirit. This potent energy instantly wakes you up in a way never before experienced and is capable of spontaneously bringing forth exceptional healing, remarkable vitality, tremendous mystical awakening, and the most jubilant bliss. The more you experience the sacred vibration and its ecstatic pulse, heat, and electricity, the more spiritually cooked, emotionally inspired, and creatively charged you become. This is the experiential foundation of Sacred Ecstatics.

The Bushmen long ago found that you are unable to get spiritually cooked and receive the sacred vibration without a strongly felt personal relationship with a beloved other, someone embodying the originating force of creation. Rather than get sidetracked by philosophical arguments concerning definitions and explanations for or against God, they implicitly recognize the practical, natural resource offered by relating to God as a loving parent, close sibling, soul mate, or best friend. A familial rope of emotional connection facilitates a direct, heartfelt relationship with the numinous.[4] When such a relationship is strongly and undoubtedly felt, you are said to have a rope to God and it, in turn, delivers the vibrant pulse to an ecstatically empowered life.

When your heart longs for the beloved creator, a fiber of sacred emotion arises. This contributes to the formation of a mystical rope. All the degrees and forms of sacred emotion you experience constitute the fibers, strands, threads, and strings of your rope to God. Over time, these relational lines of connection proliferate, expand, and intertwine to become strongly felt as a rope that connects you to the ineffable mystery above. When this rope is firmly established, it stands ready to send the rippling sacred vibration into your body.

---

[4] The Ju/'hoan Bushmen speak of both a father God and mother God as well as God's children (see Keeney and Keeney, eds., *Way of the Bushman*, 2015). What matters is not any preferred age or gender of divinity, but any strongly felt familial relationship to the source of your spiritual being.

The physical embodiment of sacred vibration towers over all talk and thought. No matter how much a conversation may address, encircle, and roam around spiritual topics, you must return to the question of whether you own a rope to God that enables a sacred vibration to circulate inside you. In Sacred Ecstatics, spiritual talk gives way to the ecstatic walk that takes you to the heartfelt pulse of mystery. Forming a notion is less important than waking up sacred emotion. For those who are spiritually cooked, spiritual talk "don't mean a thing" unless it has that authentic rhythmic swing, the good vibrations of spiritual electricity. As Oglala Lakota religious leader Frank Fools Crow stated, "When a person is right with God, he always has a special feeling. When I am curing I feel a charge of power and am excited" (Mails, 1979, 207) and "Sometimes it feels like energy or electricity when it is moving in and through us" (Mails 1991, 51).

This vibratory current trembles, quivers, shivers, wiggles, jolts, quakes, shakes, and moves you when it chooses to do so. You should be ever ready for the sacred switch to be turned on so that spiritual energy of the non-subtle kind (meaning there is no question about its presence) may arrive. If you wonder whether you have experienced the sacred vibration, then you haven't. If you recognize the truth that this statement delivers, you may be trembling with the very mention of it.

Elder Richardson, a preacher in a southern African American church, once said, "And when He answers you, the *vibrations* of the Holy Spirit begin to just go out there—you know, *like the earth when it trembles!*" Glenn Hinson, the scholar who recorded Richardson's comment as part of his fieldwork, tried to understand what this preacher meant: "I just sat there, saying nothing, thinking about those 'vibrations' that ride the words of prayer. The words themselves don't change. But they gain a mystical, affective force, a force infused by the Spirit." As Elder Richardson further explained this, "The vibrations shake the mind, but *speak* to the heart." As "blessed vibrations" flow through a whole congregation, only those sufficiently prepared receive it in their bodies. The "holy touch" is how sanctified parishioners discuss this experience and, though not everyone in a sanctified church will feel it, "all will recognize the telltale 'signs of the Spirit' in those whom the Lord has chosen to bless" (Hinson 2000, 69–70). While there is debate over whether this kind of blessing is available for everyone who seeks it versus those who are chosen, we find that anyone who is sufficiently prepared will be spiritually touched in some life-changing way, though the particular nature of this experience is always governed by divine administration.

The sacred vibration is not merely a subtle vibration or an occasional feel-good tingle, though it may sometimes include these forms. It more frequently feels like powerful electricity surging through you, sometimes arriving as an instantaneous shock and at other times like an ongoing, steady flow. When you are significantly charged with the sacred vibration you lose any calm, cool, and collected composure as you are moved, danced, shouted, and sung by a force greater than your own will. You also feel like you are fully alive with endless creative energy and perfectly in the groove without fear or concern. As one young man told us, "Drugs can't deliver anything close to how this feels. I just forgot all that boring stuff once I experienced the good God vibration." On a more amusing note, a woman named Henrietta Gant was so excited after receiving the holy spirit that she exclaimed, "Ah didn't eat nothin' the whole day—I didn't even take coffee—and Ahm crazy about coffee, coffee is my whiskey" (Kerr and Mulder 1994, 159). Nothing turns lives around more rapidly and thoroughly than getting juiced by an ecstatic boost of the highest spirit.

The sacred vibration takes you past the desire for more psychological self-awareness, contemplative understanding, religious doctrine, and secular commentary. Once you receive it, you automatically step into a radically different way of being in the world. Here the highest meaning of life is not found in spiritual discussion, but in the ecstatic drumbeat of soulful percussion. The spiritual revolution that awaits you is the journey from psychological talk to an ecstatic walkabout in the wilderness of mystery. Once you have been spiritually cooked, you find that you are creatively lifted by the inspiration behind creation, somatically empowered by the vital force of life, able to hear and feel divine resonance, and emotionally touched and physically moved by the electrical current of infinite love. The sacred vibration installed within can wake up at any time to literally give you a jolt, shiver, or tremble. This happens whenever you encounter the same vibratory creative force present in music, art, poetry, dance, theatre, or any other profound performance, especially when experiencing the expression or touch of another person who also carries the inner pulse. The sacred vibration is inseparable from your Kalahari-inspired rope to God, and it instills a new kind of compass or reference point. You naturally gravitate toward people, places, and performance situations that are alive and crackling with vibrant spiritual energy. Like the Kalahari foragers of old, you become a hunter-gatherer of the sacred vibration, someone skilled in the original way of tracking God.

More than anything, the sacred vibration fills you with an immense love that embraces the whole wide world. A numinous lightning bolt brings a flash of firepower that spreads expansive affection without interest in the argumentative dogma of religion. Consider this report from Charlie, a man born into slavery in Davidson County, North Carolina:

> Then, like a flash, the power of God struck me. It seemed like something struck me in the top of my head and then went on out through the toes of my feet. I jumped, or rather, fell back . . . I ran to an elm tree and

tried to put my arms around it. Never had I felt such a love before. It just looked like I loved everything and everybody . . . I can't tell you what religion is, only that it is love . . . There is no such thing as religion, for it is love and a gift from God. (Johnson 1969, 45)

The elder Kalahari Bushmen interviewed in Namibia say of themselves, "We are hunters of God's love and, when found, we share it so it becomes large enough to embrace the whole world" (Keeney and Keeney 2015, 107). Motaope Saboabue, a Bushman healer from Botswana, elaborates how this feels after a dance that hosts this kind of piercing love:

> At the end of a dance you are very happy. The next day while resting, I will dream and thank the ancestors, and I tell them that I feel love for everybody in the community. Everyone who goes to the ceremony gets an open heart and feels good about the community, even able to forgive the one who stole his wife . . . Everyone in the world can be touched this way. (Keeney 1999c, 63)

German poet Friedrich Schiller responds back to the Kalahari call with an "Ode to Joy," the poem that inspired Beethoven's final movement of his Ninth Symphony:

> Joy, beautiful spark of Divinity,
> Daughter from Elysium,
> We enter, drunk with fire,
> Heavenly One, thy sanctuary!
> Your magic binds again
> What convention strictly divides;
> All people become brothers,
> Where your gentle wing abides.

Testimony

Sacred Ecstatics introduces you to the pinnacle spiritual experience that has been witnessed and reported by people from all over the world and throughout human history. It brings trembling and joy, lights a sacred fire, radiates holy light, pulses spiritual electricity, and fills you with indescribable love. Brad had his first big encounter with this life-changing mystery when he was nineteen years old. Though he has described parts of his early mystical experience in previous books, here he describes it in fuller detail:

> I was a nineteen-year-old college student who had previously won first place at the 1969 International Science Fair and been offered a full scholarship to Massachusetts Institute of Technology. I mostly studied, played the piano, and enjoyed listening to jazz. On this January afternoon in 1971, I took a walk and was unexpectedly filled with extreme exhilaration. I felt guided to a small chapel built of stone where I entered and sat on the front pew. I immediately knew this was the beginning of the most important experience of my life.
>
> The curtain that separates intimate closeness with infinite divinity opened to reveal an indescribable glory. As this took place, a concentrated, pulsing fireball of energy gathered at the base of my spine and began its holy climb with a steady advance, like molten lava flowing upwards. The liquid fire rose and radiated a blazing emotion that broke my heart wide open. With flowing tears, I entered the waves of a vast ocean of love. At the same time, I noticed that my mind was being connected to a reservoir of timeless knowledge. I felt an unusual readiness for any request or question

that might come my way. I was filled with a blessed assurance and certainty that exceeded my previous belief and faith. Above all else, however, was the burning, expansive love that continued to intensify. This was the beginning of my life as a hunter of sacred ecstasy.

My body trembled, quaked, and shook with a force I had never known possible. There was nothing subtle, calm, or quiet about this inner force. I learned firsthand that there is an incredible mystical power, a sacred vibration, and an electric-like current that, once directly experienced, changes everything. I knew that no matter what I would do in my life, what was most important is that it be administered through this remarkable life force hookup. When I enact this practical truth, all is well. When I forget this, I suffer and am lost.

During the night when I first met the mystery light, I was fully aware that I was being prepared to heal and teach what had been instilled inside me. I also received a foretelling that I would spend decades as a spiritual traveler, both to actual geographical places and visionary realms, in order to meet and rejoice with others who had been spiritually cooked in this luminous fire. That would come later.

Steadily and assuredly the inner ball of fire advanced until it finally reached the crown of my head and came out in front of me as an external white light. It took the shape of a luminous egg that was about my height, close to the front pew on which I sat. I stared into this numinous luminosity and, transfixed by sacred emotion, I saw a figure standing with open arms. An outpouring of streaming rays of illumination brought further exhilaration and jubilation. I recognized that this was the divine son, the mystical sun of the holiest light.

As Jesus stared into my eyes, he spoke: "Come home, my son. I am the way and shall be with you and in your heart always." I was flooded with the kind of religious sentiment described in the lyrics of hymns I had heard sung by my father and grandfather who were country preachers: "Blessed assurance, Jesus is mine . . . What a friend we have in Jesus . . . Oh, how I love Jesus." The luminous mystical Jesus proceeded to teach through numinous means. "By this you shall heal and teach. In this you shall rejoice in the Lord. With this you shall enter the Kingdom of Heaven." I surrendered all—and by this I mean all my mind, heart, body, and soul—to the precious Lamb of God. Jesus became my true guide, teacher, friend, and home base. Throughout the subsequent years he would visit, bringing whatever spiritual gift, inspiration, and direction were needed.

Jesus opened his robe that evening and said: "All of this I hold inside my robe. They belong to the Kingdom of God." I then saw a multisensory, multidimensional presentation of saints, mystics, and spiritual teachers, one after another. In this parade of holy ones, their shining eyes sent more electrical current into my heart. There appeared the Virgin Mary, Our Lady of Guadalupe, the disciples, and what seemed like an introduction to the major icons of religion and sacred tradition: Black Elk, Buddha, Muhammad, Krishna . . . it seemed to never end. While I recognized many of the divine teachers that appeared, others I would not meet until later in my life.

I witnessed and deeply felt the mystery teachings of the illumined ones. More than anything, this experience involved heightened sacred emotion. Never had I felt such extremely intense vitality, powerfully uplifting excitement, and sweetly radiating love! Only later was I to learn that the Kalahari Bushmen call this experience "receiving God's ostrich egg," the egg in which spiritual gifts are held and bestowed. Suffice it to say that I knew that night—and even now as I write this report over forty years later—that I was cooked by the fire and dissolved in the sea of everlasting love.

In the midst of this experience, the voice that I would forever serve spoke again: "I will guide you. Follow me and the light will shine brightly. If you follow your reason rather than my direction, you will get lost. Fear not, for I am with you always. You shall be prepared to express these truths and share these gifts." I was then warned that the journey would be difficult and that I would be no stranger to failure and pain. There was much to learn about how to bring this teaching to the everyday world. I would have to fall down over and over again, each time lifted back up by higher hands.

This illumination remained ablaze in that chapel throughout the night and into the late morning, around twelve hours in duration. The oval light continued to be visible to me for several more months afterward—I am not sure exactly how long because I lost track of time. What I do remember was that whenever I looked up, the light was there. During this time I often kept my head bowed, not to be reverent, but for fear that if I kept staring at the mysterious light I would be swept away and never return. In truth, I was taken away and I have not returned.

And so my spiritual journey began as an

ambassador of ecstatic transformation, a teacher of mystical fire, a shamanic pianist, an improvisational healer, a scholar of the ineffable, a luminous attendant of the numinous, and a captain of the sacred sea who is free to call upon any and all holy names and songs. I have spent a lifetime celebrating this utmost mystery and experiencing its miraculous transformative power inside many kinds of sacred mansions—from the Amazon to Japan, Africa, Bali, Mexico, Brazil, the Caribbean, Australia, and numerous stops in between. No matter where I went, after my first encounter with the mystery of divinity I could repeat the words of the mystic Ibn al-'Arabi and say that every word I have since uttered and written was simply "the differentiation of the universal reality comprised by that [first] look" (1911, 153–54). My life is testimony to the fact that the highest experience of any religion reveals the same truth held in all of them.

After this life-changing encounter with the light in the chapel, Brad searched the local university bookstore and library to find if there were any accounts similar to what he had experienced. He first found Gopi Krishna's report of a kundalini awakening, a bliss that too quickly went amiss. Brad next discovered Richard Bucke's (1969) book on "cosmic consciousness," defined as an extremely rare mental vision, realization, or illumination of "the life and order of the universe" (3). One major section of the book presents examples of what Bucke considered to be the purest visionary cases, attributed to fourteen men and no women, including the Buddha, Jesus, Mohammed, Dante, William Blake and Walt Whitman. The next section of the book provides examples that Bucke regarded as "lesser, imperfect, and doubtful instances" (254). Here he includes testimonies of Moses, Socrates,

Swedenborg, Emerson, Ramakrishna Paramahansa, and three women who were all given initials (as were a few men). One woman, C.Y.E., summarized the height of her ecstasy:

> Then the earth and air and sky thrilled and vibrated to one song . . . An infinite peace and joy filled my heart . . . all anxiety and trouble about the future had utterly left me, and my life is one long song of joy and peace. (Bucke 1969, 358)

Another woman, A.J.S., described how as a young girl she "would spend hours thumping on an old desk of [her] father's rather than play the organ" so she could hear the sound "created in [her] own imagination" (Bucke 1969, 362). Later her desire for a musical career was interrupted by a spinal injury. When the flood of mystical light finally came to her amidst much despair she heard a voice say, "Peace, be still" over and over again in the same way she had formerly heard music coming out of that old desk. After experiencing the light she gained the capacity to heal others. Each of these women, including C.M.C., found mystical light and a pervading sense of peace inseparable from emotion and song.

We regard C.M.C.'s testimony as one of the most potent and vivid descriptions of pure sacred ecstasy found in the historical literature, arguably more inspiring than the less emotionally evocative reports from the Buddha, Jesus, Abraham, and Mohammed. Her testimony caught Brad's attention because it harmoniously resonated with his own mystical experience. This remarkable woman, born in 1844, described a body filled with a cosmic portion of elation instead of a transcendent mind full of contemplation. Sacred Ecstatics follows the lead of C.M.C. and turns away from over-elevating any grand scale insight and reaches instead for a moving melodic scale, musical flight, multi-sensory light, kinetic might, and affective delight. Here you awaken the singing and dancing body with its sacred vibration, a soulful potion that surpasses any stillborn cognitive notion.

This is the major spiritual crisis of our time: everyone, especially those called to heal, teach, and lead others, is in dire need of stepping into the ecstatic fire of ineffable mystery—feeling its transformative heat instead of only envisioning its vast expanse. Your most important goal is to get spiritually cooked rather than only take an observational look. What the world needs most, dare it be boldly said, is a resurgence and renaissance of old school, Kalahari-inspired, ecstatic spirituality fostered by people who long to be set on fire by a close encounter with the infinite love that God's heart wishes to share. Nothing less can spark, fuel, and forever guide a truly spiritual life.

We invite you to be emotionally touched, wholeheartedly pierced, physically moved, and spiritually cooked by the mysterious source of all creation. Be ready, willing, and able to meet a higher power, greater mind, broader wisdom, and deeper love. We call this supreme mystery by one of its oldest names: God. It is not the name that matters, however, because you cannot think, talk, or understand your way to the utmost experience of divine mystery. What matters is the sacred ecstasy that ignites your soul.

Sacred Ecstatics follows the paradoxical crazy wisdom that you must lose yourself in order to find the greatest truth, be broken in order to be made whole, hit bottom in order to start the ascent, be weak in order to find enough strength, and sincerely recognize your smallness as the requirement for experiencing the infinitude of it all. Without a rope to God it is more likely that your actions, though well intentioned, will be guided by ego and forced by willpower rather than naturally brought forth through numinous, luminous connection. Willpower never lasts long and leads to existential burnout, whereas sacred ecstatic power perpetually gets stronger. The compass of ego doesn't lead to the mystical egg that hatches an ecstatic life, nor does personal desire alone have the spiritual fire needed to get you cooked.

Abandon the quest for personal mastery that places you at the center of the universe. Rather than trying to take control of your destiny with exaggerated wishful thinking or self-help strategy, get knocked to the humbling ground by the fullest realization that you are always limited, easily lost, and typically powerless to do much about it. This is the human condition. You must stop the endless excuses, futile explanations, cheap distractions, meaningless exits, and false starts. Only then can the mightiest spiritual alchemy do its job and alter your life.

Let us review what preceded C.M.C.'s spiritual awakening. This excerpt from her personal account provides a glimpse of the journey that led to her life-shaking transformation:

> An irresistible force was to be aroused which should, with mighty throes, rend the veil behind which nature hides her secrets . . . I had been living on the surface; now I was going into the depths, and as I went deeper and deeper the barriers which had separated me from my fellow men were broken down, the sense of kinship with every living creature had deepened, so that I was oppressed with a double burden. Was I never to know rest or peace again? . . . The pain and tension deep in the core and centre of my being was so great that I felt as might some creature which had outgrown its shell, and yet could not escape . . . it was a great yearning—for freedom, for larger life—for deeper love. There seemed to be no response in nature to that infinite end. The great tide swept on uncaring, pitiless, and strength gone, every resource exhausted, nothing remained but *submission*. So I said: There must be a reason for it, a purpose in it, even if I do not grasp it. The Power in

> whose hands I am may do with me *as it will!* It was several days after this resolve before the point of complete surrender was reached . . . At last, subdued with a curious, growing strength in my weakness, *I let go of myself!* (Bucke 1969, 324–25)

You too must let go of yourself and surrender to the highest call. Only then can you find your way to the mystical rope. After you take one sincere step toward it, as Bushman healer Motaope Saboabue says, "That line just takes you" (Keeney 2003b, 62). The rope is already present, waiting to grab hold of you. Further movement is made possible by the installation of a sacred flutter — the inner wings of an ecstatic vibration that lift you to the brightest light and hottest fire.

Your trickster mind will challenge you to think that you already know enough about spirituality or that you are close to finding it all through the means you have been using. You may have certificates and licenses proving this claim, or even be socially identified as a local healer, mystic, shaman, or teacher. Your bookshelf, like ours, may hold numerous volumes on spiritual knowledge. A single experience of the spiritual fire of sacred ecstasy, however, is worth more than a million spiritual words. Until you enter the old-fashioned spiritual heat and get home cooked, "mystery," "ecstasy," and "divine" will be nothing more than words on a page or concepts in your mind.

Again, it is impossible to get near the utmost spiritual power without forever afterward shaking with ecstasy at the mere mention of it. As the late Mother Samuel, one of our friends among the Shakers of St. Vincent, put it:

> When I talk about spiritual things, I can feel something vibrate. It comes to me as a shivering. If you don't feel this vibration, then the Holy Spirit is not with you. Whenever it comes into you, you're on fire with the

power of God. You can't be sitting down and be cold and tell me that you have the Holy Spirit. When you contact Him, you get filled with something that makes you move. (Keeney 2002, 73)

Brad conducted over thirty years of fieldwork with the Kalahari Bushmen and found he couldn't talk for long about ecstatic experience without one of the elders starting to tremble, shake, and then break into song and dance—sacred ecstasy always overtakes talk and hermeneutic pursuit. This is true for everyone we have ever met who has been pierced by an arrow, nail, or spear of higher power, the sacred vibration of divine n/om love that alters your whole being. Once it resides within, talking or even thinking about this ineffable mystery or transformative dynamic triggers the inner force to re-awaken. This outward expression of inner fire is the most reliable indication of whether someone has been ecstatically cooked.

Vijayakrsna Gosvamin, born in West Bengal in 1841, came from a Brahmin family and both of his parents often became ecstatic. By the age of six, he was dreaming of saints and later as an adult he would often start spontaneously singing hymns and trembling whenever he felt a god, goddess, or sage around him:

> We used to feel that he would always dance in a new manner . . . sometimes he would shout, or sometimes he would be drenched with tears. Or sometimes sweat would fall from his body in streams . . . Sometimes each limb would quiver fiercely, of its own accord. Sometimes, as soon as he raised a hand, it would begin to shake so quickly that we were astounded at seeing it. (McDaniel 1989, 68)

Any authentic encounter with numinous mystery, higher power, or infinite divinity, no matter what tradition hosts and names it, delivers a vibratory current that lives inside your body forever. It reawakens whenever you feel emotionally touched by anything holy. The sacred vibration we underscore is not another concept to add to the spiritual tower of babble. It is a mysterious force from the original source that has set lives on fire for thousands of years. Nothing else can so readily and broadly fill the universe with ecstatically joyful celebration. It is time for the return of this most precious ecstatic firepower that gives rise to mystical illumination, universal love, heartfelt wisdom, and trembling jubilation.

Sacred Ecstatics:
The Recipe for Setting Your Soul on Fire

This book is a guide to the basics of Sacred Ecstatics—setting your soul on fire, becoming spiritually cooked, receiving your rope to God, and hosting the sacred vibration. Our approach is based on Brad's more than forty years as an ecstatic healer, mystic, shaman, and spiritual teacher. It also pays homage to the lineages of the Ju/'hoan Bushmen of southern Africa (Keeney 1999b; Keeney 2003b; Keeney and Keeney 2015), Caribbean shaking traditions (Keeney 2002), the Japanese tradition of non-subtle energy medicine called *seiki jutsu* (Keeney 1999a; Keeney and Keeney 2014), the earliest sanctified and holiness churches, and other ecstatic shaking medicine traditions with whom we have deep relationship (Keeney 2007).[5]

The next chapter introduces a key tool of Sacred Ecstatics—the spiritual thermometer. It provides a way of keeping track of the spiritual temperature, revealing how the heat of ecstatic emotion climbs with each step closer to the divine. Sacred Ecstatics teaches you to do more than alter your temperament and nomenclature; it

---

[5] Also see *Shaking Out the Spirits* (Keeney 1995), *Bushman Shaman* (Keeney 2005), and the *Profiles of Healing* book series edited by Bradford Keeney.

asks that you raise the spiritual temperature. Without exception, you must get spiritually cooked to receive all that infinite mystery can offer.

In part II we address the sacred recipe for setting your soul on fire, the means through which you become spiritually cooked. This basic recipe, whether followed in individual prayer, a healing session, or a community gathering, is depicted as moving along this trajectory:

By using the term *recipe*, we are inviting you to create something through specified action. Keep in mind that the recipe for a pie, cake, croissant, or soufflé does not highlight contemplation, reflection, or dialogue. The latter too easily distract, block, or delay having a taste of a delicious preparation. Follow the Sacred Ecstatics recipe instead of only ponder what it might mean. This recipe has been setting lives on fire throughout the world for thousands of years. Its instructions bring you the practical art — rather than the story, interpretation, or theory — of becoming spiritually cooked.

In part III we examine the unique experiences that arise as part of a spiritually cooked, ecstatic life. This includes "visiting the spiritual classrooms," the extraordinary visionary experiences that are a vital mystical resource to ecstatic spiritual traditions. Here we differentiate visionary dreaming by its spiritual temperature and describe what is unique about mystical experience that is hosted inside ecstatic spirituality. Finally, we conclude with a chapter on the "four changing directions," addressing how the Sacred Ecstatics life embraces constant transformation and movement through diverse aspects of experience that include mental acuity, creative fluidity, absurd activity, and ecstatic combustibility.

This guide to setting your soul on fire and becoming spiritually cooked provides a sure means of finding and staying on the highest road to sacred mystery. From the view above, this road appears as a line or rope, and can function as both a telephone line and a power line. With it you can communicate with the divine and receive spiritual electricity that empowers your life. As a rope it can also grab hold of you, place you on the highway, and guide you to the ultimate spiritual destination. We welcome you to discover the oldest and most reliable way of resuscitating your spiritual life through the sacred vibrations that move body, mind, heart, and soul. Get ready to be rocked and rolled, trembled and tumbled, flung and sung as you are thrown into the ecstatic triumvirate of fire, light, and vibratory power. Step toward the infinite room of mystery and allow its mighty force to pull you in.

Bow before the *mysterium tremendum*, not because you are supposed to, but because its bodily felt, awe-inspiring vibration can pull you into the big room where unexplainable transformation is found. Sing, not because you are a mighty shaman or powerful magician, but because you are thrilled to be no less and no more important than a sparrow ready to have your heart pierced by a holy arrow. Dance not because you are antsy or artsy, but because you are deeply inspired and moved to pray for a ray of heavenly sunshine. Go past distinguishing between God and Goddess and get to the "Holy Yes" where masculine and feminine never stop mutually bringing forth one another inside the greater generative process of sacred creation. Play because you are waiting to be more creatively expressed on the divine stage. Surrender all, not because you desire to be godly, but because you wish to be small enough to enter the mystical eye of the sacred needle and be sewn as a thread into God's rope that connects the whole of creation.

It is easy to get off course during your life journey; it takes very little to throw you out of whack. Without a divine hookup, there is little hope for getting retuned, reoriented, relit, recharged, and back on track. Without a rope to God, your soul cannot catch fire. The numinous gravitates toward experiential diversity rather than universal conformity, expresses creative improvisation rather than habituated routine, and welcomes the arousing energy of changing, fascinating rhythms rather than the boring drone of a metronome. Reducing the essence of mystical, shamanic, healing, or spiritual experience to any singular magic bullet—whether it's body posture, hyperventilation, sonic beat, incantation, redundant affirmation of belief, talisman, botanical plant, magical tone, mystery chord, or movement form—can no more lead a person to the ineffable than devotedly rubbing a piece of ivory can make a person a concert pianist or piously stroking a brush can yield a master painter. Aim to enter the whole room of the numinous rather than assume that any fragmented part provides a shortcut to the vast mystery from which it came.

Once inside the big room it also becomes clear that there is no need to give excessive importance to differentiating healers from mystics, shamans, and spiritual teachers. These are all interrelated roles, functions, expressions, experiences, and means of being in relationship to creation's ongoing creative change. Spiritual jobs are better fulfilled when they arise spontaneously through being spiritually cooked rather than through purposeful choice, presumed entitlement, and socially appointed professional title. If your soul is on fire, then you stand ready to step into any spiritual role because they are simply different transient forms of the same underlying truth—the various ways in which mystery is expressed in situations calling for its holy medicine, visionary wisdom, mystical teaching, and ecstatic fire. Be less concerned about a named title and simply embrace what's spiritually vital. Focus on being transformed into a vessel for the infinity of divinity to have its say and perform its play.

In summary, the purpose of getting spiritually cooked is to find your rope to God, receive its sacred vibration, and then get out of the way to allow the mystery of life to perform through you, its instrument. Follow the recipe for setting your soul on fire and all else will come naturally. Welcome to the most direct path to the one endless smile of sacred ecstasy, the unchanging face of everlasting grace.

Going to the Crossroads

Serious enthusiasts of the blues, the genre of music that arose and thrived in the fertile soil and soul of the Mississippi Delta, are familiar with the story of how an aspiring musician becomes an initiated performer. Though there are different accounts of the ritual, all share the theme that you must get yourself to "the crossroads," a non-ordinary intersection of two roads found in the mythically musical and tastefully soulful Deep South. There you bring your guitar (or perhaps a harmonica, piano, tambourine, rattle, or other musical instrument), and at midnight a mysterious spirit arrives, takes your instrument, and tunes it in a non-ordinary way. When it is handed back, you find you have been transformed as well. Sometimes it is said that the devil takes your soul and you are given the blues in return. The more important truth is that you require a pilgrimage to an otherworldly place that hosts the most profound tune-up capable of making you an instrument for expressing awakened soul.

As you go deeper into this spiritual journey, you find that the different roads bring together more than a tuned instrument and initiated musician. It is also a meeting ground for the sacred and the profane, God and the devil, life and death, and spirit and flesh, among other fundamental opposites and experiential contraries. At the crossroads these dichotomies come together as related complements rather than solitary occupants battling over which side is dominant. The swing toward longing for belonging after seething for separation brings a pulse that inspires soulful rhythm as well as a mystical friction that can spark a mojo fire. In this tectonic shift of juxtaposed sides your spiritual heart starts to beat as your earth-shaken body is taken to meet and greet mystery. At the spiritual crossroads you face the choice of whether you will continue with life as you know it or cross over to the other side where your soul can be set on fire, making you ready to reenter your everyday as a heart warmer and spiritual fire setter—a good match in a musical, mystical matchbox.

Are you ready to go to the crossroads? Is your suitcase packed for the journey to higher attunement? Are your instruments by your side and are they prepared to be handed over to unseen, though powerfully felt mystery hands? Don't forget that you and all your natural gifts constitute the instruments, including your humming, drumming, speaking, singing, movement, gestures, handiwork, skill, craft, art, and any other resourceful means of expression that are part of your life, whether already discovered or waiting to be found.

Getting ready for the crossroads includes emptying yourself of unnecessary baggage. Don't get weighed down by carrying too heavy a load. This refers not only to material things and spiritual paraphernalia, but also includes over-packed words, dense understandings, heavily laden beliefs, overblown rituals, and excessively ornate practices. Travel light. Bring the smallest suitcase.

We recommend finding a small matchbox—the tinier the better. Place a single small match inside it, along with a miniscule strand of thread and the smallest pebble you can find. Add one other small thing that makes no sense as to why you would put it in the box. This is all that you need to carry with you, each item a symbolic invitation for a whole multi-faceted relationship with mystery: a match that strikes an ecstatic fire, a beginning strand of your rope to God, a small pebble to honor the importance of smallness and self-temperance, and something unexpected that invites the further expansion of mystery in your life. This is your Sacred Ecstatics shamanic tool kit, medicine bag, spiritual bundle, and mystical suitcase.

We strongly encourage you to do more than only think about this task. It is critically important that you actually conduct it! When you take action that is radically new or does not readily fit inside your daily routines, acknowledge and celebrate the fact that you are going outside your box and stepping into expanded experiential territory. If your mind resists, then do it anyway to help escape the habitual way thought can tie you in a knot. Be more curious and follow the tug of a rope that is trying to pull you into a different reality. Enact this with your fullest sincerity and desire to get closer to the greater unknown. Assume this: the matchbox you have been invited to hold already resides in mystery. It is waiting for you to catch up to it, strike its match, and take the first step toward setting your soul on fire. Everything you bring to the crossroads is in need of being spiritually cooked so you are prepared for a soulfully blessed life.

Some of the old-time blues musicians were told that when you are at the crossroads you must read Psalm 136 at the crack of dawn and not run away as storms and strong winds come near. In the recitation of, "O give thanks unto the Lord; for he is good: for his mercy endureth forever," we are reminded that, in spite of lingering darkness and fierce storms, there is always a remarkable blessing in the making. It is available when you stand in the middle of it all, jubilantly expressing gratitude as you wait to get spiritually struck by lightning, ecstatically set on fire, and musically brought the sacred emotion that inspires your mystical instrument to sound a soulful celebration.

Brad once visited a reclusive retired anthropologist named

Junior who had devoted himself to researching juke joints and blues musicians from the Mississippi Delta. Brad found him living in a dilapidated shack in the backwoods near Tullos, Louisiana. Junior said that he knew for a fact that the crossroads exists. "It is real. They took me there. The old bluesmen drove me to the spot where two roads cross. I found a white stone waiting for me in the intersection." He gave that stone to Brad and said, "Here, it's now yours. It is your time for the journey." Today we say to you, it is your time to visit the crossroads where you can make yourself available to enter spiritual mystery. The small pebble inside your matchbox awaits your arrival. Prepare yourself for soulful percussion, spiritual combustion, and vibratory conduction, as whole life reconstruction unfolds without interruption. There is a highway to mystery found at the crossroads. Are you on it?

2

The Spiritual Thermometer

The most important conceptual tool offered by Sacred Ecstatics is what we call a spiritual thermometer. It gauges the degree of spiritually inspired emotion circulating inside you. The hotter the spiritual temperature, the closer you feel to the numinous source of creation and the more deeply touched and moved you are by its penetrating joy and creative life force. No matter what tradition you follow, Sacred Ecstatics invites you to take your spiritual temperature: Are you emotionally distant from ineffable mystery and cooled off by lifeless practice and soulless expression, or are you ecstatically trembling, shouting, singing, and dancing with heartfelt bliss? While there is a time and place for every degree of temperature from hot to cold, a spiritually cooked life requires ongoing reentries into the hottest spiritual fire where sacred emotion replaces detached observation, rhythm surpasses word, song takes over story, and body dance transcends mental trance.

When you go past a primarily cognitive form of spirituality and instead step wholeheartedly and whole*bodily* inside an atmosphere of higher mystery, everything suddenly comes remarkably alive with the pulsing, sizzling force of creation and its emotive power of transformation. Only then may your body be infused with the sacred vibration, filling you with extreme joy. This vibratory current and ultimate elation further ignites a burning passion for the divine, whose name you now are delighted to proclaim in any or all its forms. An encounter with this "infinite fire of love," as St. John of the Cross referred to it, is what sets your soul ablaze:

> This flame the soul feels within it, not only as a fire that has consumed and transformed it in sweet love, but also as a fire which burns within it and sends out flame . . . and that flame bathes the soul in glory and refreshes it with the temper of Divine life . . . This fire, as it is of infinite power . . . burns everything according to the degree of the preparation thereof . . .
>
> And since God is an infinite fire of love, when therefore He is pleased to touch the soul with some severity, the heat of the soul rises to such a degree that the soul believes that it is being burned with a heat greater than any other in the world. For this reason it speaks of this touch as of a burn, for it is experienced where the fire is most intense and most concentrated, and the effect of its heat is greater than that of other fires . . .
>
> And it is a wondrous thing, worthy to be related, that, though this fire of God is so vehement and so consuming that it would consume a thousand worlds more easily than natural fire consumes a straw of flax, it consumes not the spirits wherein it burns, neither destroys them; but rather, in proportion to its strength and heat, it brings them delight and deifies them, burning sweetly in them by reason of the purity of their spirits. (Tyler 2010, 53)

If you imagine an actual spiritual thermometer with a scale of temperature markings, the highest degrees indicate that you are spiritually on fire—burning with "sweet love," "bathed in glory," and refreshed by the "temper of divine life." In contrast the lowest degrees on the thermometer indicate spiritual freezing, a temperature at which you feel distant from the divine, are somatically absent of sacred vibration, and reluctant to emotionally express a hallowed name. Here there is little motion or emotion while concretized beliefs, literal interpretations, and fussy discussions prevail. In this frozen zone, more attention is paid to word and text than directly felt experience. The finger is made more primary than the moon to which it points, to borrow a well-worn Buddhist teaching. Similarly, debating the meaning of three letters—"g," "o," and "d"— is regarded as more important than feeling the numinous mystery that word is meant to evoke.

The difference between the hot and cold temperature zones is illustrated by the experience of a Christian missionary in Namibia who handed some Bushman elders a Bible and said, "You can find God inside this book." They were puzzled and after opening its pages replied, "Why is your God black and white and stuck on paper?" To the Bushmen, God dances and sings to spiritually cook them and is not frozen into static words. Whenever you resort to the emotionless recitation of doctrine or the passionless performance of ritual, you are spiritually lifeless and emotionally cold. This can be as true for Christians as it is for Buddhists, Jews, Hindus, Muslims, New Age and New Thought practitioners, as well as indigenous shamans. In contrast, spirituality that is alive and on fire fosters the highest and most intense sacred emotion. When it doesn't, you should seek emergency care for your stopped spiritual heart—the ecstatic defibrillation that gets you pulsing with life again.

Elder Richardson refers to ice-cold spiritual practitioners as "dead folk"—describing those who don't clap or shout and put no emotion or invigorated expression into their spiritual worship. As he says: "God don't want nothing dead. He wants you alive" (Hinson 2000, 160). To come alive you must go past the soulless articulation of words, silent contemplation, and passive observation. Instead, deeply *feel* the presence of sacred mystery and encourage ecstatic passion to escalate so it can set fire to your speech, move you to clap your hands, and get you dancing down the aisles.

Contrary to what some people say, heartfelt sacred emotion is the engine of spiritual locomotion. Without it, you won't find your way to the "infinite fire of love." When emotion initially awakens, words become freer to creatively roam, bringing forth more metaphorical, lyrical, and poetic expression. Continue to thaw with increased emotion and your body begins to move and dance as music arises with a soulful beat. When the spiritual temperature gets hot, the trembling, jumping, quaking, and shaking begin. At some point the heat reaches its peak and you naturally start to cool down. The sacred vibration lessens, everyday speech and thought return, and words become dominant again, though you still carry the afterglow of time spent in the fire.

One sign of having been spiritually cooked is that even at cooler temperatures you are less interested in dressing or addressing sacred experience with incessant abstract verbiage and convoluted explanation. Any attempt to linguistically coat or conceptually encapsulate the numinous does little to warm the heart and holds you distant from feeling the fire of mystery. While chilly interpretive discourse may provide entertaining insight for some, it comes with the risk of freezing, numbing, and leaving you isolated in the spiritual tundra.

Imagine Sufi mystic Dhu'l-Nun hearing any long-winded attempt to define, classify, or explain the ineffable and responding, "Whatever you imagine, God is the opposite of that." Ibn al–'Arabi joins the conversation and adds, "Deliver us, O Allah, from the Sea of Names." Then Chuang Tzu reminds you, "If you try to know it, you have already departed from it." Accept the invitation of A. W. Tozer to "follow the insight of the enraptured heart rather than the more cautious reasoning of the theological mind." Avoid the distractions of heady abstractions as you remember the words of As Abu Sulayman-Ad-Darani: "When the mystic's spiritual eye is opened, his physical eye is closed; he sees nothing but God."[6]

When your mind and its discourse box spiritual experience into tidy definitions, separate categories, and grand taxonomic schemes, you assuredly are on the frigid and rigid side of things. Avoid solely situating yourself as the observer, narrator, commentator, interpreter, assessor, diagnostician, taxonomist, judge, critic, or play-by-play analyst. When thought and speech reign over your experience of the present moment, you are kept spiritually refrigerated. This is when you are most prone to irritation by the invocation of certain religious names while pleased by others. Put simply, when you are hung up on semantic preferences, your spiritual temperature is too low. The alternative is to leave the spiritually cold name game of a textually overfed mind behind and let your heart lead with a precious kind of emotion. When the spiritual temperature is high enough, your communication shifts to the universal language of music, the surest means of expressing higher emotion. Song best conveys infinite divine love with its widespread grace, absolute forgiveness, and unconditional sharing. A close and intimate encounter with the source of all creation bankrupts your desire to

---

[6] These interspersed quotations, along with some others that will appear later, come from renowned spiritual teachers familiar with the spiritual fire:
Dhu'l-Nun cited in Reynold A. Nicholson. *A Literary History of the Arabs.* London: Forgotten Books, 2013 (original work published 1907).
Arabi cited in James Lee Christian. *Wisdom Seekers: Great Philosophers of the Western World.* Belmont, CA: Wadsworth Thomson Learning, 2001.
Chuang Tzu cited in *The Complete Works of Zhuangzi.* Translated by Burton Watson. New York: Columbia University Press, 2013.
Tozer cited in Alister W. McGrath. *Faith and Creeds: A Guide for Study and Devotion.* Louisville, Kentucky: Westminster John Knox Press, 2013.
Abu Sulayman-Ad-Darani cited in Nicholson.
Elizabeth Barrett Browning. *The Poetical Works of Elizabeth Barrett Browning, Complete in One Volume.* New York: T. Y. Crowell & Co., 1870.

argue over what to name it and whether to claim, exclaim, or defame it. As Rumi proposes, "Close the language-door, and open the love-window." When you must use words to speak of the sacred, reach for the poetry rather than the taxonomy. Poem and song reveal rather than conceal the ubiquity of divinity. Elizabeth Barrett Browning writes in her poem, Aurora Leigh:

> Earth's crammed with heaven,
> And every common bush afire with God:
> But only he who sees takes off his shoes.

All spiritual experience takes place along a temperature gradient that ranges from freezing cold to sizzling hot—thermodynamics that are more felt than understood. There is a time and place for cooler temperatures that include contemplation, conversation, and intellectual workouts that sharpen the mind. At the colder end of the thermometer, the naming and framing mind reigns. Here you find yourself in a continuous effort to mentally focus, conceptually settle, and yet dialogically unsettle mind's rigidities and dualisms. This is where the meditation-focused traditions are found whose primary aim is to discipline the mind in order to awaken to the boundlessness of reality. Ecstatic traditions, however, most highly value an ongoing reentry into the central hearth of the big room where a spiritual fire clears out a cluttered head, sets free a stuck body, and opens wide a loving heart. We live in a time when stillness, mindfulness, tame talk, and cool composure are overemphasized at the expense of shaking bodies, singing voices, untamed expression, and ecstatic emotion. Both cold and hot spiritual ways value the vast infinity hosting life—the main difference is the meditator peripherally observes it while the ecstatic jumps into its fire. Now is the time to meet the other side of the spiritual thermometer.

Many spiritual teachers and religious leaders do not want you to know about the higher spiritual temperatures where elevated sacred emotion is found. You likely have been advised—implicitly or explicitly—to never explore the heat where refrigeration immediately meets defeat. Most people are embarrassed and even horrified by the very idea of accentuating emotion and its natural somatic expression, fearful that the body might get ahead of the mind and become out of control. Here the major religions are more alike than different with their shared fear, diminishment, disqualification, and dismissal of emotion, especially feelings of the extremely joyful kind that inspire spontaneity. As mentioned in chapter one, though many religious founders may have initially felt the heightened ecstatic emotion of awe-inspiring mystery, this original raw and thawing experience was typically afterwards replaced by an emphasis on interpretation and a runaway proliferation of texts.

Nothing agitates a ritualized, textualized, standardized, and institutionalized religion like a blissful outbreak of high emotion. Buddhists, Christians, Jews, Hindus, Muslims, and New Thought practitioners, among others—with exceptions provided by heretics and outcasts—all suggest to varying extents that one primary goal of spirituality is to achieve mastery over the emotions and dampen body excitement. Despite doctrinal diversity among religions there is a ubiquitous underlying premise that heightened emotion and its somatic excitation obstruct access to an elevated spiritual state—a placid, equanimous higher consciousness held in a still body. Sacred ecstasy, the felt experience of being close to the source and force of creation, is very often ignored, feared, banned, or simply forgotten in favor of elevating the mind as the only tool capable of liberating the mind and controlling or transcending the body's emotion and motion.

The mind's quest to liberate itself from itself is claimed to bring the highest mentally held realization, something that has little emotional expression or body kinetics involved. The Dalai Lama, for example, in conversation with a group of scientists and psychologists, argues that the highest spiritual development is the ability to cultivate mental discipline to free oneself from "negative emotions" (2003, 26). Unfortunately, this focus on disciplining the mind in order to manage or overcome troubling emotions has resulted in missing an alternative and historically tried-and-true approach: the use of emotionally inspiring music, rhythm, and free body movement to ecstatically transform one's whole condition. Rather than always remain in a cold spiritual temperature where mindful means prevail, move to the spiritual fire where ecstatic means utilize rather than pathologize the arrival of unpleasant feelings. Contrast the Dalai Lama's approach to emotion with that of Bushman doctor, /Kunta Boo:

> The same power [n/om or sacred vibration] that changes a person's emotion from love to anger can also change the anger back to love. To keep healthy, healers must help the feelings keep changing. Everyone will feel angry from time to time, but a problem rises when it stays stuck. We get sick when we stay stuck in these dirty feelings. *We shake to help those things move.* All the different feelings are in a circle that must keep going round and round. (Personal communication with Bradford Keeney 2000, emphasis ours)

Excluding emotion and dismissing other natural somatic ways of being in the world, traditions that lack ecstatic thermodynamic know-how end up promoting practices that go against the grain of how we are physically and spiritually built. Rather than attempt to envision high mystery with a clear (i.e., cleared of body) mind, plunge inside it with all of your sensory-motor operations at full throttle and maximal excitation. The mind, which is not separate from the body, will spontaneously fall in line when the spiritual temperature is high enough to melt any fabricated divide. What almost all religions miss, lose, forget, erase, or censure is that your body cannot *not* move, *not* sense, and *not* emote. Trying to cease or "transcend" these natural operations cultivates an unnecessary ready-to-be-heady disembodiment that misses the full spectrum of mystical experience.

Even though you might think you have already experienced the heightened ecstatic emotion of spiritual heat, it will most likely come as a shock when you are really set on fire. As Evangelist Dorothy Jackson described her first experience:

> And when the Spirit really did come, it like to scared me, crazy. Yes, it was—I can't express it. I can't put it into words. I knew that it was the Lord. Cause I've never felt nothing like that in my life. The joy! The fulfillment! The explosion! The everything—was there! And I had longed for that. (Hinson 2000, 143)

In his autobiography, *Living with Kundalini* (1993), Gopi Krishna was also taken by surprise when he experienced his first kundalini awakening in 1937 after years of meditation, and again when it happened to him a few years later. While seated alone in meditation concentrating on the image of a lotus flower, Krishna felt himself "bathed in a light and in a state of exaltation and happiness impossible to describe" (3) and carried to "a supersensory plane where, caressed by lustrous waves of indescribable rapture," he was "immersed in the boundless ocean of unconditioned being" (265). He later discovered that although many teachers in India talked about kundalini, few had mastered it or could provide him with practical know-how: "Accomplished masters of Kundalini Yoga, always extremely rare, are almost non-existent now . . . it is no wonder that a detailed account of this strange experience is not available anywhere" (Krishna 1971, 132).

After Krishna got up from his meditation cushion he didn't know how to practically relate to the newborn vibrant energy within him. He soon felt "restless and disturbed" with a sense of "detachment" and "indifference" that lasted for days and then months on end (5). Unable to sleep or eat after his second kundalini awakening, Krishna grew so ill over the course of three months that he almost died. These extreme negative effects or so-called "kundalini accidents" do not happen among the Kalahari Bushmen who have worked with some of the most powerful energy—what they call "n/om"—for thousands of years. We posit this is because they have a drastically different and more effective approach to both igniting and hosting sacred ecstatic experience. Namely, n/om is held in a communal atmosphere that accentuates the singing, clapping, and dancing of trembling bodies. Once these healers or n/om-kxaosi feel n/om awaken in the belly, it is immediately transported to the heart via songs that evoke the joy, longing, and love for their ancestors and Sky God. When n/om reaches a boiling point it is never forced to reside inside an individual's still body, but is shared and circulated with everyone present. N/om is transmitted by physical touch and vocally produced sound. Though the healers' bodies may feel physically tired after a long dance, they and the whole community feel emotionally, relationally, and mentally attuned—and ready to share a meal. Gopi Krishna experienced his kundalini awaken with no song, dance, or community available to greet and circulate it, therefore missing the sustainable and shareable bliss of a Kalahari outcome. Kundalini misfires are not so much accidents as they are a consequence of missing practical know-how regarding how to handle its firepower.

Sacred Ecstatics does not seek an idealized and romanticized pure consciousness that is achieved by an individual practice isolated from others. It seeks spirited interactions wherein higher emotion is naturally emergent, readily immanent, automatically transferable, and infinitely fulfilling with no need to yearn for the transcendent escape hatch. Your marching orders are being shouted from on high: "About face!" Turn away from any "abouting" that perpetuates doubting the importance of whole embodiment. Don't just think, talk, or write about your relationship to the numinous or its mystery will immediately disappear and not be felt. Virginia Woolf wrote: "One can't write directly about the soul. Looked at, it vanishes." The only way to stop the looking is to start cooking. Follow Willa Cather's definition of happiness: "to be dissolved into something complete and great." Sacred Ecstatics invites you to traverse the full range of spiritual temperature and venture into the higher degrees where spiritual cooking takes place. There is found the dissolve into oceanic joy, the fulfillment, the ecstatic explosion, the infinite fire of love, and everything else you have longed for.

First and Second Creation

For the Ju/'hoan Bushmen, the spiritual heat from the sacred fire is found and experienced inside "First Creation," the original realm of mystery where life began. As Bushman storytellers explain, First Creation was (and forever is) a mythical time and place of inexhaustible vitality where everything constantly changed from one form to another, whether it was a lion into a giraffe or an eagle into a snake (Keeney and Keeney 2015). In this morphing Garden of Eden there was no sickness or death because the constant changing brought continuous rebirth, transformation, and renewed health to all of life. The pulse of this changing is a sacred vibration, the heartbeat of creation that is most strongly felt in the fire of sacred ecstasy. First Creation, or *G≠ain-g≠aing≠ani*, is perhaps the first name used by human beings to indicate the whole spiritual universe, the original Bushman village in the sky, and high heaven itself. In other words, First Creation is the home of the original creator, the primary mover and shaker behind all creation. It is similar to Hinduism's Brahman, the ALL-permeating-all that includes both being and becoming. It is also akin to the providence of divinity that George Fox, founder of the Quakers, refers to when he describes "the greatness and infiniteness of the love of God, which cannot be expressed by words" (Fox 1952, 21). We simply call First Creation "the big room" because it is the vastest space in which to house your life.

According to Bushman wisdom, any important spiritual experience requires reentering the heart and hearth of First Creation. This is not accomplished through calmly sitting still while filled with a contemplative insight *about* vastness that is absent of emotion and detached from an intimate relationship with the sacred. The Bushman way of reentering First Creation involves no techniques of concentration or any means directed at the mind. The whole of you must act—engaging a special mix of rhythm, singing, and movement—to kick-start the emotional walk that takes you deeply inside First Creation for an ecstatic homecoming. Getting spiritually cooked refers to your being *immersed in* rather than *removed from* the changing or N!o'an-ka|'ae of First Creation, the creative force of the universe that is somatically felt as a remarkable sacred vibration inseparable from heightened sacred emotion. Once you experience the vibration's pierce, installation, and final settlement in your body, the changing of First Creation forever lives within you.

As the Bushman story continues, at some point Second Creation arrived to cast names upon the changing forms of First Creation. Assigning names had an unexpected consequence—it made the changing stop. Bushman storytellers like to say that some animals were still in the process of morphing from one form to another at the moment their name was given. This is why the horse today still has the eland's hoofs. Second Creation, or *Manisi n!a'an-n!a'an*, did more than freeze-frame whatever change was taking place; it stopped the dynamic that had before prevented sickness and death.

The agent behind naming and conceptual framing is called "trickster" by the Bushmen, or what we also refer to as "trickster mind," the means of handling language and thought. Trickster mind can put a name, frame, and persuasive spin on anything, whether good or bad, and this makes it an unreliable guide for the most important matters in your life, including finding your way back to First Creation. As the Bushmen warn, you must be careful with trickster because you never know whether it's helping or hindering, healing or hurting, clarifying or confounding, leading or misleading you. And whatever it's up to, without notice it can turn at any moment. Always be careful whenever your trickster mind provides assistance because soon it may offer troubling resistance.

Trickster naming becomes addictive when it feeds the insatiable appetite of a hungry-to-know mind whose ongoing assignment and sorting of names tempts you to regard this as the primary way of being in relationship to the world. Rather than enter into the nameless changing of First Creation mystery, you perpetually stand outside it as a "spin doctor" who ascribes a name and frame to all experience. This act of interpretation creates the "known world" of Second Creation that is construed by mind. On the one hand, trickster is a blessing when it helps you find the comprehension that inspires invention, a scheme that serves a dream, the right words to comfort a friend, or a strategy that helps you function more efficiently inside the required routines of daily life. On the other hand, trickster can be a curse when it pretends to be totally in charge of your reality, boxes you inside limiting assumptions, filters away unknowable mystery, or blocks you from feeling heightened emotion. You are best served by continuously alternating between the partial perspectives of constructed frames and the unframeable, inflammable infinity of divinity's mystery where all is a dynamic creative flux that is felt but never boxed inside thought. Temporarily reside amidst the seemingly (though illusory) stable forms of the "naming world" while frequently taking a plunge into the eternally changing forms of the "creating world" of First Creation where everything is shaken free, recreated, and transformed over and over again.

When you linger too long outside the spiritual fire and changing of First Creation, a kind of amnesia sets in and you forget that the big room of mystery is your true home. As James Thurber humorously wrote, "Sixty minutes of thinking of any kind is bound to lead to confusion and unhappiness" (1966, 328). If trickster knowing solely occupies the throne of your being, then vitality, creativity, and wondrous mystery will be missing from your experiential landscape. Sacred Ecstatics brings you this special delivery message from First Creation: "You too easily get accustomed to living inside the small rooms of Second Creation, even though you feel the pinch. It's time for you to truly 'go outside the box' to receive rather than only conceive and perceive the exhilarating freedom of the big room. Your mission is to act in order to loosen and release all names, discovering you are always moving on the waves of the nameless Tao, indistinguishable from the eternal, infinite sea."

The relationship between First and Second Creation is paradoxical—they are distinct while at the same time inseparable and interdependent. When you talk about First Creation inside Second Creation, you momentarily bring a stop to its changing, creating the illusion that First and Second Creation are separate and in opposition. On the other hand, Second Creation can enter into the unbounded space of First Creation and find itself altered there. The spiritual crossroads is found where the boundary of Second Creation—mind's naming, knowing, and understanding—meets the ineffable that is not distilled or stilled by any trickster talk, trick, or treat. At this sacred intersection you may cross over into First Creation where healing and transformation take place through felt contact with the changing of creation. Here any stuck situation is instantly subject to change and there is no end to new beginnings.

Whether you know it or not, you live inside the eternal dance between First and Second Creation where each takes its turn encircling the other. To get back to the source of ultimate spiritual transformation, always return to the crossroads and choose the road that takes you to First Creation, the mystery place of God's down-home cooking. Here all Second Creation forms, including you and all your views, are placed back inside First Creation's wall-less infinitude, higher altitude, and wider latitude. At some point, you inevitably cool down and step back into Second Creation again where trickster's constructed knowing returns to prominence. In these continued back and forth crossings and their reversals of encirclement you find the vastest range of human experience.

A healer, shaman, teacher or any other anointed spiritual helper brings those with suffering to First Creation where a direct contact experience with the mysterious pulse of whole creation is made possible. To heal or spiritually help others you must place at least one foot inside the big room of First Creation where change and transformation reside. To find your way there you need a divine rope to pull you in. All authentic spiritual pursuit requires this rope, its pulling, and transformative passage. Follow the tracks of St. John of the Cross and find yourself able to say later, as he did, "I entered, but I knew not where, and there I stood not knowing . . . I stood enraptured in ecstasy" (St. John of the Cross 2007, 267).

The Temperature Range of Spiritual Experience

The higher degrees of spiritual temperature reside within First Creation while the lower degrees belong to Second Creation. The midpoint between the hot and cold zones of the thermometer is the crossroads or place of transition where sacred emotion and its expression starts to warm up or cool down depending on whether you are entering or departing the spiritual fire. There are numerous experiential changes associated with the climb up the spiritual thermometer. Here we list various ways of describing them:

Cold→ Cool→ Temperature transition→ Warm→ Hot

Second Creation → Crossroads→ First Creation

Small room→ Rhythmic transport→ Big room

Textual interpretation→ Emotional evocation→ Experienced change

Literality→ Metaphor→ Poetic verse→ Music→ Joyful noise

Hallowed name→ Aural sacramental bridge→ Mystery beyond names

Purposefulness→ Surrender→ Spontaneity

"My will be done" → Hitting bottom→ "Thy will be done"

Dissociated mind and body→ Healing→ Embodied wholeness

The journey up the spiritual thermometer requires exiting a small room of trickster knowing by getting on board a spiritual means of transport that heads to the big room of mystery. Soulful rhythm (fast or slow) is the vehicle — the auditory and bodily felt spiritual train, plane, ship, canoe, bus, or car—that moves you forward. When your spoken word hops on board this kind of rhythm it is taken to the changing, the sacred vibration of n/om, seiki, and holy spirit that resides in First Creation. In this voyage your vocal expression moves from literal to metaphorical speech, poetic verse, and sacramental song, along with the ecstatic shouts that fly past words.

Literalism is found in the coldest region of Second Creation where language is largely absent of rhythm and misses the moving variation of meaning that sprouts from creative metaphor. In a chilly climate you find the proliferation of dueling dualities, oppositional positioning, either-or war, and taxonomic taxidermy. Literalism gets you stuck proving what is real and what is not, including what is really good and what is really bad. This orientation is too "thingish" and leads to emotional hardness, the exaltation of the "real" over whatever your heart might feel. Mind thinks it is the whole reality show and the body is easily forgotten or presumed to be subservient to mind. The way out of the Second Creation freezer requires turning up the spiritual heat that enables emotion to get the rest of you in motion.

When the temperature gets warmer, rhythm awakens and strengthens as speech loosens to release word play, slippery meaning, uncommon comparison, poetic inspiration, unexpected humor, and literary surprise. Language, including the hallowed names spoken in prayer, shifts from static conceptual representation to dynamic emotional evocation. At the spiritual crossroads, Second Creation metaphors meet the rhythms that reside in First Creation. Together metaphor and rhythm mingle, forming a bridge that enables transport from one world to the other. Passage into First Creation involves this extraordinary experiential shift: *rhythm rather than linguistic meaning becomes primary*. The inner pulse of the sacred vibration eventually awakens and intensifies, amplified by heated rhythms that stir heightened emotion. Getting on board this rhythmic soul train takes you to the big room destination.

The participation of the body also changes as the spiritual temperature rises. In the coldest spiritual temperatures of Second Creation it seems as if your mind is entirely separate from your body. As the situation begins to thaw, mind continues to reign but there is more somatic awareness and encouragement of the body's involvement. In the barely warm temperature zone the body's sensations and movements are still subjected to mind's ongoing monitoring, evaluation, and interpretation. But when the heat further rises, the body moves more spontaneously and the exhilaration from this unexpected movement becomes more satisfying than the former habit of nonstop narration. Dissociated play-by-play commentary gives way to feeling carried away by rhythmically driven movement.

When the mind comes home to a moving and vocalizing body, all the phenomena of you dance together without effort, naturally guided by the rhythms and tones of song. Sacred emotion flows and grows within this blend of rhythm, tone, and movement to make the temperature rise even higher. Here the torn division of mind and body is mended in the rising sea of ecstasy. This is when the sacred vibration fully awakens, bringing the radical, ultimate transformative shift you seek: moving from the partial, self-directed reality of "my will be done" to the whole, divinely orchestrated experience of "Thy will be done in earth as it is in heaven."

In summary, the spiritual thermometer traces the transformative journey that begins with a mind-body split where your dissociated mind attempts to govern your presumed-to-be-separate body, all taking place in the cold hinterlands of Second Creation. You aim to reach the big room of First Creation and be healed, that is, made whole again. The crossroads is where metaphor meets poetic meter and becomes the expressive heater that emotionally warms recitation to convey more excitation. This is how frozen names, thoughts, beliefs, and stories thaw. Such a creative melt brings a spiritual warming that includes the body moving more spontaneously as the shifting beat further increases the heat. With the rising tide of sacred emotion, the reign of mind surrenders to the heartbeat of mystery. The song-ropes soon take over and pull you into the hottest ecstatic fire where mind and body further dance themselves into soulful divine unity and mystical community. This is the ultimate surrender of your small room self to the big room embrace of infinite love.

Adjusting the Spiritual Temperature with Music

Every ecstatic spiritual gathering has a leader attuned to noticing when it is time to raise the spiritual temperature, how long to maintain it before making another temperature shift, and when to facilitate reentry into the everyday climate. These adjustments of the spiritual thermostat are usually accomplished by changing the music that is performed. Some songs help strike a match while others sustain the temperature, bring more heat, or cool things down.

For example, during an old-fashioned sanctified black church service, parishioners express a slow-moving, improvised melodic sound called "moaning" that enables a lament to be powerfully voiced with deep emotion. People throw their troubles, worries, and suffering into the magical mix of crawling rhythm, mournful tone, and plea-worthy emotion. This bluesy prayer helps get everyone on board a religious soul train, the "train bound for glory" that Sister Rosetta Tharpe sings about in her famous blues recording of the old gospel song. Once the whole congregation feels it has come together in this way, a hymn is introduced that picks up a faster beat. It is this change in music and rhythm that lifts them from sorrow and launches a process of spiritual miracle making, transforming past sadness into a newborn joy for the felt presence of God. The transmutation of human suffering into sacred ecstasy is nothing less than the alchemical shift from heavy psychological lead to luminous spiritual gold, achieved by the transition from moaning to spirited hymn singing. This process is accomplished by rhythmic rather than interpretive means. As the rhythmic wheels of the communal train turn faster they inspire more ecstatic emotion and body locomotion. The old spiritual, "Every Time I Feel the Spirit," describes this journey: "There is but one train on this track. It runs to heaven and then right back." This kind of song track picks you up when you are down and takes you up the spiritual thermometer, returning you with joy in the heart and fire in the soul.

Once you cross into higher spiritual heat, more intense ecstatic expression takes place that is called a "shout." As some African American parishioners interviewed in the early twentieth century described it: "I shout because there is a fire on the inside. When I witness the truth, the fire moves on the main altar of my heart, and I can't keep still," In general, "shouting is but the outward manifestation of an inward joy" (Johnson 1969, 11). All ecstatics reach for this inner heartfelt joy, a special kind of explosive happiness that arrives when you are ignited by spiritual fire.

When a gathering is spiritually cooking at a fast pace, the leader may at any time switch the music to a slower song that now increases the emotional intensity because it conveys even more longing for divine intervention. This change may precipitate another temperature spike as extreme emotion pours from the deepest open wells of the devoted heart. The infinite fire of holy love is viscerally felt in such moments of spiritual excitement and exalted praise. Prayer transforms from asking to longing. As Mahatma Gandhi said, "Prayer is not asking. It is a longing of the soul . . . It is better in prayer to have a heart without words than words without a heart." As the temperature peaks, a mysterious spiritual power pours forth and touches those ready for holy alteration:

> [It] can draw a saint's feet into the exhilarating steps of holy dance. It can empower a preacher's faltering words with wisdom and revelation. It can summon from the throat a shout of praise and jubilation. It can lead the tongue to revel in the phrasings of an unknown, celestial language. And it can push a singer to voice lyrics never before heard by mortal ears. (Hinson 2000, 3)

When the service is finally ready to start cooling down, carefully articulated prayers bring the emphasis back to the spoken word. The keyboardist's musical accompaniment to the preacher's talk also contributes to calibrating the spiritual temperature and regulating the congregation's participation. This can help slow down movement and quiet things down. At any time, however, a surprising wild shout, an unexpected exclamatory drum roll, or a keyboard's sudden blast of an arousing sound may raise the temperature again. It is unpredictable if and when such a turnaround will happen, but when a gathering goes through many rounds of spiritual cooking for hours on end, parishioners say that they had a "Holy Ghost party." The movement up and down the spiritual thermometer continues until the service brings everyone back to earth, readying them for reentry into the everyday that is waiting for them outside the church doors.

Music is also the means for regulating spiritual temperature in the Kalahari. With polyrhythms and improvised melodic embellishment, Bushman singers know the purpose of clapping and singing is to spiritually heat things up and get the healing dancers moving. The strength of emotion is what increases the singers' volume and triggers more improvisational variation in their singing, which further turns up the spiritual heat. In an ecstatic dance, Bushman healers do their best to encourage everyone to whole-heartedly sing and clap. When a healer starts to get cooked, the community immediately notices and this inspires an even more enthusiastic performance. In general, when either a clapping singer or a dancing healer is set on fire, the flames spread to everyone present. In this shared circulation of spiritual heat it does not matter who or what causes the temperature surge—a clapping hand, singing voice, dancing body, or trembling touch. Everyone contributes in all kinds of ways to raise and circulate the spiritual heat of sacred emotion.

For Caribbean Shakers, the spiritual heat in a praise house is regulated by the shifts between slow and fast music as well as specially toned rhythms. A designated "spiritual captain" is in charge of calling out the songs that sustain or alter the spiritual temperature. At the height of heated expression, a song may turn into a guttural sound that expresses improvised percussion. This so-called 'doption or adoption by the spirit may overtake a melody or it may rhythmically accompany the song that inspired its emergence. In this ecstatic tradition, songs are regarded as the pathways or lines for spiritual traveling while rhythms are what fuel the journey. When the community sings and makes rhythm together, they regard this as boarding a "spiritual ship" that takes them on a voyage to the "spirit lands."

The Bushmen similarly refer to songs as the lines and ropes used for spiritual transportation, communication, and circulation of spiritual energy. Like 'doption in the Caribbean, Bushman healers experience being overtaken by a rhythmic pulse that results in involuntary guttural sounds and intermittent shrieks or shouts. Whereas the black church in the United States has forgotten how to use songs to facilitate this wide a range of ecstatic experience, they still sing of a mainline hookup to God that enables a spiritual phone call as well as the delivery of any needed spiritual power or bestowed gift. Most importantly, all these ecstatic traditions recognize that songs are the key to transporting them to the highest spiritual realm, whether it is called a spirit land, heaven, or First Creation.

In Sufism, sacred ecstasy (wajd) also involves music and the process of *sama'* or mystical listening. Abu'l Husayn al-Darraj summarizes:

> This understanding of wajd as a spiritual state of being inspired by the audition to music—sama as the "food of love" so to speak—was based on a complicated mystical psychology of rapture and an ontology of ecstasy, the subtle relationship between auditory sensation and spiritual experience . . . (as cited in Lewisohn 2014, 44)

Sufi scholar Abu Hamis al-Ghazali further explains: "singing produces a state in the heart which is called wajd. In its turn, wajd causes the bodily limbs to move, whether the movement is non-rhythmic and the emotion be disorderly, or a rhythmic movement, in which case it is called clapping and dance" (as cited in Lewisohn 2014, 45). This mystical concert that precipitates a danced ecstasy is also found among the Bauls of Bengal whose ecstatic intoxication leads to multi-sensory experience and full-bodied celebration (McDaniel 1989). Wherever music is used to induce ecstatic emotion, we find another return to the world's oldest spiritual know-how that was born in Africa and arguably most developed by the Kalahari Bushmen. Sacred Ecstatics forever invites you to get out of the exclusively cold-and-told and step into the heat, catching the musically conveyed emotion that awakens dancing feet.

Divinely inspired music helps bring the full glory of sacred ecstasy that is always unmistakably more than a placid glimpse of spiritual vastness. Be careful what you read because many scholarly treatises on mysticism, religion, and shamanism misconstrue ecstasy as a kind of cataleptic, out-of-body state rather than the heightened emotion found in the roomier room of Rumi's heartfelt excitation. The emotionally subdued scholar's redefinition of ecstasy misses the bliss, fervor, fire, musicality, and danceability that mark its full experience. The spiritual thermometer is a necessary descriptive tool that helps distinguish between the cooler, "big mind" awakening achieved during a non-moving stance or sitting posture and the spiritually hot, soulfully sung, and wildly danced emotional experience of sacred ecstasy. We call for the unambiguous and unashamed return of heightened sacred emotion, the ecstasy whose pure joy comes from feeling a personal, intimate connection with your creator. When experienced rather than imagined, there is, as William James describes, "a transfiguration of the face of nature in [the] eyes. A new heaven seems to shine upon a new earth" (1958, 142). Here we find the one endless ecstatic smile of C.M.C.

Each ecstatic lineage has its own particular way of igniting sacred emotion and traveling up and down the spiritual thermometer, doing so through the interaction of music (melodic tones strung together on a rhythm) with body movement. This ecstatically empowered journey across different temperatures is a sensory-motor ride that has been called "riding the train to glory," "getting on board the old ship Zion," "traveling to spirit lands," "spiritual journeying," "mounting a horse," "riding a spirit mule," "climbing the ladder," and "going up the rope to God," among other phrases that indicate the shifts that carry you from cold meditative looking to hot celebrative cooking. To get on board and set your spiritual life in motion, take the action that surpasses contemplation—stand up, move, sing, and dance yourself into the hearty hearth of creation.

Spiritually Cooked Dreaming

The spiritual thermometer also applies to the world of dreams. A dream may take place in the cold zone and be filled with symbols, objects, and visual displays that fascinate the interpreting mind. Or it may be spiritually hot—filled with ecstatic song and dance and the sacred vibration they impart. So-called "sacred visions" refer to dreams that are cooked by the fire of First Creation. You wake up somatically and emotionally transformed with a heart pierced by a colossal love. Other dreams with less sacred emotional impact are mere dreams, the stuff of wishful thinking and/or the recycling of psycho-biographical material, both of which lie sleeping in Second Creation.

It is not uncommon for naïve practitioners to report that they have frequent "visions" while doing a spiritual practice or ritual that lacks any spiritual heat. It is better to mark these experiences as daydreams that involve imagination rather than the revelation and jubilation of sacred vision. We celebrate the former when it gives rise to poetry, literature, artistic expression, creative inspiration, innovation, or scientific invention. However, we prefer to reserve the word "spiritual vision" to indicate those rare experiences (typically while asleep and rarely while awake) that host tremendous ineffable mystery and the extreme emotion of sacred ecstasy. We use the term vision sparingly out of respect for the big room in which such a special transformative experience takes place.

Whenever someone talks too often and casually about visionary experience, it is likely that he or she is a Second Creation dreamer. First Creation vision doesn't inspire elaborate talk, long-winded interpretation, or exaggerated story. It powerfully touches the heart and makes you spiritually bake and shake. Confirmation of visionary authenticity is found in the way its report ecstatically affects someone who is already spiritually cooked. The spiritual heat in a sacred vision is always contagious. If other ecstatics within earshot aren't trembling when you talk about it, rest assured that it was a common dream rather than a unique visionary visit to mystery.

A dream that accentuates flying saucers, strange creatures, channeling entities, or anything that is plainly weird is better assumed to be a trickster production. Such a dream is more Hollywood than what the holy would deliver. A vision of high mystery has little to do with psyche-delic-atessen consciousness, bombastic pompousness, mystical fogginess, or cognitive grogginess. It always carries the feeling of holiness and the joyful noisiness it inspires. Does your dream make a grandparent weep with joy, a child want to hold your hand, or your partner welcome you back to the everyday with open arms? Does it inspire others to pray and sing or does it exclusively exalt your specialness? Ask whether you'd want to tell your dream to the holy ones of all religions or whether it better fits inside a gathering of workshop shamans showing off their rattles. Does your dream bring you closer to the infinity of divinity or to the guided imagery of a small conference room? Ask not what your dreams can do for you; ask what you can do to honor the source of the highest visions.

Second Creation dreamers don't know that mystical vision requires spiritual heat. We discuss this further in chapter six where numerous examples of cooked visionary experience are provided. Spiritually cooked dreams always reside in the big room where common psychological themes and established mythical content are minimized in favor of mind blowing and body shaking ecstatic emotion. Revelation precipitates celebration rather than any extended search for contrived meaning. You step away from understanding and find that standing on sacred ground in the big room results in the reception of mystical wings, musical strings, and other moving things.

Taking the Spiritual Temperature of the Helping Professions

You can take the temperature of professional people helpers and their methods—from therapy to counseling, coaching, somatic work, and spiritual healing, among others. Regardless of their orientation, psychotherapists and coaches are almost always working in the cold zone, especially those who have an aversion to welcoming emotion—particularly their own—into sessions. While clients' emotional expression may be tolerated to a degree, most schools of psychotherapy and coaching exalt words as the primary means of change, whether directed at sharing an interpretation, altering a narrative, addressing a cognitive habit, or rallying for action. This is true even when an orientation claims to emphasize emotions, because the latter are subjected to chilled interpretation rather than fired up for ecstatic transformation. When assessed with the spiritual thermometer, the different schools of psychotherapy and coaching, though they are fond of debating imagined differences, are seen to be more similar than different in that they all primarily promote what is spiritually cold.

It is possible, however, for a practitioner of talk-based approaches to thaw and melt. The first rise in temperature helps talk become more creatively poetic, carried along by an awakened rhythmic movement in the body, even if it is a barely perceptible rocking, swaying, or vibratory motion. With continued warming you become more spontaneous and improvisational with unique creative therapeutics for each session, caring less about following any strict treatment protocol or clinical model. As a spiritually warm practitioner you are more ready, able, and willing to be moved by the idiosyncratic particularities of a situation, allowing it to inspire and direct you as appropriate. Such a "model-free" practitioner is unencumbered by the straitjackets of prefabricated conduct and instead, engages in the improvisational performance of a creative artist who knows not what will be expressed.[7] As Ikuko Osumi, Sensei said of the improvisational nature of her healing: "There is no fixed system or formula for healing in seiki therapy. The therapist's body can create an almost infinite variety of techniques to meet each unique client's needs" (Keeney 1999b, 73). On the other hand, without spiritual heat your way of helping others will be too predictable, model bound, creatively dead, and empty of seiki.

Sacred Ecstatics invites you to become a more inventive practitioner of change, that is, a constantly changing practitioner who works inside the big room of First Creation. If you want to be a healer with a real working relationship with ineffable mystery, you must climb the spiritual thermometer and get cooked. The mysterious changing of First Creation instills a creative force inside you that now flows through your interactions with others. This is how you are prepared to become a big room practitioner who knows how to expand, heat, and transform. Each session enacts a tailor-made way to move through the three-step recipe that begins by making enough room for change, then ignites transformative experience, and finally returns to the everyday in an altered manner.

Sometimes practitioners are tricked into thinking that dropping spiritual names into their sessions will make their work more spiritually potent. But shifting to the language of mindfulness, forgiveness, salvation, satori, karma, reincarnation, fire, heat, spirit, spirit helper, soul, spirituality, and the like does not in and of itself carry a session into the big room. You and all your metaphors will remain cool until corrective action is taken to expand the room and raise the spiritual temperature. Once you warm up inside a broader creative space, you can talk about anything, including fishing or making paper dolls, and it will

---

[7] For more details on bringing spiritual heat to a therapy session see our book, *The Creative Therapist in Practice* (2019b).

exude soulfully heated emotion that is ready to transform lives. Cold talk about hot topics cannot heat anything. But warmer talk about any topic can precipitate a good meltdown as long as there is room to enact such a change. Here spiritual heat, with its rhythm, tone, movement, vibration, and life force, brings soul to your spoken words, making them what the Guarani Indians call "word souls" (Keeney, 2000). It is the spiritual current words carry rather than only their semantic meaning that makes them potent.

The same practical consideration about spiritual temperature also applies to bodywork. If a session is mechanically delivered and follows a preset procedure, it is going to be cold and held inside creatively restricted space. When a bodyworker is spiritually heated in a big treatment room, spontaneous improvisation kicks in so that the entire session is unpredictable to both practitioner and client. The hotter the temperature gets, the more rhythm and melodic tone enter the scene, expressed by the bodyworker herself. Whether healing is done through talk or touch, what matters most is the spiritual temperature at which it is delivered, and whether it matches what is needed in the creative expanse of a given situation — neither being too much nor too little. Again, the conceptual and methodological differences between all healing orientations, modalities, and practices are less important than discerning the spiritual temperature in which they take place. You need to get spiritually cooked before you are able to warmly speak the word souls and hand-deliver the soulful touch of big room ecstatic healing.

We have previously written about the mind-body split that the helping professions perpetuate when they legally and professionally separate talk therapy from body therapy (Keeney and Keeney, 2014). It is insane that talk therapists must act as if the body is not a part of the session, and that body therapists are directed to behave as if conversation cannot or should not be therapeutic. The voice that delivers talk is a part of the body, and the body is inseparable from all the experience it hosts, including thought and emotion. The dualism that separates treatments and restricts choice in each of them actually helps maintain the suffering of clients who come for help. It enacts and escalates the iatrogenic, pathogenic dichotomies and disassociations that underlie suffering.

The separation of mind and body, along with the professional organizations that serve this separation, are maintained by clinging to the frozen names held hostage in Second Creation. Rigid institutions that claim to preserve ethics and professionalism hide the fact that they primarily serve keeping practice frigid. It is seldom questioned whether this enforced refrigeration is ethical. Like other religions, some of these institutions were originally inspired by a creative experience that is now embalmed in the existential Arctic. The source of original inspiration cannot return to life without an act of heresy and revolution that stands up to any anti-ecstatic ethic. Practitioners must move their practice to a more spacious room where the heat can defeat whatever tries to still the changing, fragment the whole, and deaden the vital life force that both hallows and heals.

Hot Shamanism, Cold Shamanism

The spiritual temperature setting is arguably the most important assessment of anyone's spirituality, distinguishing whether or not there is any authentic emotional hookup to supreme mystery's higher power. As we discussed, even shamans who once were exemplars of ecstatic fire handling can turn cold. Shamans are either in a close relationship to the numinous and guided by its thermodynamics—their rope is strong—or they are far removed and without ecstatic emotion. Let us not forget that shamans were originally so ecstatic that outside reporters wondered whether the extreme physical movements and loud sounds they witnessed were those of an epileptic or of someone with a neurological disorder. The original ecstatic shamans were not sitting still but were shaking wildly. The very word ecstatic was originally intended to underscore this kind of spirited movement and heated emotional expression (Keeney and Keeney, 2019a).

For instance, Sieroszewski observed a sixty-year-old shaman who "displayed tireless energy" and "if necessary, he can drum, dance, and jump all night" (1896, 113). Similarly, when describing a Vogul shaman, Karjalainen saw "an energy that appears unbounded" (1921, 247–48) and Castagne watched a shaman who "flings himself in all directions with his eyes shut" (1930, 93). He goes on: "Wild animal cries and bird calls are heard . . . springing, roaring, leaping; he barks like a dog, sniffs at the audience, lows like an ox, bellows, cries, bleats like a lamb, grunts like a pig, whinnies, coos, of birds, the sound of their flight, and so on." Jochelson found that, among the Yukagir, one of the terms to designate the shaman is I'rkeye, which literally translates as "the trembling one" (1924–26, 62). Mircea Eliade distinguished those dressed in shamanic garb who are ritualists from those who, with or without costume, are ecstatics (Eliade 1964).

Shamanism cools off when it becomes ritualized, memorized, and institutionalized. The core thermodynamics of hot ecstatic shamanism has no single core method, nor does it rest at a singular temperature degree. It is always subject to the constantly unpredictable and improvised direction of a mainline rope that is attached to the source of higher power and its big room of mystery. This rope delivers endless volts and jolts of ecstatic surprise. Cold shamanism replaces the voltage of ecstasy with verbiage and fantasy. It insists on an unalterable method that dictates how a session or ceremony will begin and end, without any entry into the big room fire. Shamanism that is on fire promotes endless forms of expression from one shaman and culture to the next. Such cooked shamanism is the spiritual offspring and resident of First Creation. Remember, however, that whatever is born in the spiritual wild always risks being kidnapped and made mild by a trickster from Second Creation. There it is tamed and taught to play the mass-marketing language game with all its promised magic and fame that has no flame or holy aim.

In First Creation, spiritual lineages and world religions become more authentically shamanic, that is, true ecstatic fire handlers. In the Second Creation spiritual freezer of any institution, authorities make sure that no one departs from the preselected low and non-ecstatic temperature setting. Both Tibetan Buddhism and Christianity, along with most other institutionalized religions, have an unfortunate history of persecuting ecstatic shamans and advocates of freely spirited expression. Similarly, today's commercialized institutions of so-called neo-shamanism often discredit and distance themselves from any form of heated ecstasy. One well-known founder of a franchised neo-shamanism method told Brad that "excited emotion and wild drumming should be banned because they are too dangerous and may cause a psychotic break." This timid and frigid outlook is a clear indication that he was not spiritually cooked and never experienced the hot temperature, heightened emotion, sacred vibration, or creative changing of real shamanic experience. Without the primacy of sacred ecstasy and ownership of a divine rope your heart, body, soul, and consciousness cannot soar, roar, or exit the Second Creation door. Ironically and tragically, we find today's reinvented secular shamanism promotes the same fear and concern about wild expression espoused by early European colonists when they first witnessed indigenous ecstatic ceremonies. When you chill the feared emotional heat, the shaman's kinetic, frenetic motion comes to rest as true ecstasy and its authentically empowered journey are placed under arrest.

Nearly all traditions of spirituality have entered an ecstatic ice age. Over time each orientation found a comfortable temperature zone and prohibited a session or ceremony from warming, closing any access to high heat. Again, just like diverse forms of psychotherapy are similarly cold even when conceptually different, many spiritual traditions have the same thermostat setting despite their differences of name, metaphor, belief, ritual, and practice. A consideration of the spiritual temperature setting enables us to discern new and more experientially meaningful differences and similarities between spiritual orientations. For instance, most New Age shamanism takes place inside the same temperature range maintained inside a Presbyterian church or a secular psychology clinic. Old school hot shamanism, however, is more similar to the heated expression inside a sanctified black church or a Caribbean praise house. If you are truly a hunter of spiritual heat, you'll go where the fire is, independent of whatever name is on the sign above the door. As Rumi says, "Forget phraseology. I want burning, burning. Be Friends with your burning. Burn up your thinking and forms of expression!"

In summary, you simply cannot be a shamanic technician, clinician, musician, or electrician of ecstasy unless you own a rope to God, feel a whole body sacred vibration, frequently enter the big room, and are hungry for a fire in the bones. It is the emotionally charged somatic experience found in the higher spiritual temperatures, rather than any name you call yourself, that spiritually ripens, seasons, and cooks you. Whatever serves making the temperature hot is honored and encouraged. Impassionate talk, deadbeat rhythm, overly purposeful stillness, and sanitized routine—while possibly harmless in moderation—are always questioned and challenged by ecstatics since they too easily put out the fire, deaden spiritual work, dampen the creative life force, and interrupt profound leaps of change.

Sacred Ecstatics advocates bringing back the original definition of "ecstatic" as an indication of spiritually heated emotion that inspires creatively improvised wild commotion—the wondrous experience that can't help but take place once you truly enter the big room. In other words, we sing, "Give me that old time religion" that was once called shamanism. Sacred Ecstatics asks you to "show the heat" and "move your feet" instead of falling asleep in the rote repeat of another cold workshop retreat. Also do not mistake "setting yourself free," "doing your own thing," "letting it all hang out" or "going totally wild" as indications of ecstasy. Without sacred emotion, your motion won't soulfully swing, creatively ring, or spiritually mean a thing. The utmost spiritual experience is not meant to only make you high, but to make you feel more need for divine intervention that rescues you from trivial popular convention. You are spiritually cooked for a higher purpose: made ready to assist others who are out of spiritual steam or have lost their tracks in a spiritual blizzard. A Bushman's visionary voyage to the ancestors and God in the sky village always ends with the journeyer being told, "It is time for you to go back and help others. Go back now." Your job, once your soul has been set on fire, is to be an ordinary person who shares an extraordinary heat with those who are cold. You help thaw the spiritual ice and defrost the lost. Sacred Ecstatics reveals that souls are never in need of retrieval; they are simply in desperate need of being set on fire.

Beware Constructing a Simple Good/Bad Dualism Between Hot and Cold

We do not mean to suggest that cold temperatures are always "bad" and only hot temperatures are "good." There is a time and place for each spiritual temperature and climate. As we discuss further in chapter seven, cooler temperatures can either shrink you within a shallow banality or deepen you inside expanding wisdom. We live in a time in history, however, when vastly crazy wisdom and extremely hot ecstatic experience have been forgotten, overlooked, diminished, reined in, explained away, or explicitly banned (McDaniel 2018). People fear wild religious joy and the way it excites the body to shout, sing, tremble, quake, shake, jolt, leap, dance, rock, and roll. Do not be wishy-washy about the experiential difference between hot and cold spiritual temperatures lest you blur the important differences between spiritual recipes, their temperature settings, and intended outcomes. You must choose whether to shrink or expand, look or cook. Act in order to venture into the expanded mansion, heated emotion, and expressed explosion found in the big room.

From the perspective of spiritual temperature, ecstatics from different religions and cultures have more in common with one another than they do with their non-ecstatic neighbors who come from the same religion and culture. Again, most religions historically lock themselves into a particular temperature zone while ignoring the other degrees of the thermometer. It's possible that Buddhism became popular so quickly in the West because it maintains the same low spiritual thermostat setting as non-ecstatically calibrated Judaism, Christianity, and Islam. It offers alternative concepts and practices while keeping things at the same calm, cool, and collected temperature. Buddhism does not encourage or host spiritual heat—sacred emotion and its jubilant expression—preferring instead to cultivate an experience of big room boundlessness through silent meditation.[8] Buddhism

---

[8] Though Buddhist traditions emphasize other practices or "skillful means" involving movement and vocalization such as prostration, chanting, walking, and even work (e.g. cleaning, cooking), seated silent meditation has remained the main practice since the time of the Buddha. Buddhist chanting—accompanied by bells, drums, and other instruments—naturally evokes more emotion than sitting meditation and creates an atmosphere of awe and mystery. However, such chanting is not practically or doctrinally performed for the purpose of igniting extreme sacred emotion and affection for a divine other (despite Buddhist devotion to various deities). Any sacred

disciplines and focuses the mind as it stills the body and subdues emotion—an approach readily adopted by secular meditators who adulate mindfulness, serenity, and relaxation as peak experiences of wellbeing.

Across the globe the mindfulness of Buddhism (received from its original meditation teacher, Hinduism) is countered by the body-fullness of the African Diaspora where emotional pyrotechnics and somatic kinetics rather than calm stillness are valued. We find, however, that when African cookers stay out of the heat too long they are just as susceptible to the shrunken rooms of excessive dogmatism, literalism, fundamentalism, and ritualism found among people from other religious traditions. In other words, the expansion and heat experienced in the big room are not always effectively sustained by ecstatic traditions when they re-enter the everyday. The clearing provided by an old-fashioned Taoist-Zen sweep could readily benefit all religions as much as it did the excessive interpreting and textual attachment of its earlier Buddhist predecessors. Once the room is cleared and expanded again, however, everyone is in equal need of the African Kalahari fire where the mind sinks back into its awakened body, joyfully shaken by bliss that does not miss any part required for making life whole.

Sacred Ecstatics carefully examines the spiritual engineering (practical action and performance) of any spiritual tradition and discerns whether and how it travels up and down the thermometer. We value the wisdom that can take place at all temperature ranges, but our unique mission is to bring back the climb to the highest ecstatic heat so that it may again be valued and celebrated as a natural and wondrous part of human experience.

---

ecstasy experienced by Buddhists throughout history has been an exception rather than the achievement of Buddhism's defined practical goal.

The Spiritual Thermometer is the Rope to God

With each progression up the rope to God, the spiritual temperature rises as sacred emotion strengthens. For all practical purposes, the spiritual thermometer is another way of talking about the divine rope, staircase, or ladder. Remember that it also functions as a spiritual power line, holy telephone line, and miracle-lined path to mystery, among other metaphors. When this main holy vine or mystery pipeline takes root inside of you, the sacred vibration pours through whenever required. It's also like an electrical cord dangling from your body that needs to be plugged into an outlet, hooking you up to the main power source of electricity that is both spiritually direct and alternating. You go to the crossroads hoping to make connection with the higher power station. The current flows from the big room generator and rejuvenator of First Creation where you are immediately charged upon entry. Once connected, you walk back to Second Creation hoping your power line does not become disconnected. This line must be strong and always plugged in, ready to deliver its spiritually empowered charge when needed.

Bishop John, a Caribbean ecstatic Shaker from St. Vincent, defines this mysterious phone line and its conveyance of spiritual electrical power:

> It's a natural communication with the Holy Spirit. It's like having a telephone line that direct-dials to your God . . . It's also like turning on the electricity, bringing forth a current in the line. The power of God is an electric force that comes into your body. When the power takes you, you cannot resist it. It's like lightning . . . I vibrate from my head right down through my body. I feel jolts of electricity . . . I feel I can throw this power to the people. (Keeney 2002, 102–105)

If you get out of the way and don't interfere, spiritual electricity comes through automatically inside First Creation. When you try too hard to bring it forth, this purposeful intentionality blocks the current or pulls the plug. Piety, self-righteousness, moralism, rigid precepts, non-situational ethics, and presumptuous inflexible understanding also weaken the connection, as can a lack of appropriate reverence, under-confidence, lazy apathy, and insipid empathy. Fools Crow had this to say when asked what blocks a person from being in direct communion with the Creator, Wakan-Tanka:

> Doubt, guilt, reluctance, fear, selfishness, wanting to tell Wakan-Tanka how and when it ought to be done . . . Our reason must be that we want to be helped so that we can help others. There must be nothing selfish in this. Wakan-Tanka's wish is that we do for others, and we are taken care of . . . I heard a song on the radio which included the words, "I did it my way." This is nothing to be proud of, and the person who follows that way of life cannot be happy for very long. (Mails 1991, 51–52)

Become familiar with the practical basics of "spiritual engineering," the know-how of lighting up your life with spiritual electricity. Traditional Brazilian healer, João Fernandes de Carvalho, described how he accessed and was renewed by this kind of sacred current and its means of communication:

> The pearl that is within me doesn't belong to me. It comes from a larger dimension . . . It belongs to God. It feels like a force or electric current that moves through me when I pray. My rosary works like a telephone line to God. These experiences enable my faith to be reborn every day. (Keeney 2003a, 19)

Making the natural connection to the big room power station is so simple that even a child can accomplish it, but be humbled by the fact that your mind's habitual shenanigans will often try to pull the plug. It is time for you to find out how to better cease and desist the ways in which you disrupt or block the ecstatic current. Begin by turning away from "doing it your way" and learn to surrender to the higher and mightier wisdom of your creator. This includes paying less attention to everything you think you need to understand, dialogue, debate, contemplate, elaborate, or imagine about yourself and your relationship to spiritual matters. Pride and arrogance, as well as excessive self-deprecation and doubt, equally contribute to short-circuiting the power cord. That which evokes vast mystery brings you down to the size that better hosts the ecstatic prize and its felt surprise — the electrical heating and jubilant greeting from the rope to God.

Setting Sacred Words on Fire

Once you are spiritually cooked you discover that sacred books can be read while cold or hot. A cold reading readily leads to the entrapment of entangled interpretation, while a hot reading converts words into holy bread that satiates the ecstatic appetite. A warm relationship with a sacred book provides a nutritious dose of what brings you close to mystery. Make sure your heart is warm and your spiritual eyes wide open before opening a sacred book. Then proceed to heartily receive a leavened feast.

We invite you to get out your special matchbox and prepare to light a fire. To get ready for this mystical prescription, perform an uncommon form of spiritual warm up. Sing a children's song in a sacred manner, chant a prayer with an imagined foreign accent, take a vow to bow before the next breeze, jump up while feeling down about your troubles, or whistle a tune to both sides of the moon. Consider taking a walk around the room in a counter-clockwise direction as you say, "I am unwinding whatever binds me from stepping toward the big room."

Next proceed to open a sacred book of your choice and select one sentence at random. Feel free to repeat this three times and then choose the most fascinating literary line. Perhaps you will open the Torah, Bible, Quran, Vedas, Tao Te Ching, Upanishads, The Papyrus of Ani, Bhagavad Gita, or Buddhist sutras. Once you find your chosen line, immediately take the match out of your matchbox and strike it, allowing the flame to come near the sentence. Look through the flame and burn the words of that sentence into your mind. Then blow out the match and write down the sentence on a special piece of paper. Immediately rub the charcoal from the tip of the burned match over these words to remind you that it is possible to receive a life sentence that brings you closer to the infinite fire.

Go through the next twenty-four hours partnered with these specially heated and charred words. Carry them with you. Sing the sentence as a new lyric to either a song you know or in a free-form melodic improvisation. Remember that words must hop on board a rhythm if they are to help bring you closer to the spiritual heat. Feed your belief that this performance both empowers and is empowered by the mystery fire on high. Finally, choose the hottest word in the sentence. Repeat this word to yourself as often as you can throughout the day. Know that after the sun goes down you will set the whole sentence on fire by burning the piece of paper. Recognize that you are learning to creatively handle multiple mystical levels of spiritual fire. Repeat this exercise several times a week. Don't forget to provide a new match for your matchbox, keeping it ready for the next round of spiritual cooking.

Close your eyes, trigger your felt longing for mystery, and imagine jumping into the ecstatic fire that can spiritually cook you. As Rumi advises, be a "well-baked loaf" that is "served to your brothers [and sisters]." Later he asks, "Isn't it time to turn yourself into a temple of fire?" Recall how God spoke to Moses through a burning bush while the Buddha taught, "Just as a candle cannot burn without fire, [people] cannot live without a spiritual life." Jesus announced, "I have come to bring fire on the earth." Centuries later, Pierre Teilhard de Chardin made the prophecy, "Someday, after mastering the winds, the waves, the tides and gravity, we shall harness for God the energies of love, and then, for a second time in the history of the world, man will have discovered fire." At the end of the day, Hafiz summarizes what it's all about: "Our progress on this Journey can be measured only by the intensity of our love, the living flame that illumines all life." Rumi echoes back to help keep you on track: "Set your life on fire. Seek those who fan your flames." Open the page of a sacred book to receive your life sentence, light an ecstatic match, set every mystical level on fire, get spiritually cooked, and find yourself a charred bard no longer barred from the heavenly starred sky!

Part Two

The Recipe for Setting Your Soul on Fire

3

BUILDING THE BIG ROOM

The Sacred Ecstatics recipe, whether conducted during a home spiritual practice, a healing session with a client, or a ceremonial group gathering, is structured like a three-act play that moves through a beginning, middle, and end. You first make enough room to experience the numinous — whatever impedes felt contact is cleared away. Through the skillful handling of words, the spiritual masonry of prayer, and the gradual increase of sacred emotion and its inspired expression, the "room" hosting your experience expands. Once it has been built, you commence the second step of the recipe where heightened emotion precipitates the trembling, quaking, and shaking familiar to the ecstatic mystics, saints, shamans, and healers. This is when spiritual cooking with its soulful singing and dancing naturally takes place. Finally, the third step of the recipe highlights a prescription for unique creative action that carries the experienced transformation back into your everyday. In summary, you must build a big room, get spiritually cooked, and then share your expansion, warmth, and altered action with the world.

The next chapters present the recipe for setting your soul on fire. In the beginning, the existential room of your life must profoundly expand. You must establish a space that is vast enough to hold the most powerful life-changing spiritual experience. If you build it, the numinous will come. However, if the room you are in is not large enough to welcome and host that which awakens sacred emotion, then nothing you do—including going through the motions of prayer, song, and dance—can light a spiritual fire. While this may seem obvious, it is actually one of the most difficult skills to master in the ecstatic transformative arts. Nothing big can happen unless a big room has been built. Make room for infinity and divinity will follow. This may be the most revolutionary act of Sacred Ecstatics: give up trying to change yourself or others and instead change *the room*. Do so wherever you are—make the surrounding existential space broad, deep, and high enough for the miraculous to happen. Bring down the walls of Jericho and make room for the entire universe. This is step one of the Sacred Ecstatics recipe where you must roll up your sleeves and get to work as a mystical construction worker.

Gary Holy Bull describes how the Lakota elder, Frank Fools Crow, could render any room sacred no matter how humble:

> Old man Fools Crow would pray in the basement of a metal shanty and it would be like praying in the middle of the most beautiful place in the middle of the prairie. We should never forget that wherever we pray, that spot becomes the center of the universe for that moment. (Keeney 1999a, 86)

Fools Crow made the room bigger by the way he sincerely prayed. Old-fashioned religious action is what turns a tiny closet into the cosmic prairie. It makes "one little room an everywhere," to borrow a phrase from English poet, John Donne. The opposite is true as well. You can be in the largest physical space with all kinds of sacred ornamentation and still find yourself in a cramped room if you personally have not erected a big room inside your heart. Building the big room requires exiting existential landscapes that are fully occupied by self-centered concerns that choke the oxygen needed to light a spiritual fire. Move instead toward the biggest picture that includes the Creator of all creation. Begin with a sincere prayer like that offered by Lakota Chief Yellow Lark, "Oh, Great Spirit, whose voice I hear in the winds, and whose breath gives life to all the world, hear me, I am small and weak, I need your strength and wisdom."

It is not enough to contemplate an abstract infinite universe where you are some kind of spiritual astronaut floating around in higher consciousness. Such an imagined journey usually takes place in the same small mental screening room that projects whatever images satisfy the reigning monkey mind of your "kingkongsciousness." The required expansion primarily refers to making enough room for you to *feel* the sacred rather than only conceptualize or envision it. If holiness is not felt, then the room needs to be made larger. You need to both build a big room *and* step into it with your whole body. Impassionate outside viewing misses the experiential immersion that ignites sacred ecstasy, the sought heartfelt closeness with the Great Spirit whose eye is on the lark, sparrow, and all who pray and sing in both need and praise.

Building a big room leads to a major part-to-whole existential adjustment: Every aspect of your life becomes realigned as an active part or *part*icipant in the big room of mystery, rather than your erroneously pretending to be the whole show with no room for anyone else, let alone the divine. When you take your rightful place as a small part inside the greater whole, it is analogous to the firm push against your back that provides a spinal realignment, brought forth with a chiropractic "pop." A joyful noise and ecstatic spark take place the instant you shift your spiritual alignment with the divine spine, the rope to God.

Many conventional spiritual practices, so-called shamanic methods, and healing protocols take place in a small room where the sacred is reduced to being a tool or power that is harnessed and directed by the practitioner. The quick and easy-to-learn techniques offered by the spiritual marketplace disregard the more important skill of building a room that is able to host higher empowered change. What typically takes place is a small room, trickster-led imitation of the real thing. Compare this to the Guarani shamans who won't even tell a story, let alone attempt healing, until they have built up a sacred context through several days of singing, praying, and dancing. As Ava Tape Miri told Brad:

> Before I tell a sacred story, I usually dance to prepare myself for three or four nights in the sacred hut, called the *nande ru rog*. This is required before I teach sacred knowledge. When someone comes with a sickness, I must also prepare myself. It makes me ready to receive a dream that contains the necessary directions for the cure. (Keeney 2000, 40)

You cannot viably enact spiritual work within a shrunken, shallow space by merely adding spiritual words or ritualized action. You must build a big room whose far-reaching sacred foundation is surrounded by an atmosphere of complex, always perplexing divinity. If your spiritual home is built upon the bedrock of infinity, it will be able to host whatever spiritual blessings and gifts are meant for you and withstand any storms and challenges that come your way. Ask yourself what foundation and container house your life: a flimsy card table holding a house of cards where you reign as king or queen, or the enduring rock on which stands the big room of mystery?

Moving from Small Glass to Vast Sea

A Zen story about an aging master who grew tired of his apprentice's complaints illustrates the importance of living inside a big room:

One morning, the master sent his apprentice to get some salt. When the apprentice returned, the master told him to mix a handful of salt in a glass of water and drink it.

"How does it taste?" the master asked.

"Bitter," said the apprentice.

The master chuckled and asked the young man to take the same handful of salt and put it in the lake. The two walked in silence to the nearby lake. Once the apprentice swirled his handful of salt in the water, the old man said, "Now drink from the lake."

As the water dripped down the young man's chin, the master asked, "How does it taste?"

"Fresh," remarked the apprentice.

"Do you taste the salt?" asked the master.

"No," said the young man. The master then sat beside this serious young man and explained, "The pain of life is pure salt; no more, no less. The amount of pain in life remains exactly the same. However, the amount of bitterness we taste depends on the container we put the pain in. So when you are in pain, the only thing you can do is to enlarge your sense of things. Stop being a glass. Become a lake. Better yet, become a vast freshwater sea."

Everyday minor irritations, more challenging difficulties, and major suffering all bring an invitation to enlarge the space that holds your experience. If you are not careful, an emphasis on relieving pain and alleviating symptoms can distract you from the vast sea and throw you inside a small glass where the bitter taste keeps you focused only on your troubles. For instance, consider what happens when others prompt you to join them in discussing "issues," "problems," "disturbances," "funks," "upsets," "setbacks," "calamities," "catastrophes," or any other name for life's "bitterness," whether it is regarded as theirs, yours, or shared. It is easy to get caught in a vicious cycle that continuously salts the conversation with bitter talk. This might include detailing what books, therapists, or coaches have advised, as well as specifying historical details, meanings, and stories about the concern, hypothesizing underlying causes, and anything else that revolves around the bitter theme.

Without being aware of it you place your suffering, which is actually only a *part* of your experience, inside too small a container where it gets over-concentrated and magnified until it appears to be the illusory *whole* of your life. Inside this constricted and condensed space, everything tastes bitter.[9] The first step of Sacred Ecstatics is to reset your relationship with the universe so that you return to residing inside the whole mystery of life. Here is found a multitude of experiences that will likely still include the bitter salt of suffering, though it is now in the company of other important ingredients and seasonings such as humor, play, invention, curiosity, exploration, creative tinkering with the unknown, experiments with God, and all the rest of life's too often forgotten possibilities. It is important to note that we are not suggesting that suffering doesn't exist or should not be addressed. We are suggesting that any partial experience, whether bitter or sweet, is better related to as a *part* rather than the whole of life.

---

[9] Supplementary content to this chapter has been articulated in books we have written specifically for the field of psychotherapy. It is beneficial reading for anyone conducting a session, whether they call themselves a coach, consultant, counselor, therapist, shamanic practitioner, or spiritual healer. For those seeking more detailed and elaborated discussions of the three-act structure with its construction and circular movement of distinction, indication, and contextual frame, see *The Creative Therapist* (Keeney, 2009), *Circular Therapeutics* (H. Keeney and B. Keeney, 2012), *Creative Therapeutic Technique* (H. Keeney and B. Keeney, 2013), *Recursive Frame Analysis* (H. Keeney, B. Keeney, and Chenail, 2015), and *The Creative Therapist in Practice* (H. Keeney and B. Keeney, 2019b).

When partial experience becomes inflated (whether regarded as a problem *or* solution, failure *or* success, darkened shadow *or* enlightened halo), life seems over-seasoned with a singular ingredient that makes it taste too bitter, foul, or sickeningly saccharine. Furthermore, trying to squeeze the whole universe inside a small glass called "ME" is incredibly exhausting, alienating, disorienting, and disheartening work. An inflated self that resides in a deflated container gives rise to all manner of spiritual dis-ease, the discomfort found from living in shrunken headquarters. If you don't have enough room to ecstatically move about, your mystical muscles atrophy, your heart loses it soulful beat, and your head aches as it tries to put on the brakes to what can never be stopped — the underlying changing force behind life itself. Instead of taking your troubles to the big room of First Creation, any negative experience is held hostage in a Second Creation small room where trickster gets busy naming, framing, and blaming it on psychological dysfunction, personality disorder, chemical imbalance, astrological misalignment, family consternations and constellations, spiritual dis-ease, metaphysical foul breeze, and so on. This is how trickster reduces your life to traumatic pathology rather than shakes it free with ecstatic seismology.

Realignment that resituates you inside the vastest whole brings the snap, crackle, pop, and spark that lead to a whole reality change. Only this kind of room adjustment makes the impossible dream possible, including a sea that parts for your safe crossing into mystery. Realigning, resituating, resetting, refreshing, and re-seasoning the whole of your life requires re-building and reentering the big room where whatever was previously too inflated, magnified, or exaggerated is now made a well-proportioned part again and put in its rightful place. The expansion of the big room resets both the whole and the parts of you, readjusts your relationship to the vast experiential universe, clears the stage, cleans the slate, and prepares the way for a new beginning in a more ecstatic life where spiritual cooking brings more light and delight than small room mirror looking.

Step one of the recipe asks that you first cease all habits of conversation, thought, and action that keep you in a small container. Then proceed with the most important spiritual journey of them all—a voyage to the big room where higher mystery power heals all schisms, that is, makes everything hallowed and whole again. Get out of the little glass, the tiny room, the miniscule ceremonial circle, the miniature church, the microscopic ashram, and the small universe holding them all. Even leave behind the unnecessary choice between maintaining a positive or negative attitude, exalting the former while vilifying the latter. Make room for both and then make even more room to notice how each always brings the other along! Balian (shaman) I Gusti Gede Raka Antara from Bali told Brad:

> I learned that good always comes with the bad. They are in the same home. If some good happens, look out for the bad. I have learned to respect both sides and to work carefully within the space that holds them. (Keeney 2004, 88)

Don't get caught in a small room that exclusively searches for solutions, maintains non-critical outlooks, projects wishful affirmations, and obsesses over fostering the right intentions. These life themes are simply too experientially limited, one-sided, and creatively cold compared to the broader container that hosts unbounded experiential diversity and complexity. The big room welcomes the contrary partners of suffering and joy, the long-term marriage of problems and solutions, the fraternal twins of dark and light, and the parental duo of negativity and positivity. Instead of chasing the fantasized monasticism of isolates who live separate from the world, encourage both sides—inside and outside—to dance as equally involved partners who interact with a relational embrace that includes every other opposite conceived. Without contraries, as William Blake proposed, there is no progression—no means of interacting, differing, contradicting, counterpointing, harmonizing, blending, splitting, embracing, rejoining, changing, transforming, morphing, and dancing in the greater vastness. Go all the way to the big room where interacting relations rather than separated monads live. Why limit yourself to the miniscule shot glasses and thimbles of individual psychology, self-improvement, selfish prosperity religion, non-ecological spiritual isolationism, socially uninvolved secular monasticism, or the like when you can live inside the infinite realm of the big room?

In summary, no matter what struggles come your way, act in order to expand rather than shrink your surroundings. Never forget that some of the wisest and most cooked spiritual people also had lives of great hardship. Head for the big room adventure rather than only chase the small room ease that has never cured spiritual dis-ease. When the room containing your life is big enough, whatever you spiritually need arrives without asking. This is the hidden and most often silenced secret of existence—get into the big living room where everything immediately falls into its changing place. There you receive the spiritual sustenance you need to face and embrace the ups, downs, laughter, frowns, and surprising turnarounds that take you on the most exhilarating ride of your life.

Skillful Talk

Step one of the recipe begins in the cooler temperatures and smaller rooms where talk and thought are the primary operations. Here you must wisely use words to widen, deepen, and heighten the space. Practically speaking, your speech should attend to whatever expands and warms rather than shrinks and chills. This can include off the charts humor, wild creativity, absurd kidding, unimaginable inspiration, or irrational surprise. While it is not always necessary to be extreme or encourage an outlandish dream, make sure you introduce enough of a difference that brings a noticeable ripple to the pond. Reach for whatever might shake and release you and others from cramped existential quarters. As we noted in chapter two, to turn up the spiritual heat you must move from the constriction of hardened dualism and clichéd literalism to the expansion of metaphor and creative evocation. Whatever maintains your imprisonment inside small-framed living should be teased apart and jiggled loose.

It cannot be emphasized enough that simply adding spiritual words to a conversation or interjecting a symbolic action (e.g. reciting an incantation, reading a scripture, lighting a candle, burning a sage, or bowing) does not in and of itself build the big room. Spatial expansion comes from the skillful introduction of expansive metaphors and their ongoing linkage over the course of the conversation. If someone comes to you for help, simply recycling the previous Zen parable or talking about smallness and vastness will not necessarily deliver that person from trickster's tight grip. Talking about big things in a small room usually shrinks whatever vastness such talk was intended to evoke—even deep spiritual truths then sound more like clichés, bromides, and platitudes. Often the initial room is too constricted and cold to immediately introduce ritual, prayer, or anything that seems spiritual. You must first take an exit from the immediate shrunken situation.

For example, we had someone tell us at the beginning of a session, "I am very sad because I have not experienced God." At that moment we faced the temptation to get sucked into a small room that would keep his life riveted to the theme of "sadness" or the equally small room that would overanalyze the ontology of

God, the philosophy of deism, or the theology of religious experience. We, however, regarded the client's communication as a metaphor about bitter salt in need of dilution rather than further concentration. Whether you are a spouse, parent, son, daughter, friend, neighbor, teacher, coach, therapist, or healer—further emphasizing a person's psychological state, interpretation of reality, or going to battle with whatever metaphorical salt is in hand will diminish rather than enrich the stage on which life is performed. Instead, we addressed the grander action theme of "finding God" and asked, "Where have you searched for God? Have you looked in religious buildings or at the smiles of children, the songs of birds, or in a jar of honey? What about your backyard garden, the local music store, or the best ice cream shop in town? Where have you been looking?" This immediately opened, expanded, enriched, and enlivened the room. Notice that we did not respond by saying, "Don't be sad, God is everywhere and always with you." That statement does not connect with the man's experience and therefore would not serve as a bridge from the current constricted situation to a roomier space. The initial response, including the metaphor(s) introduced, must both match and mismatch the situational moment—partly fitting and partly not fitting the present context. This stretch between common and uncommon experiential territory is the bridge from one room to another. Moving on with the session, we next surprised our client by asking whether we should continue our talk in a nearby park, bakery, or even a theatre adding, "Perhaps it will be easier to find God there, rather than in this room." It mattered less whether he understood or was confused by this inquiry. What was more important is that all of us experienced the room become more alive as its existential reach expanded.

Keep in mind that it is not necessary to bring people to an actual sacred geographical place in order to feel a surrounding mystery, though it may sometimes help. The big room also does not have to be explicitly named. It is something that experientially manifests as the ongoing weave of metaphors enables more and more of life to be included rather than excluded. Again, you can't just name this expansion by saying, "Let's take this to the big room," and then expect to instantly experience yourself inside it. You have to walk toward the big room while building it — a conversational journey whose metaphors surprise, further link, and continuously expand rather than redundantly bore, increasingly fragment, and repeatedly shrink. When you hear someone's plea for help, above all else recognize that this is voiced inside a small room. Don't get sucked into that shrunken space and only deal with its broken parts; act to change the whole room. Introduce unknown ideas, unexpected action, unimagined possibilities, and unmet inspirations lying outside the small room walls where truly mysterious actualities reside and preside. Rather than fight and fuss with suffering in a small glass, take an exodus to the big lake, sea, and oceanic bliss where expansion liberates constriction. Here metaphors and themes subsequently arise to bring more life and further expand the room as it pulls you further inside.

Consider again the previous example of a client frustrated by an unsuccessful quest to experience divinity. Later in the session when the room had sufficiently expanded we asked him, "Can you imagine how frustrated or bored God must be with human beings? If you were going to do something to lift God's spirit, what would it be? Would you consider painting "Hello!" or a one-of-a-kind sacred symbol on the top of your roof? Would you fly a kite that carries a personal invitation asking God to have lunch with you? If you're really serious about making a divine connection, you have to be willing to do something odd for God. Maybe you should forget your own sadness and do whatever you think would make God smile."

The same kind of expansive handling of an uncomfortable downslide in life also applies to how you house an uplifting victory. Any enjoyable success, whether it involves career, finances, family, or spiritual accomplishment, brings the same choice in regard to existential container as personal disappointment and failure. The most important consideration is what room will hold your experience: a small room entirely filled by you and your presumed knowing or the big room with space for more people, all of nature, and the gods without any understanding standing in the way? Are your conversations focused only on observing and evaluating your life, determining whether you are succeeding or failing, happy or unhappy, healthy or sick, prosperous or poor? Or are you inside the big room evaluating less and experiencing more of the whole mystery show with all its spirited emotion, commotion, and change?

Building the big room requires a progression from "observing" to "serving" — going past constant self-assessment (and assessment of others) and instead taking action that moves your life and your relations with others to a more lively creative space. Move from small room mindfulness to big room soulfulness. If your daily conversations are fixated on attracting desired outcomes, repelling bad influences, catching positive vibes, cleansing negative energy, and the like, then you are still in a small room container. Outside the mind's puddle of names and scramble game lies the vast, multicast body of the uncharted sea.

It is important to develop a discriminatory nose that can smell whether the room of your experience is shrinking or expanding. If you can't discern whether you, another person, or your interaction is in a shrunken box versus a wide-open expanse, then you will find it difficult to raise the temperature enough to get spiritually cooked. Don't underestimate how skillful talk can contribute to expanding the room. There is extraordinary transformative power in the kind of conversation that opens, extends, lifts, and deepens life — and most importantly, makes you and everyone present ready to make the subsequent leap into the spiritual heat.

Take My Hand

The beginning conundrum in any sincere spiritual journey toward the big room is this: you can't easily pull yourself up by your own bootstraps, using the thought, talk, and action found inside a small room as the means of escaping it. It is not possible to skip step one of the recipe—where the room gets bigger and you get smaller—to jump into the spiritual cooking of step two. To escape a small room and experience expansion requires first giving up your seat on the throne of an imagined isolated kingdom. Recognize your limitations, *feel* the need for divine help, and then ask for it; all of this is required to ignite an ecstatic fire.

Guarani shaman, Tupa Nevangayu, describes how he readies himself before healing: "When I put myself into a prayerful attitude, I speak with great humility, acknowledging that I am nothing as a person. I confess that I am simple flesh made of dirt. This attitude helps to make me a cradle for the soul" (Keeney 2000, 61). This kind of prayer is not a strategy for feeling mystically empowered, spiritually righteous, morally superior, or piously inflated. Nor is it a trick to rally the forces of the spirit world to do your bidding. It is also not "a pity party that wallows in feeling shitty," as an old medicine woman once told Brad. Rather such an attitude is sincerely felt as a transformative truth inside the big room, bringing the peace and exhilaration of smallness, as well as the tenderness that enables your heart to be pierced and soul set on fire by the greater all-ness.

Often people who come to Sacred Ecstatics long to be spiritually cooked but soon find it difficult to get to the big room fire, realizing they don't feel a sufficiently direct or intimate connection to the divine. It is far better to truly face and feel the absence of this connection than to rationalize it away. You have to get real honest in order to get reeled in by the Big Holy. More than anything, you need to sincerely *feel the need* for help from a higher hand. This wisdom request is expressed in the lyrics of the classic gospel song by Thomas A. Dorsey, "Precious Lord, take my hand; lead me on, let me stand." Without exception, and independent of the spiritual tradition followed, those who are able to build a big room are holding onto a holy hand, praying to be led in the right direction. Asking for divine intervention with sincere contrition is experientially required to expand the room of your life, but such need must be felt rather than momentarily imagined. Feel the need and then further deepen that feeling by putting it in a soulful song. Music is the purest and surest means of expressing the longing of the heart.

If you must, go ahead and try again to be the captain of your soul until you bankrupt, exhaust, and extinguish every particle of belief that you can build and pull yourself into the big room on your own. Only in this defeat are you made ready to feel that nothing else is left to do but reach toward the heavenly sky and wholeheartedly ask that a higher hand lead you on. Don't mess around with lesser spiritual entities, deities, ghosts, spiritual hosts, and forms that seem cool and trendy to your mind. Reach for the highest and most trustworthy embodiments of holiness with whom you can feel a personal relationship. In other words, be less inclined to ask for help from a fantasized "power animal" or a "channeled spirit." Why take another trip on trickster's merry-go-round when you can be in touch with the indisputable holy ones that ancient wisdom keepers relied upon?

The further away from the main source your prayer is sent, the less you receive in return. For instance, Black Elk's prayers first addressed the highest power before he cited any of its relations. The same was true for Frank Fools Crow, who advised people to ". . . remember and think about the closeness of Wakan-Tanka. If you live in this wisdom, it will give you endless strength and hope." Pray first to the Creator, and then allow this higher source to introduce you to a distant relative if that is the Creator's will.

Praying to the creator as a heavenly parent or grandparent helps your mystical umbilical cord—your rope to God—emotionally come to life, and this assures that more blessings will be felt. While it may pique your curiosity to imagine asking an entity from another planet for cosmic insight or to imagine the ghost of Jung tutoring you in mythological understanding, it is less likely that you will call upon them if you or your loved ones are in desperate critical need. Reach instead for the utmost hand whenever you seek the mightiest help, wisest guidance, deepest inspiration, and warmest friendship.

Your own suffering, and that of others, is a reminder to search for a solid bridge that can carry you across troubled waters. Ask yourself right now, "Whose hand do I wish to hold in the most troubling times?" The right answer to this question must be felt in the depth of your heart and inspire a tear, giggle, wiggle, or song rather than an abstract thought. The moment you stop being the boss of you, admit you're lost, and faithfully plead for help, the small room walls collapse as a holy hand grabs hold and pulls you into the big room. Building the big room requires that your hands be held by a First Creation carpenter's hand, someone familiar with the nails of n/om. They are needed for the construction of a mystical house of ecstasy that is beyond all scientific measure and earthly pleasure.

Spiritual Masonry: Laying the Right Cornerstone

Building the big room involves clearing away whatever blocks your having an intimate encounter with divinity. As always, this requires taking action—asking for a higher helping hand to bring a broom and help you sweep. This special combination of human action and divine assistance is assembled in prayer, the core activity of nearly every religion. Prayer is communication with the ineffable, whether it is asking for help, expressing devotion, or expressing deep emotional affection. In terms of spiritual engineering, prayer lays the stones of a foundation capable of holding up the infinite. Whether spoken, chanted, or sung, the prayer words chosen, their sequencing, weaving, and the emotional tone and rhythm in which they are expressed are equally important in this spiritual masonry. Not just any prayer will work. Saying, "God, please give me the winning lottery number" does not lay the same foundation as "The Lord is my shepherd; I shall not want." Do not ask for specific experiences as if you are ordering goods from a catalogue, and don't try making a deal or placing a bet with a wheel of fortune. God and the universe do not exist to serve your desires, especially when the latter usually lead you astray. It's easy to see how ridiculous it is to pray for an expensive car or a vault full of gold, but you should be equally careful about praying to receive spiritual gifts, titles, and achievements. Such a personally defined request may inadvertently render spiritual experience a commodity, implying it can be ordered on demand by consumer command. Voice a wisdom-saturated prayer that assuredly aligns you toward the big room and then get out of the way. This is what is meant by the phrase, "getting right with God."

Introduce yourself to the utmost spiritual law of attraction: big rooms attract profound wholeness and small rooms attract trivial partiality. As the room expands, so does the nature of your prayers. Hence you are protected from making petty requests as you move away from ego's shallow wishing well. Here we find that the New Age/New Thought belief in the power of intention and attraction simply makes a monstrous part–whole error. It is the room holding thought that attracts, not any particular thought inside it. Divine-centered contexts attract sacred mystery and make your emotional relationship to the numinous stronger, whereas self-centered contexts attract more inflation of your trickster mind while cutting off reception of higher gifts that may include bitter lessons as well as sweet blessings. Before making a prayer, make sure your room is big enough to receive a more wholesome reward.

The cornerstone is the first stone set in the construction of a foundation, and all other stones are laid in relationship to it. Start with the right stone and you end up with a foundation strong enough to hold the big room. If the first stone isn't right there is nothing you can do afterwards that can build the foundation you need. Unless you are already thoroughly spiritually cooked, it is best to not trust your choice of words to get a prayer started. After all, your mind will most likely only want to keep you in the smallest space where it already rules over your status quo. Instead, turn to the prayers that have endured the ages and belong to a wisdom lineage whose mystics, saints, rabbis, preachers, teachers, gurus, learned cuckoos, devoted kneelers, and de-schooled healers lived inside the big room.

For example, when one of the disciples asked Jesus how they should pray, The Lord's Prayer was offered. It begins with the cornerstone, "Our Father which art in heaven, hallowed be Thy name." Here you are situated in a masterfully aligned part-whole setup right from the start, accomplished by suggesting that you are a spiritual child in relationship with a heavenly parental figure. At the same time, the latter's name is made hallowed, and this declaration lays down the first sacred building stone. The next line of the prayer, "Thy kingdom come; Thy will be done, in earth as it is in heaven," extends the ground floor by setting what takes place on earth inside the big room of heaven. The request that guidance be administered by "Thy will" openly declares that God is in charge rather than your small room mind. Note that it is not only the words of this prayer, but their sequencing that contributes to building the big room. You first set down a sacred cornerstone and as other stones are added to the prayer you build upon the space created. By the time you have set earth inside heaven and yourself along with it, you are ready to be fed otherworldly bread. Notice that "give us this day our daily bread" is not uttered in the beginning because you are not yet in a room big enough to receive its nourishment. In addition, no bread can be made until the spiritual temperature is hot enough for cooking. You first must feel the need that you are among the least before you can knead the flour and add the yeast that yields wonder-working flour power. By the time you get to the supper table, your heart and soul are ready to be fed holy bread, bringing forth an experience of extraordinary love. You are then able to do what you couldn't do before—easily love everyone, including your next-door neighbors and faraway enemies.

Holy bread is the sacred vibration, n/om, seiki, or the holy spirit that carries intense sacred emotion, an infinite fire of love so great that it surpasses all reason. It enables you to forgive your debtors as your spiritual parent forgives you through an immense, unconditional love that pours from the biggest heart. "And forgive us our debts, as we forgive our debtors." In other versions of the prayer the word "debt" is "trespasses," which refers to people violating any boundary, whether stealing, inflicting harm, or claiming that which is not theirs to claim. In some versions of the prayer the word is "sin," so you forgive other's sins as your sins are forgiven. The important point here is that after being fed the sacred emotion of divine love, you are so spiritually cooked and filled with ecstatic joy that you are able to lovingly forgive all of creation, including those who have trespassed on your life, are indebted to you, or have sinned in ways that harmed.

You will soon be returned to the world, recognizing that trickster mind will try to pull you back into a small room. This is when you pray, "And lead us not into temptation." The temptation is to exit the big room and return to the small containers, bottles, boxes, and rooms. Shrunken living encourages the false impression that you are bigger than you actually are. That is how you are led to "evil," the desperate acts and "eye for an eye" just-ice of someone trapped in a small room and out of divine alignment. Pray to avoid such experiential shrinkage and emotional detachment from infinite mystery—"protect us from evil." Finally, remember to lay the last stones that are a reminder that the whole of your life takes place inside the vastest space. The big room shall always be the residence and source of higher power and ecstatic glory throughout time: "For Thine is the kingdom, and the power, and the glory forever and ever."

Any of the classic prayers of the world religions help you lay the first cornerstone of the big room if you sincerely speak them with an open mind and pierced heart. The beginning of Black Elk's prayer also gets you started right: "Grandfather, Great Spirit, once more behold me on earth and lean to hear my feeble voice. You lived first, and you are older than all need, older than all prayer. All things belong to you . . ." Again, the names spoken in a prayer must be made hallowed and this only happens when you are made hollow—empty enough for vibratory spiritual power to come through you. When you're empty, you become a temple, and when you're feeble, you pass through the eye of the needle. The prayer of St. Nicholas of Flue also helps clear the ground for building the big room:

> My Lord and my God,
> remove far from me whatever keeps me from You.
> My Lord and my God,
> confer upon me whatever enables me to reach You.
> My Lord and my God,
> free me from self and make me wholly Yours.

The beginning act of Sacred Ecstatics—the first step of the recipe for setting your soul on fire—requires laying down the cornerstone of a hallowed name to build a sacred foundation whose holy verses erect the universe where communion with the divine is made possible. During this construction process you find that the big room only comes together if you infuse your expression with steadily increased doses of affection. As you build the big room, you are drawn further inside it. This is what brings transformational realignment—you become a full-fledged, fully activated participant inside the whole of creation. When you start praying, you are in Second Creation and it is you who is voicing the prayer. When the prayer room is sufficiently expanded and heated, it becomes charged with a sacred vibration that carries you nearer to the center of the room. Prayer then speaks, sings, and dances you. Make prayer more than a part of your life; make it the whole room. As Guarani elder, Tupa Nevangayu (in Keeney 2000, 62) states: "the life of a shaman is the life of prayer. This is most essential. If a shaman prays hard enough, the gods will come to give what is needed."

The Rope to God is a Song:
Your Link Between Earthly Ground and Heavenly Sky

The rope to God describes exactly what a Bushman n/om-kxao sees when the room is vast and they are cooking at a very high temperature. In the spiritual fire of First Creation you may envision a thread, string, cord, or rope. It is attached to your body and goes straight up and down, serving as a link between earthly ground and heavenly sky. In a sense you are like a puppet with a string that is pulled by the puppeteer above. Remember again that this same line of connection is also used as a spiritual telephone line and an electrical power line through which spiritual current is sent—an all-purpose, multitasking spiritual rope. It is the experienced (rather than merely conceptualized) divine axis of the spiritual universe. Its means of communication, power, transport, and guidance is something strongly felt by the whole body rather than only realized as a state of consciousness. The rope is made of sacred emotion and it sets your ecstatic climb in motion.

When you have a strong rope you are more reliably guided by higher power and better able to sustain presence in the big room. However, any time you lean toward trickster ideation your "rope to God will bend," as Bushman elders repeatedly point out. To straighten out the rope, you must do something you may have previously overlooked because you were never taught its mystical importance: you must sing a sacred song with all your heart. Elder Richardson of the sanctified church reminds us, "Without song, one stands in constant danger of stumbling down the path of error" (Hinson 2000, 3). Here we find an important teaching that is often ignored or forgotten—the vital importance of song. Without vibrant singing, your rope to God is too easily weakened and bent by trickster. When song is strong it makes thought bow to serve higher emotion. Without a song, emotion cannot become strong enough or be sustained long enough to rein in mental drift or its unruly rule. Any beginning spark or small flame of sacred emotion is too quickly and easily put out unless it is sufficiently amplified and fed by music, the most conductive means of emotional conveyance. Song is what empowers a healer or spiritual leader to perform sacred activity. As Guarani elder, Tupa Nevangayu, concludes: "The power of our shamans comes directly from the songs" (Keeney 2000, 88).

Pythagoras depicted the universe as an immense musical instrument with a single string, a monochord, connected at its upper end to spirit and at its lower end to matter. In this stretched cord between heaven and earth, the universe manifests itself as music. When your heart is tuned and ready, the angelic choir and the music of the spheres are heard. Join in and take a vibrational ride upon a melodic line. The rope to God is the string of this mystical, musical instrument. When plucked, you feel your heart touched, and because you are part of the string, you are also trembled and sung. The Sufis are Pythagorean-like string instruments, as are the Kalahari Bushmen and the Native American medicine people whose songs bring a personally felt relationship with the Creator and all of creation. Without a string, you cannot become a spiritual instrument, song, or vibration of prayer that trembles and sings with God.

The Bushmen regard the multi-string rope to God as the most important gift you can ever receive. As Motaope Saboabue describes its appearance, "When you dance and get hot, you will see the rope hanging from the sky" (Keeney 1999c, 61). /Kunta /Kace emphasizes, "The rope is the most important thing we know" (Keeney 2003b, 80). It is physically felt as a mysterious pulling. It is what pulls cooked speech, rhythm, music, and movement out of you. When it is said that you "own" a rope to God, it means that you "own the feeling" for and "own the songs and dances" from God. When the rope awakens, ecstatically lit song and dance spring forth.

Sacred Ecstatics begins with building a big room and then shifts to a top-down orientation—once inside the big room, the higher power flows down the rope from its source above. Anticipate the day when this rope will actually get a hold on you. Like a Bushman, you may receive "tappings"[10] from the rope, enabling a unique kind of tactile communication. You might feel a tapping on

---

[10] The Bushmen regard the body as a kind of alphabet and dictionary, referring to how they feel "tappings" on their body that provide communication with their surroundings. For example, a tingly feeling on the thumb indicates that a lion is near, while a tapping on the arm or shoulder is a message that a desired animal for hunting, such as an eland or kudu, is ready to be found (see Keeney and Keeney, 2015). In Brad's work in the Mississippi Delta region of northeast Louisiana, Brad found African Americans still aware of some of these body tappings in their everyday lives. Many people are familiar with the itch in the palm of your hand that signals that a gift will soon be received. In addition, it is not uncommon in a charismatic church service for a person to feel an invisible tapping on the shoulder, an indication of a divine house call.

your shoulder or a tingling in your leg as you are reminded to pay attention to something important. Through this rope, all things needed come to you. Wait for the spiritual electricity. It's coming down. Wait to get your instructions. They're on their way from up above. Pray to be changed, heated, charged, illumined, pulled, and led by your rope to God.

The size of the diameter of your rope depends on how strong it is, that is, how cooked you are. A weak cord looks likes a thread. As it gets stronger it appears as a string, and with further spiritual cooking it finally becomes a rope. Brad has seen the rope to God as the size of an elevator cable. He has also seen it so large that it held a whole church in the midst of angels, thunder, and lightning. Like other Bushmen n/om-kxaosi, as soon as he starts walking toward that cable, he takes a smooth visionary ride all the way to the big room of First Creation. It is less important that you see the rope; what is more important is *feeling* its tugging and pulling as it delivers the rhythmic pulse of soulful prayer, rhythmic chant, melodic song, and celebratory body movement. The rope to God is the link to everything sacred. It is absolutely required in order for spirituality to have any higher aesthetics and deeper ecstatics.

When you receive a rope to God, the sacred vibration is simultaneously instilled. Both arrive together. No rope, no sacred vibration. No sacred vibration, no rope. When you have both a rope and sacred vibration, something else takes place that is usually the biggest surprise of all. This is the moment when a new kind of soulful music is powerfully born inside of you. Sacred music is the living voice of the vibrational current that surges through your channel to divinity. Once you find your rope to God you realize that a sacred song is not merely entertainment or a familiar means of emotional excitement. It is the carrier of spiritual heat and holy electricity—conveying the sacred vibration of all spiritual power. "Precious Lord" and "Hare Krishna" both deliver a spiritual force of nature that can only be wholly appreciated in the hottest fire. If you don't have soulful, rhythmic music flowing through you, then there is no spiritual heat, no sacred vibration, no spiritual power, no rope to God, and no residency inside the big room of mystery.

There is a truth to saying that above all else, the installation of an inner divine jukebox is the most important spiritual gift. It is even accurate to say that music itself is the rope to God. The Bushmen have no ambiguity about this—a song is indistinguishable from the rope. Recall the prophet Isaiah's proclamation: "For ye shall go out with joy, and be led forth with peace: the mountains and the hills shall break forth before you into singing, and all the trees of the field shall clap their hands" (Isaiah 55:12). As Frank Fools Crow taught, the act of singing a holy song is what makes you a hollow bone ready to receive spiritual power.

Sanctified practitioners declare, "Song ranks as much more than 'just another' realm of expression. Song stands apart, vaulted to the very pinnacle of heavenly favor. In the eyes of the saints, song reigns as the chosen channel of celestial expression." God is also said to favor music and "reigns over all as the ultimate master of music" (Hinson 2000, 110). Even St. Augustine said, "He who sings, prays twice." Sanctified practitioners often prophesy, "There will be no preaching in heaven." Heaven is surely more like a concert hall than a lecture hall where spoken word hands itself over to music. Music is heaven's main activity, and what Hungarian composer Franz Liszt considered to be God's means of communication. When you stand inside the voluminous mystery room, you are infused with sacred song. The most powerful and magical spiritual gift is not a magic wand, hocus pocus incantation, healing formula, fairy dust, entheogen, talisman, medicine bundle, flying drum, glowing rattle, or power object; it is a special kind of song. The Guarani shamans say: "A sacred song is called *pora'i*. It is probably the greatest gift a shaman can receive. It is the shaman's link to the gods and to their powers" (Keeney 2000,

74). Tupa Nevangayu warns that shamans must continue to honor this musical gift because temptations will arrive to minimize its importance and block its reception:

> You have to be careful when you are receiving a sacred song. Evil knows when this is happening. It sends temptations so you have to be very strong when the spirit gives you any kind of gift. The sacred songs and sacred gifts bring good to the world, and evil doesn't want this to happen. Evil tries to stop you from being a shaman by throwing challenges at you. Many shamans leave their songs because of the way evil interferes with their life. (Keeney 2000, 74)

Trickster mind will try to make every argument it can to convince you that music is only one means, gift, tool, practice, or pathway to spiritual experience and that other ways are equally effective and strong. We join the ecstatic lineages that regard the soul itself as music and believe that without a song, you are lost. Furthermore, any diminishment of song's importance is an indication of separation from the divine. True soul retrieval is bringing the music back to someone who has lost touch with the way it can help everyone get spiritually cooked and feel the heated ecstasy that musically pours inside God's room. Shakespeare (*Merchant of Venice*, Act V, Scene I) concludes,

> The man that hath no music in himself, Nor is not moved with concord of sweet sounds, Is fit for treasons, stratagems, and spoils; The motions of his spirit are dull as night, And his affections dark as Erebus. Let no such man be trusted. Mark the music.

Joan Halifax also emphasizes the central importance of song as she speaks for the diverse shamans found throughout the world:

> As the World Tree stands at the center of the vast planes of the cosmos, song stands at the intimate center of the cosmos of the individual. At that moment when the shaman song emerges, when the sacred breath rises up from the depths of the heart, the center is found, and the source of all that is divine has been tapped. (Halifax 1991, 30)

Though the initial use of skillful talk and the stonemasonry of prayer lay the right cornerstone and expand the space, without a song you can't fully move from the colder temperatures of Second Creation to the spiritual heat of First Creation. A healer without a song remains spiritually cold and is not ready to heal or reel in others. A shaman without an emotionally evocative song is a pretender whose imaginary trip is missing the right rope grip. A preacher without a song can't open the hearts of a congregation. A spiritual seeker without a song has not entered the big room nor has the spark to light the dark. It matters not whether the song is heard as the holy sound of *Om* or the spirited singing of an old hymn, a newly minted tune, or the thrilling wild trill of a Canadian loon. The sound of the big room is music that conveys so much heightened emotion that its sacred vibration permeates the universe, including your flesh and blood. This passionately and tenderly sung high emotion is the throbbing heart, bobbing body, bowing mind, dancing bones, singing tones, and soul trombones of sacred ecstasy.

Forever Expanding Sacred Ground

Lakota elder Frank Fools Crow taught that you must become a "hollow bone" through which spiritual energy can move. To do this you must build a big room as you sweep away the inner chatter, questions, and dialogues that elevate trickster knowing.

When the hollow bone or hollow pipeline is clogged or the sacred ground is littered by rampant naming, interpretation, argumentation, and written law, as it was for the scribes and Pharisees, then access to divine mystery and its life-giving creative power become blocked. This was behind the admonition of Jesus when he said, "But woe to you, scribes and Pharisees, hypocrites! For you shut the kingdom of heaven in people's faces. For you neither enter yourselves nor allow those who would enter to go in" (Matthew 23:13). The conceptual clutter must be cleared and the inner space hollowed to enable the hallowed power to flow through.

Trickster mind serves one purpose: carving the whole fabric of life into discrete parts that can be sorted and re-sorted in any multitude of ways, an operation that can both help and hinder. Trickster may hold up a piece of anything that might attract and seduce and then tries to persuade you that this cutout part is the whole goal, outcome, truth, and holy grail you seek: "It's this, not that!" "It's here, not there!" "It's them, not us!" An emotionally felt rather than conceptually imagined trip to the big room immediately unsettles any and all of this kind of fixed conclusion trickery. Consider this wisdom voiced by Ralph Waldo Emerson, "People wish to be settled; only as far as they are unsettled is there any hope for them." The divine asks you to not only be unsettled and shaken loose, but to keep building an ever-expanding room that holds more and more mystery, doing so even when your mind protests. If necessary, tell your mind that your heart has decided to revolt so that your soul may gain an extra volt.

Brad experienced many spiritual traditions around the world and he found that each lineage offered something important that was found missing in the others. In Japan, seiki jutsu revealed the wisdom that comes from offering the least conceptual elaboration and discourse other than the occasional mention of a cosmic mystery that cannot and should not be over-discussed. Its greatest teacher and practitioner, Ikuko Osumi, was also devoutly religious. She had two altars in her prayer room—Shinto and Buddhist. Brad prayed with her, facing each altar and bowing before each tradition. She implicitly taught that when you move on the seiki bench without bowing to the largest mystery, you remain in a room too small for seiki to be fully present.

When Brad was led to finding and initiating a project to restore the oldest printing of the Zohar (annotated ancient books on Jewish mysticism which were discovered in a closet in Venice), he found another way of freeing the kernel of mystical light from its husk. In particular, a sacred word holds a spark, but its shell must be carefully removed in order to reveal the light and set the fire. Visioning the Sufi teachings of Ibn al-'Arabi, Brad was shown that people whose hearts are illumined and awakened by the divine are members of the same overarching mystical family. Whether praying with Hindu priests, shamans of the Amazonian rainforest, Zulu sangomas, or healers in the northern mountains of Argentina, remote farms of Mexico, or small villages of Brazil, he found that they were more alike in the ways that matter most. Everyone that the mystical rope led Brad to meet was a person ecstatically on fire and undisturbed by anyone else's religion or way of naming the primary source of creation.

At the same time, Brad discovered that there were largely unknown ecstatic spiritual traditions that had a unique contribution to offer the practical art of spiritual cooking. Whereas the seiki bench can help liberate you from excessive naming and the proliferation of trickster talk, it lacks the robust, combustible singing that touches the heart and further raises the spiritual temperature. In the Kalahari you learn to sing with others, and this gets you hotter than is possible when alone on the seiki bench without song. The more cooked you get, the more your spiritual audition awakens and for the first time you really hear that the gospel songs of the sanctified black church are actually powerful n/om songs, an infusion of old African ways into deep root truths about unconditional infinite love. While singing and dancing down the church aisles, you are then taken on a spiritual journey to even older Kalahari times, and you realize that its ecstatic knowhow has been lost in most other traditions, including those of Tibet, Japan, Europe, the Americas, and elsewhere.

At the same time, something remains lost or not yet found in the Kalahari. When things cool down, the post hoc chatter of mind, attributed to trickster, too easily diminishes the vastness of Kalahari sand with superstitions that lead to unnecessary precautions and ritualized preventions. The latter end up inhibiting heat more than defeating any agent of harm. The same happens in other ecstatic contexts, including the sanctified and holiness black churches of the United States, especially when the spiritual temperature doesn't get hot enough to reach the vastest love which is free of word-governed rule and inflexible order. Like the Shakers who stopped shaking and the Quakers who stopped quaking, people get easily entangled in mind's naming that blocks subsequent entry into the big room. The narrowly interpreted life then quashes the ecstatically performed broad way.

In the midst of ultimate mystery, anything and everything are free to keep changing and cross-pollinating. Persian sages deliver the extraordinarily heartfelt poems that reignite the dance of loving God. Here Islamic *kalam*, divine speech, meets *word souls* voiced by Guarani shamans. Both point to the Kabbalistic Tree of Life, now holding Bushman holy firewater ready to quench the thirst of a Buddhist monk sitting in a lonely cave wanting to take a stand and cast off his robe. In the outbreak of the St. Vitus dance another Kalahari saint is speared, and the Holy Mother is seen again not far from where nature is worshipped through hugging a tree, praying on a branch, and diving into baptisms of fire, water, earth, and sky.

Do you see, hear, smell, taste, and feel the divine movement here? Inside the big room of the Ouroborean whirling serpent every moment is always the first spin of creation, including the birth, death, and resurrection of the changing religions whose embodiment resides inside the minutia of infinite mystery. Here one spiritual form appears and disappears on a vastly breathtaking stage, each called to enter and exit as an incredibly transformative—though always unnamable—force behind creation brings ALL tingly things forth. Heed the prayer of Swami Veda Bharti, "May God's hand continue to sculpt your heart into the most beautiful and ever-new forms." In this morphing, empowered by the divine, it is not the spiritual dilettante, consumer, or thrill seeker who is in charge. There is a higher tower of power directing the shifting names and grounds on which holiness springs forth to germinate movement as it terminates anything stuck. Yield to this impossible-to-freeze truth and honor, celebrate, and love this mystery and all its holy names. Find again the hot, bright, pulsing truth voiced by Meister Eckhart: "Theologians may quarrel, but the mystics of the world speak the same language." As Ibn al-'Arabi professed this inclusion:

> O marvel! A garden amidst the flames! . . . My heart has become capable of every form. It is a pasture for gazelles and a convent for Christian monks, and a temple for idols and the pilgrim's Ka'ba, the Tables of the Tora and the book of the Koran. I follow the religion of Love: whatever way Love's camels take, that is my religion and my faith. (Ibn al-'Arabi 1911, 67)

Move on your seiki bench, praise the Lord's name, dance with the Bushmen, rock and sway with the prayers in a synagogue, whirl like a Sufi, get swept by a koan, and be ready to express all ways of becoming spiritually cooked. But first build the big room, enter it, and expect the divine to call you out and act around, upon, and through you. Be not concerned about the form or how long the change will last, leave, return, feast, or fast. Only request this in the big room: "Thy will be done." Don't worry if you are at a prayer meeting on Wednesday night, a sweat lodge on Friday, and singing Hare Krishna on Sunday, as long as you are moved and swung by your rope to God, equally ready to sing Fats Waller's verse, "Ain't nobody's business if I do." Move toward the fire that mystically and musically lights the dark and run away from any silent, still, and dark claim of unemotional enlightenment that is absent of song. Ignore any unnecessarily imposed sensory restriction, emotional constriction, and spiritual refrigeration. At the same time, be as grateful to be an immovable boulder as you are if called to be a rolling stone, hollow bone, or tuning tone. Allow the divine to take your dust and throw you to the wind, for however long and in whatever way, according to the universal will, ultimate testimony, and supreme law of the highest awe.

Make the most room you possibly can for the divine. It may be that the more religions you can authentically honor and love, the vaster your big room becomes. Brad once received a phone call from the daughter of a chronically ill man. He had only a few weeks remaining in his life. A renowned physician, Dr. Crowley was in his eighties and had lived a successful life. He was known for several inventions in anesthesiology, was a friend of Frank Lloyd Wright, and was an accomplished painter. When Brad met him, Dr. Crowley said he wanted to resolve something before he passed over. He told Brad his amazing life story:

> I am going to tell you something that my wife, children, and grandchildren have never heard. I read about you, Brad, and was led to call upon you because I think you can help me. My father was from Ireland and to escape poverty and find a better life for his family we immigrated to the United States. My parents eventually

landed in South Dakota where my father worked until he barely had enough money to purchase a small piece of land where he could farm. The land he wanted to obtain was owned by neighboring Lakota Indians. He went to their elders and asked if he could purchase a plot. They responded, "This land is our Mother. How can we sell her?"

My father went away disappointed but he was determined to get that land because times were hard and without land his family risked possible starvation. He came back several weeks later and asked, "What would it take for you to give me some land to live on?" The elders saw how serious he was and said they would get out the *chanupa* or sacred pipe and pray about it. "Come back next week," directed one of the old men. The following week, the elders told my father that they had decided to give him a piece of their land.

"What's the cost?" my father asked. An elder replied, "The cost of you having a piece of our Mother is you giving us a piece of your family. We will take your newborn son in exchange for her." Desperate to survive and support his family, with a broken heart and no other apparent choice, my father gave me away to the Lakota.

I grew up reared by medicine people. They taught me about their holy ways. The name given to me was Iktomi, the name of the trickster spider that holds special medicine, for I had a relationship with nature that included my being able to speak to the animals and cure them. My children still wonder why the birds and animals would come up to our front door and wait until I came out and spoke to them and sang some songs. This was what I was taught and who I am.

When I became an adult, I left the reservation to go to school, eventually becoming a medical doctor. I never told anyone where I came from. I married, raised a family, and had a career. I also become a devout Catholic and raised my children in the church. Now that my days are numbered, I ask you to hear what has burdened me. My question is this, "How can I exist in two different spiritual traditions? Is this a conflict?"

When Dr. Crowley asked this, he seemed to voice the question for Brad as well, since Brad had been called to participate in so many different spiritual traditions. Brad's answer to Dr. Crowley was for both of them. Without thinking, Brad felt connected to his original experience of spiritual fire and sacred ecstasy and replied, "God is big enough to hold all kinds of prayers, rituals, and songs. In His house are many mansions." Dr. Crowley smiled and replied, "Yes, of course."

Brad then noticed that Dr. Crowley's children and grandchildren were standing in the hallway listening, weeping with joy and amazement, for they had never heard any of this about their father. They always wondered why, when they visited the reservation, the old timers would say "Wakan" ("sacred") when their dad walked by. Dr. Crowley was holy and these holy people could sense it, as could the birds, deer, horses, dogs, bears, and other creatures.

Dr. Crowley and his family asked Brad to help perform his funeral. Brad did so in an Irish Catholic Church with the help of an open-minded young priest. There they celebrated with pipe and Bible, sage and holy water, visionary song and hymn, all being of equal importance and relevance to this man's life. Dr. Crowley lived in a big room that was larger than either a Catholic cathedral or Lakota tipi, while including room for the truths and expression of both.

It's time to bring greater immensity to your life, to release you from any small room constriction and place you upon sacred ground within the big room. We invite you to make this your new mantra: "First, go to the big room." Say this as often as possible. Make it a banner on your wall. Anytime you have an important decision to make, immediately say these wisdom words, allowing them to point you to the big room for making the decision. Discipline yourself to stop thinking about the right decision, right understanding, right cure, or right action. Instead, go to the big room. There the right question arises as does cooked thought, vibrant emotion, and anointed deed.

We are going to introduce an alternative metaphor that points to the big room, vast sea, and infinite mystery. It refers to a tremendous African desert called the Kalahari. This name is derived from the Tswana word *keir* that means "the great thirst." If you wish to set your soul on fire, become spiritually cooked, and quench your greatest thirst, know that you must mystically walk on Kalahari sand.

First, go procure some sand. You will need a little less than a cupful. Spread some of it on the top of a table or surface area that is near your bed. Place your matchbox on this sand while saying out loud, "In the big room, this is sacred Kalahari ground." Each morning when you wake up, place the tiniest pinch of sand inside each shoe. Pray this heartfelt request: "Precious Lord, take my hand as I walk on this sand, and bring me home to the big room." Then take each step that day as if you are walking, leaping, and dancing in the Kalahari. You truly are if your room is big enough for the changing of First Creation to make it so. Remind yourself that since the universe may be found in a single grain of sand, you are unquestionably walking upon the infinite. If doubt creeps in to shrink the room, follow the Bushman way and sing a tune. It's time you mentally appreciate, emotionally own, mystically activate, and ecstatically celebrate the sacred shifting sand—the vibrant changing within the big room—upon which you walk each step of your life.

4

GETTING SPIRITUALLY COOKED

Raising the spiritual temperature is inseparable from amplifying sacred emotion, the heightened joy that both inspires and is inspired by heartfelt praying, soulful singing, and spirited dancing. The special blend of intense emotion with rhythm, melodic tone, and movement awakens the sacred vibration, the ineffable spiritual current that feels like a fire in the bones. Once this fire is burning, step two of the recipe is in full effect as anointed gifts and roles come to life. These include the "pulling" of sickness in healing, the "pushing" of the sacred vibration in transmission, and the various forms of numinous communion, all made possible by spontaneous sound making, divinely willed song catching, involuntary body shaking, improvised celebratory dancing, and automatic vibrational touching. More than anything else, getting spiritually cooked is an immersion in an exhilarating higher atmosphere that aligns all of you with the divine. It leaves you transformed with an uncontested desire to return again and again to get cooked in the big room fire.

Getting spiritually cooked is the pinnacle experience of Sacred Ecstatics, and the recipe is all about getting you to the fire. The first step builds the big room whereas the last step brings you back ready to live in a radically transformed way. In the middle is found the strongest heat, the place of most dramatic alteration and highest transformation. This is when your soul is ignited and you feel the most alive you have ever felt. Once the fire is lit, spiritual cooking happens without contrived effort. In the vast grace of heated space, the divine is unambiguously in charge and whatever is needed takes place naturally and miraculously as long as you follow its lead. This is when you feel sacred ecstasy, the incredible joy of having a rope to God and being an instrument of its sacred vibration.

There is no way you can ignore the most basic operating premise of the oldest ecstatic spiritual tradition on earth: like the Kalahari Bushmen, you need a rope to God in order to get spiritually cooked. You can never become a true spiritual instrument unless you have been pierced, speared, hooked, or caught by divinity. A sanctified parishioner describes it this way, "Before God can use a man, that man must be hooked in the heart" (Johnson 1969, 19). With this heart-to-heart rope between you and the Creator in place, anything is possible. It can suddenly turn an ice cube into a sizzling flame, immediately empower a whisper to be as mighty as a roar, or readily reveal how an attention getting howl is simply chilly and foul. Once inside the big room, anything can shift, change, morph, or transform. In general, you cannot predict what spiritual temperature you will reach or how you will express yourself once your soul catches fire. Spiritual cooking and all its inspired expression happen beyond your control. It is your rope to God that regulates the ecstatic thermostat and wisely guides your action. Therefore, have no attachment to any outcome other than striking a match, catching fire, and getting cooked.

Striking the Match

In addition to expanding the room, the main operation of step one, you must also take action to raise the spiritual temperature until a fire ignites. It won't work to simply imagine that you are cooking while sitting there cold and still. Nor can you expect the leader of an ecstatic gathering to do all the work while you passively observe, hoping to suddenly burst into flames. Sacred Ecstatics is an "all hands on deck" experience. If you want to get cooked then do not hesitate — make your best effort to do your part to help start a fire and keep the room vast enough to host it. Do this in concert with others instead of acting independently — be a part of the group synchrony that creates a mutually enhancing symphony.

Such fire setting includes spirited hand clapping, thunderous foot stomping, soulfully aligned body rocking, highly contagious vocal chanting, uplifting bursts of shouting, heart-thawed choral singing, mood-altering humming, rhythmically thrilled drumming, deeply rooted praying, inventively crafted word playing, finely timed rhyming, any combination of these, or other spontaneous forms. For the seiki jutsu masters of old Japan, piercing sound staccatos, energetically released shrieks, and loud wall pounding help stir up the seiki and strike the match. In the Bushman way, singing and clapping get the Kalahari spiritual fire started. In the sanctified church, the match may involve an emotionally charged, rhythm-infused prayer, a singing, ringing, fire-flinging sermon, or a stirring rendition of an embellished, heart-enhancing gospel hymn. The particular means of igniting a spiritual wildfire are often unpredictable and always subject to change. What remains constant is that you aim to wake up and amplify the emotional current of the sacred vibration.

During the first step of the recipe your actions are more deliberate than spontaneous as you conduct the disciplined, purposeful work of building a big room. When the space is nearly expansive enough, you enter the transition point between steps one and two. Here you oscillate between self-directed willpower and the spontaneity inspired by feeling a higher power at work. After the match is struck and the fire is burning, all action becomes effortless and involuntary. During step two you let go of yourself and get out of the way so a higher means of control takes over. If you have previously received the sacred vibration, it now wakes up and automatically causes your body to tremble and shake. It's as if your rope—curled up in the resting position—springs to life and is thrown straight up to the sky and plugged into the electrical outlet on high. If you haven't been cooked before, simply stay on board the rhythm that gives your mind a reprieve and keeps moving you forward. No matter how many times you have made the ecstatic journey, always enter the big room as if for the first time—a child of God with a beginner's mind and a beginner's heart.

Once the fire is burning you are swept away by the tidal waves of intense sacred ecstasy—"waves of joy and gladness," the "rapture of love," and the "all of one endless smile" described in C.M.C.'s testimony. In the beginning of step one, however, how you act is more important than what you think or feel. Don't begin by complaining, "I am tired and weary and don't feel like doing anything" or "I am not inclined to clap my hands or dance because my shoulder was aching this morning." This kind of declaration anchors your presence inside the small room of a magnified self and its obsession with self-assessment. You have to do all you can to help expand and heat the room. Ecstatics advise that if you don't feel like singing, start singing anyway and "sing until you feel it." Once a fire commences, singing becomes effortless. As sanctified parishioners describe it, all expression is then "controlled by the Spirit rather than the self. At the moment of anointment, the self ceases to be a player. The only 'artist' in this devotional drama is the Spirit" (Hinson 2000, 145).

Heartfelt and soulfully expressed prayer also provides a good match for starting a fire. Pour your heart's longing and deepest need for God into the prayer until you feel its emotion energetically move throughout your body. Building up the emotion of devotion matters more than excavating the meaning of words and the interpretation of texts. Heat a prayer until your rising emotion hits an ecstatic threshold where an incredible reversal of praying is experienced. You start in the cold where discipline, effort, and willpower are required to do the work of prayer. But as you and the prayer climb the thermometer together, all this reverses and you suddenly feel prayed and played by the divine with no effort on your part. In the small room, you do the work and bring life to prayer. In the big room, God takes over so the prayer administers ecstatic life to you.

In the first physical movement of bowing before mystery, kneeling for prayer, clapping both hands in praise, shouting a response, or singing a song, you enact the first strike of a match. Simply remembering that you are already within the reach of God can be enough to create holy combustion. This is not just a conceptual recollection; it is a body memory of how it feels to be close to the burning bush and forest fire of divinity. As the gospel song says it, "God don't need no matches; He's fire by himself!" At the same time, you are the match, and the more friction there is in your life the better chance of getting a spark out of you. If you are too comfy and luxuriating in wealth and health, you may need to be roughened up around the edges by some old-fashioned suffering. If needed, look around and notice the suffering of others, realizing how the same could easily happen to you or your loved ones. Feeling ultimate joy requires also feeling the desperate suffering that renders you more tender tinder. The more you experience the ever-present coldness and darkness of the world, the more you will desire to come as close as possible to the warmth and light of a heavenly fire. Take hold of an ecstatic match and start the motion of swiping the match head against the rough edge of your life. With the right contact between sacred conviction and everyday friction, an ecstatic fire is ignited.

Without exception, the heat of spiritual pyrotechnics is raised, intensified, and further amplified by sacred emotion, your personal heartfelt relationship with the divine. If you do not feel such a connection, then feel your longing for it. Start with whatever sacred emotion you presently feel, remember you previously had, or long to own and then try to amplify it. Do this by regarding sacred emotion as a *call* for more jubilation and *respond* by voicing an appropriately matched celebration. There is a delicate balance here, because if you either underplay or inappropriately exaggerate your celebratory response, it will be incongruent with the degree of emotion you feel and this can short circuit the amplification process. Voice a sincere and wisely measured response to whatever sacred emotion you can muster, and then let the intensity of your next response increase just enough to effectively raise your feelings. The natural magic that takes place is found in how sincere celebration lifts the emotion it celebrates, which in turn, lifts your next enthusiastic response. This mutual escalation between felt emotion and expressed celebration fans the flames of the spiritual fire.

Such a circular interaction is the classic "call and response" found in ecstatic spiritual gatherings. This form is also found in music when one musician plays a phrase, followed by another musician answering back with another phrase that is neither an exact repetition nor too divergent, but a difference that continues to inspire another creative difference. Such a back and forth, mutually amplifying interaction was carried throughout the African Diaspora by enslaved Africans. In the United States and Caribbean it blended with the "lining out" method of call and response hymn singing spread by Protestant immigrants from England and Scotland, later called "Dr. Watts" style in the African American church (after English hymnodist Isaac Watts). John Wesley Work's study of African American folk music concluded that this music is organized so "rhythm arouses emotion and emotion arouses motion" (1915, 38). To elaborate this for Sacred Ecstatics: the pulse of ecstatic rhythm awakens exhilarating emotion and this in turn excites the vibration, trembling, and shaking of body motion. Once the call and response wheel of circular interaction is turning, each of its elements is simultaneously the cause and the effect of the others, perpetuating an ever-increasing rise of powerfully charged rhythm, musically conveyed sacred emotion, and celebrative physical commotion that transport you to ecstatic spiritual heights.[11]

At the first sign that you are moving toward a more expansive room, enthusiastically greet that movement. Feel free to shout, "Hello! Hello!" like the Shakers in St. Vincent whenever they feel a sudden closeness to the spirit. Or make room for a loud staccato burst of excited sound to emerge, like the *kiai* yell of karate or what Osumi Sensei would similarly release when seiki arrived. The further you go inside the big room and feel its vibrant pulse of life, announce your welcoming praise with more celebrative excitation. Strike your spiritual match and set in motion the virtuous circle of calling and responding that ecstatically escalates with each exchange. This is how you keep turning up the spiritual temperature.

Ecstatic traditions typically emphasize group interaction rather than solo spiritual practice. It's simply a matter of practical spiritual engineering—it is much easier to start and stoke a fire with other people rather than on your own. When you hold another person up in this same celebrative way, the spiritual temperature rises for both of you. The spirit becomes contagious and more easily spreads. Hinson elaborates:

> I asked Elder Richardson to plot the course of an anointed sermon, moving from his introduction in self to his climax in the Spirit. He started by noting, "I'm never willing to get out there on my own," [referring to

---

[11] For more a more detailed description of the call and response of emotion, motion, rhythm, and tone see our book *The Spiritual Engineering of Sacred Ecstasy* (2018).

the need for the whole congregation to clap, shout, and sing] "ever inviting the Spirit to shift the sermon into high gear." (2000, 160–61)

If you find yourself caught in the small room of narrating mind and unable to feel the spiritual heat of sacred emotion, try paying less attention to your inner talk and instead turn outwardly to clap and sing for others. By this we don't mean shifting your attention to observing other people. Instead you should be serving what helps them cook, especially holding up the leader(s) of the gathering. Take action to lift up others while curbing the calm and cool spectation that leads to cold separation. Participate rather than cogitate—this is what helps ignite and spread the spiritual fire for all who gather. While there is a time and place to light a match on your own at home, it is easier to generate spiritual heat and get cooked when you effectively interact with others, whether it's with one other person or many. Even interacting with a video or audio recording can help bring you inside the ring of fire. You must step inside a *coordinated* call and response that celebrates as you raise the spiritual temperature with rhythm, tone, movement, and emotion that steadily bounce back and forth. One of the reasons we enjoy conducting healing sessions in front of a group is because everyone's participation helps ignite, intensify, and spread the flames. This enables everyone to get cooked, not just the person having a session. Spiritual cooking with others is the ultimate spiritual enactment of human interdependence. It is a powerful experience that brings the relational web of life from abstract notion to experiential fruition.

When someone pretends, imitates, or fakes spiritual cookery, its chill of inauthenticity and egocentricity can threaten to bring down the spiritual temperature, tempting you and others to slide back into small, judgmental mind. This also happens when there are spectators in the room who are there to analyze and criticize rather than ecstatically catalyze. Their presence can easily throw you off. Some ecstatic traditions enlist a person for the spiritual job of "surveying" the ceremonial room, looking, listening, and feeling for any kind of distracting influence. If an outsider is not joining or supporting the gathering in an appropriate way, he or she may be helped, coached, or even asked to leave. This kind of caretaking of the big room and its spiritual temperature often takes place in ecstatic communities all over the world. However, whenever someone or something distracts you, you can also choose to shout, sing, dance, clap, or pray with more intensity and overcome any distraction that threatens to cool you down. The spiritual battleground is nothing like the gladiators of Rome or the Star Wars of good-versus-evil forces. It is the battle over cold and hot spiritual temperature, and the tug of war between a small and big room.

During the first moment that you catch fire you may appear like a fish the instant it has been hooked. You may jerk like your body is startled and trying to pull away from the fishing line. This is a natural response and a good sign that you have been spiritually hooked and are being reeled further into the heat. You notice that something has got a hold on you and that you are headed to the big kitchen frying pan. When this initially happens it might bring such a surprise that it triggers your narrating mind to quickly return and interrupt to ask, "What is happening? I feel something. Is this it?" Or, you might internally evaluate and declare, "This bliss is incredible! I wonder how long this will last?" Shifting the emphasis to a talking head that comments on what is taking place, whether with criticism or gratitude, disconnects you from the ongoing flow of spontaneity and whisks you back into a small room. This is a slide down the spiritual thermometer—you stop being cooked and fall back to a chilled trickster word spill. Whenever the ineffable grabs hold of you, surrender and do not resist, allowing sacred emotion to rise. Do this by staying on board and inside the coordinated rhythm, tonality, movement, praying, or singing around you. Be more intimately involved with and playfully attached to your body sense, movement, and emotion in spite of any spiritual advice that comes from emotionally chilled, immobile, body-negating teachers who forgot that they never got hot and were never spiritually cooked! Let the rhythm and music pull you further into the next ecstatic groove. Your mind must step down from its throne and allow your whole body to receive and express a downpour of emotion.

In summary, getting spiritually cooked begins with the kind of expression that strikes the match, starts the engine, switches on the light, and pushes the start button. As the room expands, enthusiastically celebrate to bring a corresponding emotional rise in the spiritual temperature. Set in motion this virtuous circle whose uninterrupted turning makes the room bigger and the temperature hotter. In this spinning mystical wheel of ecstatic emotion, celebratory commotion, and spirited motion, you climb the rope to God. Once the fire is lit, the engine is running, and you are caught and reeled into the big room, it is then only a matter of letting the higher power work on you, doing so until you have been cooked through and through. When your cooking time is done, you are thrown out of the fire to go back to the world again.

Keep it Sweet

If, during an ecstatic event, a person begins screaming as though possessed or acting out the "release of trauma" and the like, this is not spiritual cooking. Such a person has not crossed into the big room of First Creation but is acting out inside a smaller container of experience. Non-joyful chaotic agony, weirdly dissociated conflict, and awkward displays of power are not associated with sacred expansion and spiritual heat. Unfortunately, these outcomes are often misconstrued as a strong, authentic experience by newcomers to spiritual cooking. But true ecstatic transformation, including the welling up and release of sadness or grief, is always spiritually soft and sweet, even when its expression is extremely amplified. As a rule of thumb, the higher the spiritual temperature the more that movement, sound, rhythm, and joyful emotion are beautifully and smoothly synchronized — this is what makes the sacred vibration stronger. Once you are ecstatically awakened, all unseemly movements recede in favor of enacting the grace found when performance aesthetics and emotional ecstatics are coordinated and choreographed by the highest inspiration.

The overly purposeful and exaggerated quality of erratic, involuntary motor movement is too often assumed to release something undesirable. This notion is widespread among some chill-informed teachers of physical therapy, somatic therapy, psychotherapy, and New Age healing workshops. They naïvely advocate a pathology-focused orientation that primarily aims to purge or exorcize a hypothetical pathogen, the reality of which is more created than removed by the treatment method. In other words, these teachers fail to realize how such constructed, simplistic assumptions about the cause and cure of suffering builds a small treatment room with little to no room for spiritual heat, sacred emotion, or a higher means of moving transformation. Guard against promoting the idea that a bad spirit has inhabited you or another person, or that a previous trauma — psychology's modern word for "bad spirit" — is struggling to remain inside. Remember that, once built, the stage that spotlights "possession" or "stored trauma" is a setup that calls for the scripted action that fits this kind of misdirected uninspiring drama.

Ultimate joy is always found in the ineffable transformative flames of the big room. This is where suffering is spontaneously, ecstatically, and jubilantly transformed. If you are wailing and writhing in pain like a Hollywood movie scene about demon possession, you aren't being cooked and your spiritual temperature is way too low. Whenever we witness behavior that is absent of elevated spiritual affection we either ignore it or simply remind everyone to "keep it sweet." If it does not pierce the heart or evoke joy in others, then it is spiritually cold and held inside a small room. Such unseemly and unfriendly conduct will more likely cool things down and threaten to sink a spiritual ship. The cold spiritual temperatures that include exaggerated displays are what the Bushmen call "being stuck at the lowest station of power." Members of the sanctified church wisely advise that the spirit is never out of control. It has higher control, for "God is not the author of confusion" (1 Corinthians 14:33) and "Neither does God lead you to act unseemly" (1 Corinthians 13:4–5). Those familiar with the emotion of sacred ecstasy know that spiritual cooking brings the elation of higher elevation with its fine cultivation of ecstatic and aesthetic know-how. Rather than a mushy, messy, random, dumb free-for-all, spiritual cooking is a high art requiring skill to move you from a know-it-all, show-it-all chill to the naturally sweet, mystically attuned, and socially shared thrill.

A Joy Better Felt Than Told

A true sign of getting spiritually cooked is that you feel the happiest you've ever been, far surpassing anything you could have previously imagined was possible. As /Kunta /Kace describes this: "The feeling is so intense that you feel your heart breaking and opening to everything in the world" (Keeney 2003b, 77). /Kunta !elae says:

> When I get close to the Big God, I feel his heart. It makes me want to be good to all the people. When I am touching someone with this power, I feel my heart touching my father, my grandfather, and all of their

ancestors, all the way to God—that's when I feel everyone's heart. (Keeney 2003b, 81)

Similarly, Guarani elder Ava Tape Miri describes his initiatory experience that came after ceaseless praying, singing, and dancing: "I cried all night long during this period of intense dreaming. It was the beginning of my new life . . . I began dancing and singing all the time. I was filled with the spirits and a new life" (Keeney 2000, 28). Without a doubt, getting spiritually cooked brings the ultimate emotional flood of sacred ecstasy, an intense bliss that brings on a performance that uplifts, but never drifts into the banal. It's an experience "better felt than told," a phrase that shows up repeatedly in earlier African American religious testimony. As Henrietta Gant asserts: "Ahm tellin' you religion is better felt than it ever was told...[You] jest so happy...you feels like you could leap over walls an' run through the troops." (Kerr and Mulder 1994, 159). This phrase is also found in the hymn by the same title, written by H.R. Jeffrey in 1885: "Blest was the hour that heav'nly fire / Lit up my darkened soul...No tongue can tell the joy I felt / 'Tis better felt than told." If you aren't ecstatically happy, then you are most likely too cold and chatty. Just remember that "told" rhymes with "cold," and in order to feel the indescribable big joy you must let rightly timed, sweetly rhymed words rise above all else said to help you leap heart-first into the big room.

Zulu sangoma, Vusamazulu Credo Mutwa, told Brad that an initiate into their healing ways seeks "the hidden power of eternity and the force that lay hidden amongst the stars" (Keeney 2001, 46). A profound encounter with this power inevitably leads to a new kind of joy. Credo reports:

Now what is this power? It comes to you in a strange way. When you dance, you dance in a circle stomping your feet firmly against the ground and kicking your feet. You must kick your feet high and shake every inch of your body. When the dancing reaches its height, a strange spell comes over you. It feels like you are no longer dancing but like you are floating in air. You are one with the earth and the sky, at once. You continue to dance. And then a strange thing bursts from the small of your back. A pot full of hot water suddenly jets up from the small of your back between your buttocks right up your spine to the top of your head, where it explodes into space and seems to float toward the stars. Your vision changes. Your mind suddenly flies . . . I can't describe it any other way than to say that you feel as though you are one with every animal, tree, river, stream, and mountain on earth. You feel united with creation . . . I was filled with this great joy. A joy so intense that I wished I had arms long enough to embrace the whole world. I felt as one, but yet I felt as many. I was one human being, and yet I was many, many more. Suddenly, my heart also felt a deep sorrow. I heard people crying from far away. I also heard people, thousands of them, laughing far away . . . I felt I could run outside and embrace that tree or that cow grazing next to it. (46-47)

Credo reported this inexplicable joy to his teacher:

Great one . . . I feel like embracing everything outside this village . . . But I hear people crying in my ears, and I hear people laughing. What is this? Am I going mad? . . . Great Father, why do I feel as if I should embrace everybody? (48)

Credo's teacher, Felapakati, replied:

> Because you are everybody. This is what a true *sangoma* should be. You should feel like you are everyone and anyone. You are a white man, a black man, and a colored man. You are an Indian. You are a priest. You are a thief. You are everything. (Keeney 2001, 48)

Big room joy—sacred ecstasy—is so strong that when experienced, you may wonder whether you will pass out from the intensity. It is mighty enough to miraculously "turn all sorrows into lasting joy" (John 16:20). Such high emotion is not like any kind of familiar happiness. Hot spiritual temperature hosts the entire spectrum of human emotion that includes the despair of sadness, the pain of suffering, the glee of victory, the ache of longing, the thrill of love, the heartbreak of loss, the trembling joy of ineffable bliss, among other combinations and permutations, all morphing and mixed together. In the early days of so called "experimentalism" and "experientialism" of the Protestant church, hymn writers like Joseph Hart and William Gadsby valued songs that communicated such emotional complexity to the heart. They regarded the simultaneous experience of weeping and joy to be confirmation of authentic spiritual rebirth and renewal. The multi-leveled, combinatorial emotion of sacred ecstasy holds and remolds every trial and tribulation. Its elation vibration is a non-static love dynamic with an extraordinarily vast heart reach.

The utmost exhilaration radiating from this special mix of sacred emotion and expression can dissolve any opposition, discern the highest resolution, surpass any human solution, and offer the transformation that defies all explanation. As it floods the heart, it can also induce seemingly impossible physical feats such as this performance reported in the 1800s:

> During this time of spiritual revival, Elder William Reynolds, of Union Village, Ohio, at the age of sixty-

five, started the ecstatic practice of turning cartwheels from his home to church, sometimes turning over fences. He did this every Sunday for three years. (Mavor and Dix 1989, 197)

Similarly, the sanctified black church had its pew jumpers:

It took some good ones to hold [Aunt Kate] down when she got started. Anytime Uncle Link or any other preacher touched along the path she had traveled she would jump and holler . . . The old ones in them times walked over benches and boxes with their eyes fixed on heaven. God was in the midst of them. (Sobel 1988, 143)

At a sanctified church service in Algiers, Louisiana, Brad was once so spiritually on fire that his arms and back were bent over backward, his palms and feet flat on the floor as his torso aimed toward the ceiling. He looked and danced like a super-happy crab, an impossible physical feat for him, something usually only seen in the performance of a Chinese acrobat. In the big room, formerly impossible things are surprisingly possible, but their value is not found in how far your body can physically bend but in how its movement reflects the exploding joy within. Such bliss makes you unable to cogitate, contemplate, speculate, postulate, narrate, or verbally regurgitate. It cuts to the chase so you don't waste another moment before diving deep to avoid the heaps of word-stacked beliefs.

While ecstatically heated emotion provides the highest intoxication, there is never an injurious hangover. Being "drunk on spirit" leaves you with a steady sacred vibration that is wonderfully aligned and delightfully tuned. Experiencing the numinous, ineffable, infinite, spirit-filling divine brings bright clarity to the mind and sound musicality to the heart, together providing trustworthy guidance in your everyday. After a dance in the heavens, you are made ready to walk and talk wisely on earth.

Upon entering the big room and moving close to its fire, wonder, splendor, and joy, you reach a level of experience that is beyond description. If you stay around long enough to get ecstatically lit, you will not hesitate to dedicate the rest of your life hunting the sacred vibration that thrives on spiritual heat. One man said of his experience during the miraculous — though brief — days of spiritual cooking at the Azusa Street Revivals in Los Angeles (1906-1915): "I would rather live six months at that time than fifty years of ordinary life . . . The presence of the Lord was so real." The first time you are set on fire in the big room you will immediately know exactly what he meant. You'll discover that six months of what Paramhansa Yoganada called "ever-new bliss" is worth an eternity of cognitive certainty about the nature of reality.

The Arrival of Song

Although intense spiritual heat can inspire unbelievable jumping, cartwheel turning, the marriage of suffering and joy, and other incredible feats, when things get spiritually hotter, another shift in spiritual gears takes place. At this moment the emphasis moves to higher frequency somatic vibrations rather than extreme gross motor movements or dramatic yogic kriyas. You move from acrobatic power to galactic, rhapsodic love, and this higher climb into the heat inspires the next surprise: super-charged vibratory singing. This vocal performance is capable of transmitting a powerful vibration to others, as it also breaks observing windows to bring you deeper into the big room's heavenly production, something reported by Barton Stone, a Presbyterian minister who observed the early Cane Ridge revivals in Kentucky in 1801:

> The subject in a very happy state of mind would sing most melodiously, not from the mouth or nose, but entirely in the breast, the sounds issuing thence. Such

music silenced everything, and attracted the attention of all. It was most heavenly. None could ever be tired of hearing it . . . [We] concluded it to be something surpassing anything we had known in nature. (Stone 1847, 41–42)

Unless you have actually experienced a song ecstatically pour out of the depths of you in this way, it is difficult to fully appreciate the critical importance and transformative need of sacred song. Scholars, for example, have too often dismissed indigenous shamans' and healers' assertion that it is their songs that are most valued and cherished above all else. Instead, outsiders impose and advance their own theoretical ideas about what underlies another person's spiritual experience. Cooked shamans and healers cannot imagine working without a sacred song. As Guarani shaman, Tupa Nevangayu (Keeney 2000, 51), summarizes this, "Through the sacred song, we [are] able to see and guide everything . . . allowing me to see what I cannot ordinarily perceive." The shaman's drum and rhythm also need a song's melody in order for the visionary rider to merge a singing-dancing body with a dreaming-traveling mind, both required for a whole soul journey. No cooked visionary experience is possible without the presence of ecstatic singing, whether before or during the vision. Let us once and for all set the record straight: Music is the highest and strongest link to mystery. Without it, you are not able to leave any small room. With it, you can soar through the universe.

The utmost spiritual ecstasy is not reached though sitting still and beholding the vastness of reality. Nor is it achieved by only shaking the body. You must also sing to wake up the heightened sacred emotion that strengthens the fire of spiritual cooking. Paramhansa Yogananda makes this same point in his book, *Cosmic Chants* (1938):

> Sound, or vibration, is the most powerful force in the universe, and music is a divine art, to be used not for pleasure but as a path to God-realization. Vibrations resulting from devotional singing lead to the contact of the Cosmic Vibration or the Word . . . Music which is saturated with soul-force is the real universal music, understandable by all hearts . . . music is the universal language of the soul's devotion to God . . . (para. 5, 16-17)

In the early days of Hillary's experiences with Sacred Ecstatics, she too couldn't fully appreciate the extent to which song is essential. That changed when she was truly set on fire for the first time. Here is her testimony:

> I remember when I first heard Brad telling people that sacred songs are the ropes that connect people to vast spiritual mystery. I accepted his wisdom on the matter but I myself could not quite grasp the literal truth of that statement and assumed he was being metaphorical. Though I am a dancer and have always felt deeply moved by music, I did not realize the extent to which sacred songs are needed for fully embodied mystical experience.
>
> Then one day we were conducting an ecstatic gathering in São Paulo, Brazil. Brad had been chanting and shouting while accompanied by a professional drummer. The rhythms were slow and soulful, and the room was charged with spiritual electricity. Our Brazilian friends were trembling, shaking, and rocking in their seats. I suddenly felt a surge of energy rise up inside me. It came up into my throat and filled me with an overwhelming urge to open my voice and sing. I

had never before experienced anything like it, yet the feeling was so natural I readily surrendered to it and spontaneously burst into improvised song. It was the first time I had ever sung in public. Normally I am not able to do more than carry a simple tune, but that morning the songs flowed from my heart so effortlessly that I was astonished by the sound of my own voice. It was as if songs were brought out of my heart and soul by a mysterious force outside my control. It filled me with exhilarating bliss. I discovered firsthand that sacred ecstasy is an emotion that wants to sing.

The more I sang the more I began to shake from within to such a degree that I could barely hold the microphone. The inner physical vibration was of such a high frequency, however, that I exhibited very little outward movement—it poured out of me as the sonic vibration of song. My singing was so full of the sacred vibration that it inspired Brad to sing in a heightened way as well. We couldn't stop this musical, mystical current and sang throughout the remaining five days. People were shaking, dancing, singing, shouting, and weeping with joy. It was a special blessing from God that we all still talk about to this day.

I can truly say that I was converted that morning—not to any particular religion or belief—but to the experience of a mysterious sacred ecstasy and spiritual current that send music through your whole being. No matter what it's called or where in the world it is happening, wherever the sacred songs are ringing and the ecstatic fire is blazing, that is where I want to be.

I now know what the Bushman doctors mean when they say that song is the rope to God. Since that Sacred Ecstatics intensive in Brazil, whenever I want to strike the match, I sing. When I get spiritually cold and need to get back to the big room, I sing. If I enter a place where people are cooking and the songs are on fire I can't help but join in. Though I am not blessed with the type of voice that can grace the Broadway stage or lead a choir, I was given the gift of being able to let the fire in my heart pour out through song. When it comes to spiritual singing it's the awakened feeling rather than any perfect performance that matters. I now quite literally experience music and song as both the vehicle that takes me to the spiritual fire and the key that turns the ignition. If there is a sacred song living in your heart, you have everything you spiritually need.

The lyrics to the 1930s song entitled "Zing! Went the Strings of My Heart," said it this way: "Never could carry a tune, never knew where to start; you came along when everything was wrong and put a song in my heart." Once you have been filled with song in the big room, you will hear this popular tune as a sacred hymn pouring wisdom from the cosmic melodic atmosphere. Ecstatic singing is arguably the truest, purest, and surest sign of being spiritually on fire. If there's no singing, there's no cooking. Stuernagel referred to this gift as a "singing heart," "heavenly heart-song," and a "music-box deep down in the soul":

> The Spirit-filled believer will also be "making melody in the heart." He will have a singing heart. Not everybody can sing with the voice, but everybody can have a whole music-box deep down in the soul. Besides, the vocal song must cease at intervals, but the heavenly heart-song can go on forever. It is the new song of heaven wafted down to Earth which will continue through countless ages. (1928, 8)

As a church member described the divine reception of song, "You do not use your mind at all. The Lord God uses your vocal organs, and words come out without your having anything to do with it" (reported in *The Apostolic Faith*, May, 1907). Zora Neale Hurston collected this visionary account involving spiritual music from a parishioner who lived in Beaufort, South Carolina:

> I went to the east under beautiful shade trees and the green was like a carpet on the ground. There was a band of people. They all had different musical instruments . . . I stood outside the ring. The director, he was a man marching time, giving the measures to the music. He just handed me a box (guitar) and didn't stop beating time. I played it. (Ecstasy— "Glory, sweet! Better felt than told! Glory!") I just went to play and went to laughing. Came through in the holiness, laughing, and shouting in the bed. That was the glorious time of my life. That was the day! (1940, 22)

It is not uncommon for someone without musical training to instantaneously play a musical instrument while under the influence of spiritual heat. In the Pentecostal movement that took place at the Azusa Street Gospel Mission in Los Angeles during the early 1900s, there were reports of songs and music spontaneously arising in the services—all "glory, sweet!" Consider this example from a woman named Jennie Moore:

> I sang under the power of the Spirit in many languages, the interpretation of both words and music I had never before heard, and in the home where the meeting was held, the Spirit led me to the piano, where I played and sang under inspiration, although I had not learned to play. (*The Apostolic Faith*, May 1907)

The role of music in awakening, conveying, and elevating sacred emotion brings considerable discussion and debate among diverse spiritual traditions. Sometimes it is ignored, toned down, rendered unimportant, or banned. Or music may be valued yet debated as to whether it hosts the right kind of melody, performance, means of listening, elicited emotion, inspired movement, and the like. For instance, among the Sufis an important historical controversy involves how one should listen to music, the act of which is called *sama'*, in order to evoke sacred ecstasy. Ernst and Lawrence (2002) propose that the role of sama' in "the spiritual progress of a Muslim mystic or Sufi adept" is defined in one of three ways:

> It may be totally excluded as inappropriate to Islamic teaching—mystical or non-mystical . . .; (2) it may be accepted as a penultimate stage on the mystical ladder leading to ontological unity, i.e., perfection, or (3) it may be viewed as the top rung on the ladder, itself the ultimate mystical experience when properly pursued. (34)

These different definitions of music's role in mystical experience correspond to the temperature range of the spiritual thermometer. In the extreme cold, music is given no importance or even regarded as an irritation to stable cogitation. When things warm up, song is a vehicle that amplifies sacred emotion, vibration, and facilitates your ascent up the rope to God. And finally, in the big room where the spiritual fire is really cooking, the rope, emotion, and sacred vibration are experienced as inseparable from song. For spiritually cooked Sufi mystics,

> . . . music was the sine qua non of Islamic mysticism. It not only helped the lover to attain a state of ecstasy in

the presence of the Beloved, but it itself was integral to the ecstatic moment. [It] absorbed the human listener into the place of music till there remained only the song. (Ernst & Lawrence 2002, 35)

Spiritual heat cooks away all exclusion, shyness, and diminishment concerning music and the sacred emotion it evokes and shares. The more spiritually cooked you are, the more musically mystical you become. Your song is reborn in the moment and fresh as an opening night performance. Hinson articulates how this is understood in the sanctified black church:

Saints say that the Spirit will never touch one of His children in precisely the same manner more than once. Hence if a singer shows the same spiritual signs—the same shouts, the same waves, the same dance—at the same place in the same song on more than one occasion, or if that singer offers the same tearful testimony—repeating every word, every gesture, every tear—night after night, then the singer is enacting a rehearsed sequence. As the saints often say, "God don't work like that." (Hinson 2000, 255)

Once you enter the big concert room and feel its heat, spiritually cooked singing begins. Allow yourself to be freed from assessing your condition and keep opening your heart to a soulful rendition of spiritually heard and ecstatically felt music. The Guarani Indians propose: "There are two types of people: [those] with a sacred song and those without a song" (Tupa Nevangayu, cited in Keeney 2000, 75). Most shamanic traditions are very clear that "You are not a shaman unless you have been given a song" and that "the deeper and stronger you are, the more often this [catching songs] will happen" (77-78). It is not everyone's destiny to receive such a song in vision or to become a shaman. However, when people have a strong, heart-to-heart connection to God, it is not uncommon for them to have music inside them both day and night. What matters most is that you keep working the steps of the recipe throughout your everyday life and trust divine providence and its means of decision, attribution, and distribution. The music will eventually arrive for whatever purpose has been chosen for you. Without a doubt you were born to have a singing heart and a music box in the soul that plays the songs of sacred ecstasy.

Healing and the Higher Energetics of Sacred Ecstatics

One primary change that takes place when the temperature significantly rises is the shift from purposeful, predictable action to spontaneous, improvisational action. In a spiritually warm (rather than blazing hot) situation where talk still remains, you more likely find yourself saying something with no understanding as to why you would think, let alone say, those words. Once the noise of psyche attractions and distractions are cleared, you become a hollow pipeline, empty vessel, and tuned instrument ready to host and share higher inspired creative expression. The Guarani shamans regard this kind of spiritually warmed talk as giving "word souls." As they describe it, "When a shaman is talking to you, he or she is giving you soul" (Ava Tape Miri, in Keeney 2000, 29). Tupa Nevangayu explains further: "For the Guarani, the word souls are the main thing. I am only a medium for the spirits who carry the word souls. We bring forth the word souls for the good of the world" (61). Ecstatic praying, singing, and dancing bring down the sacred emotion that is infused into subsequent talk that delivers the message from a higher source.

If you are any kind of healer, from an African sangoma to a Louisiana hoodoo doctor or a creative therapist, you might ask a married couple whether they ever thought of going to the bookstore and exploring a book on Tunisia, suggesting that it might help cure their romantic amnesia. Or suggest that a person suffering from insomnia schedule a fifteen-minute afternoon "anti-nap" where he should try to get more awake, doing so in an experimentally different way. If you are a spiritual teacher, you might tell a lost seeker that her "discord" is a sign of being *dis*connected from the holy *cord*. Anything is possible when you move into a big room and deliver its inspired, ecstatically heated spontaneity rather than remain obedient to the habitual routines, overused tricks, and unimaginative clichés of a trickster protocol that keeps everything small and emotionally cold.

The same is true for a shaman who is guided by a mainline rope rather than a rote method. Once the spiritual match is struck, he might unexpectedly tap his feet rather than a drum, shake his hand rather than a rattle, or take a shamanic walk around the room. Similarly, a spiritually lassoed mystic might introduce someone to a fallen leaf, turn one page of a holy book while looking at it with only one eye, or drop a pinch of salt into a wallet. Know this: you will not know what you will say or do until the moment the rope delivers it to you. If you try to imitate this spontaneity or perform it inside a small room, it will come across as false, flat, and absent of spiritual heat. The room will shrink and stink rather than expand and smell sweet, and you will not feel creatively alive. Become spiritually cooked and then get out of the way so the sacred pipeline can deliver its innovative goods. You cannot worry about how others will interpret or judge your action; whatever is inspired and suggested by a higher source must be shared. As the Guarani shaman, Ava Tape Miri, was told by an ancestral shaman in his primary initiatory vision:

> Well, my son, I have shown you how things are. Now you know what is here in the world of spirit. You must go back and tell your family and the whole world. This is for the people who believe. Don't worry if some

> don't believe you, because this is only for those who believe . . . The spirits explained to me what to do and what I needed to know . . . Learn to listen to the spirits only . . . If you listen to what people can say, you can lose your communication with the spirits. (Keeney 2000, 35-36)

With each major rise in temperature there is a shift of the ecstatic spiritual gears that is accompanied by a different body automatism or form of involuntary expression. When heated singing causes the powerful trembling of your voice to reverberate throughout your body, it activates the higher energetics of Sacred Ecstatics. You may feel a ball of energy gather and concentrate near your belly. With even hotter singing, this accumulation of lower body energy is pulled upwards, and as its rising current enters your voice it further heats and strengthens your singing. This process is yet another call and response, this time involving the sound of your vocal chords and the muscles around your belly button, where the vibration of each intensifies the other.

This energetic interaction activates an inner "body pump," something well known to Bushman healers who experience concentrated, vibratory energy travel up and down the torso. Bushman healer Kgao Temi explains that this takes place because "the rope is going through your head and pulling you" (Keeney 2003b, 76). Imagine a rope suspended from the sky going into the top of your head, through the heart, down the spine, and all the way to the ball of energy in the belly. As the rope is lifted and lowered by higher hands, the energy ball rises and falls, creating an abdominal pumping action that feels like a steam engine piston.[12]

---

[12] When a physical vibration gets on you or inside you, it sometimes happens that the muscles in the abdomen naturally contract, become tight, or cramp. This is different than the ecstatic body pump, which is an experience that

As the ecstatic pump or spiritual steam piston further strengthens, you eventually voice a guttural rhythm, what the St. Vincent Shakers call *'doption*, referring to "adoption" by the spirit. Here the polyrhythms of Africa come through the throat and are called "number one 'doption," "one-foot 'doption," or "working the pump." This is arguably the strongest vocal expression of sacred ecstasy. That it came from Africa is supported by Bell's observation in the 1870s of a dance performed in Grenada by old "Congo negroes" that was identical to the Caribbean Shakers' "number one 'doption" (Bell 1889). While some scholars hypothesize that enslaved Africans, prohibited from making drums and other instruments, were the first to use the body as a rhythm instrument, the vocalization of percussive sound was expressed by free Bushmen before any drum arrived. Therefore, it is possible that body-produced percussion was the original inspiration for *creating* a drum, rather than its replacement.

Mother Samuel of St. Vincent speaks of strong 'doption as what happens "when the Spirit gets into your body." Here is an account of one of her early visionary journeys:

> I came to a fork in the road, where a spirit was standing at the middle of the two roads and I asked where 'doption came from. He pointed to the ground and the Earth began to shake. He showed me that the stomping of the feet and the shaking of the Earth sent a pumping spiritual energy into the belly. That energy is then pumped up the body, with percussive sounds coming from the mouth. It was so powerful that I went into a top number one 'doption right there. (Keeney 2002, 74–75)

---

involuntarily happens when the spiritual temperature is very hot. Sometimes people imitate the pump or consciously try to force it to happen. As always, when action is purposefully willed to make a wish fulfilled, it blocks authentic spontaneous experience from taking place.

Speaking of 'doption, Mother Sandy, also from St. Vincent, adds:

> If you go deep into the spirit you can get the experience of 'doption. It hits you in the belly, tightens you, and pumps your belly up and down. Move when the spirit adopts you. Walk it out. Stomp your feet, swing your arms, and let the sound come out. It will sound like a drum beating inside your chest. 'Doption can show you something. It can bring you a vision or even take you on a spiritual journey. (Keeney 2002, 65)

When 'doption first brings its unique ecstatic contraction, energy compaction, and somatic syncopation, it's tempting to be worried about its extreme strength and potentially over-powering influence. Mother Ralph advises, "When you feel it, don't get scared. Don't hold your belly and sit down. Stand up and let your feet stomp the ground. You must walk it out, stomp it out in a dance for the Lord" (Keeney 2002, 87). When you experience 'doption, you are supposed to "work it out," "jump Spirit," "work penitent," or "work the Spirit" and transfer the spiritual power associated with shaking into the 'doption. This is a heightened way for percussively anointed ecstatics to generate and accelerate spiritual heat.[13] As you become a Sacred Ecstatics rhythm machine, your feet stomp like a Bushman n/om-kxao or a Shaker deep in 'doption. In its most intense form, this walking march, driven by an embodied involuntary rhythm, is called climbing the rope to God among the Bushman healers.

High spiritual heat is needed to elicit the guttural spirit-drum sounds of 'doption, with ecstatically precipitated (rather than

---

[13] Some Caribbean Shakers explain 'doption by referring to Romans 8:15 and 22, which refer to the whole of creation groaning and waiting for the adoption of the spirit.

purposefully contrived) over-breathing fueling its delivery. The stronger the beat and sound, the more powerfully the energy moves. This ecstatic dynamic is how you become heated enough for spontaneous ecstatic healing to commence. Without this high degree of spiritual cooking and its outbursts of vibratory sound, rhythmic abdominal pumping, and hand trembling, any attempt to heal will be a charade or worse, induce an iatrogenic backfire.

This is the teaching of the ecstatic healing lineages, especially that of the Kalahari Bushmen. The ecstatic body pump enables sickness to be "pulled" out of another person's body while simultaneously pulled out of your own body. Here you tacitly experience yourself involuntarily "pull" as if the tug of the rope above causes your body to pull out any sickness. If the pump isn't sufficiently activated by strong vocalized vibration, you cannot effectively pull out another's sickness. Furthermore, if the pulling isn't strong enough, that sickness might get stuck in you. "When I dance and touch someone, I shout loudly," Ngwaga Osele from the central Kalahari of Botswana once said (Keeney 1999b, 94). /Kunta !elae from Namibia adds, "When the power is in you, it can bring out the [pulling] sounds" (Keeney 2003b, 67). The "power" /Kunta refers to is n/om or what we call the sacred vibration, and the pulling requires a well-matched pulling sound. Synchronized, co-amplifying spontaneous body shaking and involuntary sound making are required for the ecstatic pulling and releasing of sickness.

In non-ecstatic healing traditions, attempts to heal via spiritual energy are carried out without benefit of knowing anything about the basic healing mechanism of the ecstatic body pump and the importance of empowered singing and spontaneous shouting. Most healing traditions simply have never heard of or experienced elevated spiritual temperature. As a result, these healers sometimes feel sick or tired after healing others. This is arguably a warning sign that you shouldn't be healing because you are not yet spiritually cooked. If you are spiritually hot enough, the sacred vibration will automatically draw the sickness and tiredness out of both you and the client, and after the session you will feel healed, renewed, and invigorated. Healers today should worry less about whether they have the right intention or feel sufficient compassion and instead focus on igniting more ecstatic passion in order to effectively pull sickness.

Energy medicine practices that advocate being calm, subdued, and quiet do not generate enough spiritual heat for a healer to remove sickness. If anything occurs in cold or lukewarm healing it is likely a placebo effect, a simple form of hypnosis, or some other variant of faith healing. Rather than advise energy-exchange taboos, these practitioners should be far more concerned about the way a calm and cool trickster mind—both theirs and their clients'—can fabricate any reality, including whether there is any energy at all in their energy medicine. Most energy medicine is not very energetic, lacks any spiritual heat, and has no meaningful relationship to being spiritually cooked. As a result, it is typically full of trickster deception. Fortunately, it doesn't have the potency to harm others, though it can promote spiritual refrigeration habits that distance all involved from experiencing the higher heat and transformative energetics of sacred ecstasy.

The outcome of a successful Sacred Ecstatics healing session or group gathering is registered by the experience of the conductor—our umbrella term for healers, shamans, teachers, preachers, or ceremonial leaders. If the conductor feels cooked, then the needed healing atmosphere for spiritual transformation was most likely achieved. Keep in mind that it takes more spiritual heat and energy to pull out a conductor's tiredness and sickness when working with a client than it does to only pull it out of the other person. Therefore, when you feel transformed in such an interaction, the same most likely happened to the client. Japanese healer Ikuko Osumi, Sensei explains that this kind of healing is a "one-being therapy" because it transcends the dichotomy between patient and healer (Keeney 1999b, 76). Both are treated in the big treatment room.

All post hoc verbalized outcome reports from anyone, whether positive or negative, should not be given too much importance. This is because trickster commentary made after the spiritual temperature has cooled brings only a partial, distanced, and usually distorted glimpse of the whole episode that took place. In addition, not everyone—including clients or patients—has sufficient discernment to gauge spiritual expansion and heat. If a healer with trustworthy spiritual discernment experiences First Creation changing during a session, then it is assumed that the room became spiritually big enough and hot enough so that whatever changes were needed were accomplished by higher hands, whether consciously noticed by others or not.

In conclusion, healing can't generate enough heat unless a healer sings with fluttering hands in concert with a pumping abdomen. This coupling of musical sound and somatic movement are required to pull out sickness. You must be musically, kinetically, and ecstatically empowered in order to heal. As Bushman doctor Twele from the Central Kalahari in Botswana states: "It is the power from the music and the seriousness of the occasion that make me feel very hot. It comes up into my head, and I feel it as a kind of steam" (Keeney 1999b, 71). Trickster healing is cool as a cucumber and tries to trick the mind into believing you are no longer in a pickle. Ecstatic healing that really cooks takes you out of the jar and throws you into the big room fire. *Remote* healing becomes *close* healing, something directly felt and heard rather than imagined from afar.

As the interaction of vibrant singing, rhythmic thumping, abdominal pumping, and body trembling become hotter, things shift into an even higher gear. At this sizzling temperature the ecstatic practitioner goes past healing and, rather than pull out sickness, she transmits and installs the sacred vibration. This is when the actual vibratory pulse of n/om, seiki, holy spirit, or the universal life force is somatically given to another person. While healing removes sickness by pulling, transmission is accomplished through a kind of pushing. The latter has a qualitatively different feeling and a higher, stronger frequency of vibration. Both the pulling of healing and the pushing of transmission involve sacred song, ecstatic emotion, vibratory touch, and spontaneous body movement. It is the degree of spiritually heated emotion and breadth of sacred expansion that differentiate their experiential nature. Transmission requires more spiritual heat in the vastest room to ignite a strongly felt rope of connection between both recipient and transmitter, enabling the sacred vibration to be mutually shared.

The hottest spiritual temperature brings yet another shift in sensory experience: you no longer experience the materiality of your body but feel as if you have become a formless, cloudlike vibration—the pulsing, luminous, numinous fog and mist of mystery. Reaching this highest temperature does not culminate in a silent, expressionless body but in becoming a pure sacred vibration whose emotion sings and dances the "one endless smile" of ecstasy. This is the rarified air of the most sanctified healers, shamans, mystics, and teachers. As Lakota elder Pete Catches hinted at this dissolving of his life: "So as I get older, I burrow more and more into the hills. The Great Spirit made them for us, for me. I want to blend with them, shrink into them and finally, disappear in them" (Lame Deer & Erdoes 1972, 140).

Rhythm Overthrows Word

The crossing from Second to First Creation, the movement from small to big room, and the rise from cold to hot spiritual temperature require an equally important mind-blowing, emotion-heightening, and body-shifting change in the organization of your experience. The verbal productions and semantic interpretations of trickster mind must fully surrender to the primacy and leadership of rhythm that is expressed by and felt in your body. In this transition you allow rhythm rather than spoken talk, inner thought, or written word to become dominant, reigning over all inner experience and outer performance. If words come, you cannot help but speak, chant, or sing them with a more soulful beat and this is what brings the next wave of heat. The elevated pulse of rhythm spontaneously pulls forth the tones and movements of more spiritually heated body expression. Ikuko Osumi, Sensei defines the spontaneous body movement practice of seiki jutsu as bringing a special life-enhancing rhythm to the body: "*Seiki taisou* [daily seiki practice] gives rhythm to your body similar to the way music conveys inspiration through vibration" (Keeney1999b, 67). Its healing and renewal promote "balancing body rhythms in daily life," which Osumi, Sensei regarded as of the "utmost importance in maintaining good health" (55).

While there is never a time when you are absent of rhythm, crossing into the spiritual heat of the big room amplifies its presence and makes it primary. The beat, both inside you and in the room around you, is more consciously recognized and somatically noticed. You are fully aware of this taking place because it brings an instant surge of energized life. The Bushmen regard this moment as *!aia* or "waking up." In other words, the arrival of rhythmic dominance is inseparable from waking up the heightened emotion and somatic motion associated with the sacred vibration, and all this synchronized commotion overwhelms, reorganizes, and sometimes shuts down trickster mind so that it can serve rather than just observe the ecstatic ride. This process is in contrast to contemplative traditions that assume your monkey mind is best reined in and quieted through silent meditation. Rather than sit still and risk catching a spiritual chill, offer the monkey the ecstatic key to a more enlivened rhythmic engine.

When rhythm is introduced, words shift from the literality of rigid names to the creative flexibility of evocative metaphor. With more rhythmic intensity, metaphors string themselves together in poetic prose. As rhythm crosses the midpoint between cold and hot, the beat of a poem overrides consideration of what its words mean. The Guarani address this transition: "For very strong shamans, the gods take over their body and voice as soon as they start to pray" (in Keeney 2000, 78). As rhythm's higher power grows stronger (though not necessarily faster), songs burst onto the scene, sometimes called heart-songs, prayer-songs, or n/om songs. Further intensification comes with changing the beat and this eventually leads to the big room boom of the somatic drum—in 'doption you become the percussive embodiment of the sacred vibration.

To get thoroughly spiritually cooked requires that you be taken over by a spiritually powerful rhythm that makes the temperature go up and helps the cooked medicine go down. As each rhythmic shift occurs you move closer to the numinous. Osumi, Sensei similarly describes the rhythmic transmission of the universal life force, seiki:

> When it is time for transmission, I experience no ego consciousness and there is no separation between my mind and body. I feel that I have become absorbed into the body of the recipient. The seiki will soon flow naturally into their body. When this takes place they will receive exactly the right amount and the whole operation will be done in the same manner as a perfectly orchestrated dance . . . At the instant of transmission, the receiver and I become one being. Our bodies and minds are brought together into harmonious unity. This is when we feel a beautiful

rhythm. (Keeney 1999b, 46-47)

There is no metronome or predictable beat in spiritual heat. Alternating, multi-layered, and complexly interwoven polyrhythms juxtapose a steady heartbeat with a shifting, sacred arrhythmia. Sanctified gospel music, Kalahari n/om songs, medicine song lines, and all the other sacred songs used for influencing spiritual temperature are potently alive and under the supervision of mystery time. These rhythms invite the body to march, dance, leap, flip, whirl, tremble, and shake to the beat of higher percussion that has repercussions for the whole of your life. Once you have experienced these kinds of fascinating rhythms get inside you, you'll find any prayer, healing session, ceremony, or spiritual gathering that lacks soulful rhythm to feel cold and spiritually dead. Likewise, whenever you are inside the infinity of divinity you won't be able to keep yourself from feeling and expressing the varying rhythms that naturally come forth when sacred emotion is empowered by the mighty duo of spiritual heat and soulful beat.

First Creation prefers syncopated ragtime to mechanized clock time because it has more changing, conveys more emotion, inspires more motion, is more interesting, and expresses more life. As scholar John Wesley Work wrote:

> "Ragtime" is an ingenious and fitting appellation for the music to which it gives its name, for it is time torn to tatters, but in such rhythmically fascinating manner as to arouse every single motor nerve of our being. That is why we like it, say what we may . . . A fresh, vigorous flow carries the life-giving forces to all parts of the system. (1915, 38)

In short, spiritual cooking is inseparable from the soulful

rhythms that underlie the music, dance, emotion, vibration, and change found in the big room. These are what "arouse every single motor nerve of [your] being" and deliver "life-giving forces" to the whole of you. Without rhythm there is no special medicine song, bodily felt sacred vibration, or strong rope to God. Forget having an imaginary conversation with God; you need something more than small room talk. What you want is a vital, real deal rhythmic relationship with God's revitalizing life force.

Think more about cymbals than symbols. Consider finding a cowbell, hi-hat, marimba, snare drum, wood block, castanets, triangle, bongos, tabla, djembe, conga, darbuka, octoban, tom-tom, timpani, bock-a-da-bock, cabasa, celesta, maraca, steelpan, vibraphone, xylophone, side whistle, apita, chimes, glass harmonica, glockenspiel, rainstick, tambourine, bucket, garbage can, metal pipe, pot, rocks, gamelan, berimbau, timbales, or piano. Do more than think about these rhythm instruments. Play them, hear them, feel them, and absorb them. Go past the word-laden humdrum, touch the drum skin, enter the rhythmic changing, and be the beat that brings heated change. Big room occupancy thrives on ragtime, swing time, and jazz time. Rhythm is the undisputed spiritual ambassador, ecstatic vernacular, and electrical capacitor of soul. With a pair of drumsticks, you can set the world on fire.

Getting Spiritually Cooked: A Contemporary Testimony

The following testimony is from a member of the Sacred Ecstatics community, Diana Jacob, a woman from Edgefield in Norfolk, England who with her husband owns and operates Wood Farm Holiday Cottages in the countryside. She received the sacred vibration—an old-fashioned nail of n/om—on the third day of a Sacred Ecstatics intensive. We present her account to give a contemporary illustration of what it can be like to get spiritually cooked for the first time. She writes:

The Day a Nail Came to Me from God, by Diana Jacob

I remember feeling close to everyone in the room that day. Most folks were throwing themselves into the flow of the experience. We were chanting prayers as a group, voicing simple lines together like, "Thy will be done" and "Anything can happen in the big room." The temperature rose as we clapped and chanted these prayers in a call and response that was interspersed with ecstatic shouts.

During this fervor, the microphone was handed to me. Noises began to spontaneously come from my throat, sounding a bit like the chanting heard in the recordings of 'doption that take place in St Vincent. I was absorbed in the rhythm.

Later in the day, during a rest break, I got irritated and upset by news about something that was happening at my farm. I felt deeply disappointed that I had allowed myself to go so quickly into a small room. So I jumped up and stood behind a friend and put my arms around her. I begged God to take me into the big room. It worked. I found myself skipping and literally hopping from one leg to the other outside as I went to meet new guests, all the time feeling very joyful.

I came back to the gathering and walked into the lounge where I saw Brad working with a young man. It was like a Bushman encounter — let's say there was a lot of shaking going on!

I have no clear memory of what happened; I was just in the midst of all this spiritual emotion and movement when I again started to make guttural noises in my throat. My body kept doubling up. Something grabbed a hold of me and moved me and made sounds through me. I didn't want it to stop. I moved over towards Brad and tucked myself under his shoulder and continued with this movement and sound as he joined in with me. He started to tell me to "Take it in" and then shouted that I had received a nail. I wasn't aware of the exact moment when this happened, but I recall that there was no punch to my stomach that I had heard about from others who had received a nail. I do remember Hillary was playing music and I felt a deep sense of happiness hearing it.

I couldn't stop the subsequent body movement and rhythmic sound. It went off and on all through the night. There was a very strong contraction and aching in my gut, and I kept doubling up all the time. I was both concerned about this new experience and yet I enjoyed it. A part of me didn't want it to stop. I knew this for sure: whatever I thought I knew before, I now know that I know nothing. This is simply an unbelievable gift from God.

Later I would say out loud to others, "Dear God, here is my hand; please hold me and show me the way, please help me keep my nail clean. Everyone, please help me keep it clean, and help me help others."

The next night I dreamed of holding other people's hands and sharing this vibration. I woke up and found myself holding my husband's hand while I was shaking—we were sharing the vibration together; words can't describe how it felt. I can hardly believe this has happened. Thank you!

In response to her written testimony which she transcribed several days after the event, Brad wrote the following account of what had happened to both Diana and her husband, Chris Jacob, who is also a longstanding member of the Sacred Ecstatics community.

> The day before Diana received a nail of n/om, the group had been enthusiastically working the spirit. Hillary and I went into 'doption and at the height of its rhythm, I went to Diana and held her hands and pulled her arms like the St. Vincent Shakers do when they transmit 'doption to another person. In the midst of this spirited fervor, Diana suddenly began to spontaneously bring forth the sound and movement cherished by ecstatic shakers. Shakers would say that she "received 'doption" which is essentially the same as what Bushmen call "receiving a nail or arrow of n/om" — both are indications of receiving the sacred vibration.
>
> I proceeded to do the same with Chris, her husband. He and I were holding each other when he also spontaneously caught the heated rhythm. He soon started chanting and singing with a quality of sound he had never voiced before. It sounded like old time moaning. Being cooked by the sacred vibration and sanctified rhythms of 'doption opened, doctored, altered, and anointed his voice.
>
> Both Chris and Diana experienced 'doption and that day a nail of n/om gently crossed the somatic divide of each. This has also happened to others at our Sacred Ecstatics intensives. Sometimes the nail or arrow only brushes against you or it remains dangling on your surface because it hasn't gone all the way through and settled inside. While this also brings a joyful ecstatic experience, it is not the same intensity as a full reception. When this mysterious carrier of higher power deeply enters you, it stays there for the rest of

your life. You then completely identify with the song, "Something Within," the first gospel song written and published by the African American gospel songwriter, Lucie E. Campbell, also known as the "mother of gospel music." Once you have experienced this "something within," you forever desire feeling it come back to life. It is a remarkable life-changing experience. After you receive it, you realize that this, above all else, is what you have been looking for in your life odyssey. Nothing quenches your spiritual thirst and satisfies your spiritual hunger other that setting your soul on fire. Let us pay homage to the lyrics of Campbell's earliest song:

Preachers and teachers would make their appeal,
Fighting as soldiers on great battlefields;
When to their pleadings my poor heart did yield,
All I can say, there is something within.

Something within me that holdeth the reins,
Something within me that banishes pain;
Something within me I cannot explain,
All that I know there is something within.

Have you that something, that burning desire?
Have you that something, that never doth tire?
Oh, if you have it - that Heavenly Fire!
Then let the world know there is something within.

I met God one morn', my soul feeling bad,
Heart heavy laden with a bowed down head.
He lifted my burden, made me so glad,
All that I know there is something within.

On Saturday night after all this took place with Diana and Chris, a small group of us gathered for another meeting in the living room. A climate of warm fellowship was in the air and prompted Hillary and I to again work the spirit. One thing led to another and the heavenly fire was relit, especially after another participant, Dominic, got thoroughly shaken and cooked.

As before, I went to Diana and together we immediately activated the experience of 'doption. She went straight into it. The nail of n/om was obviously still hanging on to her. What happened next is the difference that made a profound difference. I felt four bursts of energy shoot from the tight gathering place of energy in my body into her abdomen one after another. Each time I shouted to her, "Take it in!" Here Bushman doctors would ponder whether or not she received four more nails or whether one nail was being pushed deeper into her. Both descriptions are partly true, but it is likely something more complex and beyond description because words can't fully describe this ecstatic spiritual process. Another description is that the initial nail and the subsequent nails combined to become what I formerly heard some traditional Bushman doctors call a "mother nail." It is arguably the strongest nail that can later give birth to other nails.

Suffice it to say that with each push and shout of "Take it in!" Diana's body recoiled and absorbed the sacred vibration in a powerful way. It went deep inside her like it does for a Bushman n/om-kxao in the making. All the rest of the typical experiences followed—being drunk with n/om, barely able to walk, feeling both apprehensive and thrilled, spontaneous eruptions of 'doption, bliss, and the complete rewiring of her physical, emotional, intellectual, expressive, and soulful being. As everyone noticed, she was reborn as a woman of God, a n/om carrying, First Creation holder of the sacred vibration.

The sacred vibration thrives inside a spirited interaction with another person. When people gather for Sacred Ecstatics, spiritual cooking happens. It does so as long as there is mutually empowering ecstatic activity—each person wholeheartedly participating in a true call and response whose rhythm pulls everyone further into the fire.

There is also an important truth conveyed in saying that Diana and Chris, as a relationship, received a nail, as did the whole community that was present. The Jacobs are now able to get cooked whenever they turn the wheel of interactive prayer, song, and movement. The nail then travels in a circle that traverses both of them. Instead of circulating only inside the boundaries of one person, it loops through both of their bodies. They become held, moved, and cooked by a circulating mystical nail that comes to life during their spirited interaction.

Diana is now ready to lay her hands on Chris in a newborn way, doing so whenever she feels moved or pulled to do so, as long as she is in the big room of expanded and heated mystery. She can similarly lay her hands on her parents, children, and others. If she doesn't force anything or try to make something happen, then whatever comes forth will be naturally regulated so it is not too little or too much for the recipient. There is no need to name what takes place and there is no need to adhere to any particular form. The vibration arrives so it can be shared with friends and loved ones in a way that flows naturally and effortlessly without conscious purpose. In other words: "Thy n/om be done."

The same experimentalism is also open to Chris. He can awake up his inner nail and spiritual heat, and Diana's as well, but only with carefully aligned call and response expression. This can take place through soulful prayer or spiritually inspired song — whatever is pulled forth in the big room. In the mutual interaction of Diana and Chris, heated prayer-songs and heated vibrating nails travel through both of them. A few years later, Chris received another nail during an intensive and several months afterwards he had this dream:

> I've just woken up from a dream that ended with my hands tingling and a sweet vibration in my tailbone. All around me were the people who love me and are no longer here. As I saw each of their faces I was filled with a longing to touch their hands. I kept reaching out with my arms as each new face appeared — I didn't have enough arms and hands — and as we touched I could feel the pulsing of their particles in my fingers and in my tailbone. The longing was in my belly. This longing could only be met through touching their hands, but I did not have enough hands to touch all the sweet faces that kept appearing around me. I was weeping with both delight and longing. I'm so grateful. It's good to be home again.

Once you receive a nail of n/om it longs to be shared and circulated. This is the original way of spiritual interaction that serves higher transformation. We celebrate that in the English countryside, as well as other places throughout the world, the oldest and most powerfully felt spiritual experience is back in circulation.

The Dancer Who Received a Nail

We share the story of another Sacred Ecstatics community member who received a nail of n/om. A young man named Nathan Foster had devoted his life to ballet and had been chosen as the lead dancer in an internationally renowned dance company. Months before the performance season opened, Nathan was diagnosed with a spinal tumor and told that he could never dance ballet again or he would risk serious injury or death. With his life's purpose and passion suddenly taken away, he turned to drugs and alcohol and drifted for several years, sometimes feeling suicidal and uncertain about whether he wanted to give life another chance. Nathan's mother, desperate to help her son, encouraged him to see us. During his session, a mystical prescription came forth: We recommended that he purchase a matador costume and while wearing it, ask out loud, "Will I wallow in the bullshit or run with the bulls?" We also invited him to come to one of our intensives. At first he mostly sat in the back row and observed, but he was fascinated with it enough to keep returning. Nathan would later say that he was also softened at these gatherings by noticing how his father steadfastly provided an example of unconditional love, devoted participation, and ongoing encouragement to join in.

Then one day during a Sacred Ecstatics intensive in Budapest, without warning something remarkable happened. We placed our trembling hands on Nathan and his body caught the sacred vibration. In a fury of ecstatic touch, movement, and sound, Nathan received a nail of n/om. He did not realize that he had received this gift until later that night when he woke up feeling like 1,000 volts of electricity were surging through his body. He jumped out of bed and spontaneously danced all night. It was the first time he had danced since his diagnosis. That night Nathan was reborn as a new kind of dancer, a n/om dancer who is danced by divine mystery. This allowed his body to move in a natural way that was healing and renewing. Furthermore, throughout the night and for the rest of the week he could not stop hearing the song that had awakened inside him—"You Are My Sunshine." Since that time, Nathan has never been the same. His reception of the sacred vibration along with a song led to his anointment to heal others with his trembling hands.

Nathan learned that the spontaneous movements and sacred vibrations of Sacred Ecstatics are naturally regulated for everyone. You are moved and shaken in a way that is safe, healthy, enhancing, and perfect for you, with no need to name or understand what is happening. Unlike forcing a preconceived choreography, purposeful form, or desired outcome, spiritually heated ecstatic movement is absent of the kind of risk he would face if he pushed his body to exceed certain limits. Under the influence of the big room and its spiritual heat, the Creator takes care of you and this includes managing the spontaneous expression that comes forth. This is another reason you should never try to imitate spiritual ecstasy—forcing anything may cause an accident, whether it be a sprained ankle or a bruised ego. Let yourself be naturally moved by the sacred vibration and every motion, whether small or large, will be exactly what your body needs. Several years later, Nathan found that his tumor had unexplainably shrunk, enabling him to dance without fear. The matador had entered the big ring, one large enough for a n/om-filled bull to charge the world.

One of the most amazing things about Sacred Ecstatics is that when one person gets spiritually cooked, the heat becomes contagious. You benefit from being around others who are ecstatically on fire because it increases the odds that your soul will be ignited. This is why Sacred Ecstatics deemphasizes solo spiritual snacking and encourages the spiritual feast of community cooking. Go ahead and ask yourself: "Will I continue to wallow in the bullshit, or will I run with the bulls, joining those who came before me on the path headed to the big room ring of fire?" We have been extraordinarily fortunate to witness something that is truly unique for the world. The Kalahari sand and its campground fire are spreading. Step into this expanding numinous landscape and release whatever has held you back from the singing mail and piercing nail of infinite love.

Sacred Ecstatics: Welcome to the Mystery Show

Sacred Ecstatics follows an old recipe in an ever-new way that welcomes a remarkable diversity of sacred names, metaphors, chants, songs, dances, and endless forms of gleeful expression that permeate the many cultures, places, and spaces where we go to help people spiritually cook. Like a rolling First Creation stone, our work is continuously influenced, inspired, altered, and reinvented by each gathering and visionary journey that bring unexpected mystical gifts and teachings. At the same time we have no attachment to whether Sacred Ecstatics finds a stable form or keeps on changing. We follow our rope to God and hand our life over to the supreme conductor of all mystery because we cannot possibly know how, when, or where we will be directed to host the spiritual fire.

Over the years we have experimented with many ways of conducting intensives that last one evening, a couple of days, or a full week. We have called these gatherings by different names including the Life Force Theatre, Shaking Medicine Show, Shamanic Cabaret, Mojo Mind Spa, Rehab for the Soul, Seiki Circus, and the Burning Bush Festival. These shifting names echo the changing we experience as we enter the big room of First Creation at each intensive. From the shape-shifting theatre we might experientially go to a mystical carnival or we may land in a shaker meeting, a sanctified shout, or a Kalahari dance revival. Anything can happen in the vast expanse manse that hosts Sacred

Ecstatics.

Once in Paris we spontaneously recreated the French cabaret of the 1890s, while in London we brought back the fire of its flame-throwing preachers of the 18th Century. On another night at a historic mountain ranch in Arizona, the Kalahari dance with its way of singing, clapping, and throwing nails of n/om spontaneously broke loose under the moonlight. In New York City the ghosts of Tin Pan Alley and the great secular shamanic song catchers like Gershwin, Porter, Kern, and Sondheim graced our stage, while in Amsterdam Brad played the Mississippi blues in homage to Van Gogh's starry night of the soul. Soon after, the fervor of Franz Liszt fever was reignited in a Budapest ruin pub when a Hungarian folk dancer rediscovered his life force. Down in Mexico City, we invited Frida Kahlo's life to give testimony to the magical transformation of suffering into creative art. The Blue House she shared with Diego Rivera, with its vibrantly painted floors and walls, inspired us to tear down all boring, lifeless barriers that block us from living with more creative fire underneath a changing, endless butterfly canopy.

Sometimes we lead a group of people on an ecstatic travel track and at other times we conduct healing sessions. Or we forget the name, role, and type of charcoal to make way for an unexpected form to arise. The only thing we demand of ourselves is that we start with no plan or purpose other than crossing into the big room to get ecstatically lit and soulfully ignited. Once a match is struck and a fire is set, we simply get out of the way and let ineffable mystery have its say and advance its play. Our matchbox includes anointed music, spontaneous dance and movement, improvised chants, and spirit driven percussion. Brad is a fire-setting improvisational pianist and drummer while Hillary is a n/om dancer, chanter, singer, and tambourine shaker. All our action is dedicated to placing everyone inside the big room for spiritual cooking and serving its feast of sacred ecstasy.

Our ecstatic gatherings and audio tracks may sound like a wild mix of mystical induction, shamanic combustion, and magical theatre production. Mixing metaphors, themes, genres, tropes, lyrics, poems, prayers, chants, songs, rhythms, dreams, and rhyming streams we create a space so large that show business and mystical transmittance can co-mingle. What matters is that these musical-mystical journeys expand and heat up the room, making the stage vast, bright, hot, and transformative enough for anything to happen from visionary dreaming to vibrant well-being and whole room healing. Most importantly, when the big room really cooks, we receive an infusion of the sacred vibration that ripples throughout the celebratory atmosphere.

This is not merely wild entertainment or radical amusement. It is an example of the way the big room hosts First Creation change and moves us to and through any performance form, all in the service of spontaneous spiritual combustion. There are times when we get deeply in a groove and hang out for a while. We especially find this true for the sacred spaces of the ecstatic lineages with which we have relationship. For example, we often ride the gospel song tracks of old school sanctified black churches, reaching as far back to their earliest roots as possible. We also enter into the Kalahari way of archery and carpentry, shooting arrows and nails of mystery into welcoming hearts. Similarly, a Japanese seiki jutsu bench can float into the room and send us bobbing down the life force shiver river. We do all of this freed from the heat-constraining habits of institutionally (dis)stilled beliefs and wing-clipped practices. In other words, we are not attached to anything other than the rope to God. We aren't even attached to that idea—we are attached to catching its emotion and expressing its song.

We acknowledge, however, that when we are in the midst of any particular kind of spiritual expression, it truly feels like "this is it" or "this is our true spiritual home" and we can't imagine exiting. There are moments when we are sure we will pour

Kalahari sand in a warehouse and invite folks to a regularly scheduled n/om dance. At other times we are ready to open a storefront Holy Ghost Clinic or a seiki jutsu movement hall of non-subtle energetics. Over the years our website and physical locale often changed. We have been the mojo doctors of New Orleans, the seiki jutsu practitioners of California, the shaking medicine doctors of Toronto, the café mystics of Budapest, and the Life Force Theatre performers of New York City. It took us a while to realize that we live in First Creation (the Kalahari name for the big room we use when feeling shaky and spear-y) and that the long-term term, Sacred Ecstatics, enables us to keep all of this on a performance stage broad enough to welcome any known or unknown way of getting spiritually cooked. Since we place our hand in the hand of the First Creation changing (wo)man from the time before Second Creation name games, we allow the changing One to have his/her way with us and this means we must be open minded and open hearted enough to allow the wind of vast mystery to carry us wherever it is blowing. We might find ourselves suddenly transported to an African ceremony, a juke joint, a Viennese waltz, a Mexican mariachi bandstand, a Balinese trance dance, an improv comedy show, a circus act, a gypsy wedding, a casket-swinging New Orleans second line, a Flamenco in the indigo sky bull ring, a creative therapy arena of change, or something further out-of-the-box and not yet named. This is ultimate living, the practical and theatrical spiritual cooking enacted on the ever-changing mystery stage for every age.

We recognize that a big room First Creation production can be disorienting to newcomers, as it should be. If you are stuck believing one way is the only way or equally stuck with the assumption that one particular way can never be a worthy ambassador of the singular ropeway, then the original Kalahari changing of First Creation is going to shake you up. Rather than resist and raise your fist, reach out to meet, greet, and grasp a welcoming ecstatic handshake. Sacred Ecstatics may irritate word trumping and Bible thumping Christians even though we sing old hymns with heart and soul. We are not moved by any admonishment of emotion in favor of the stilled and overly tilled word. We also may equally irritate New Age evangelizers who are rigidly gluten-free, sugar-free, and God-free. We simply dismiss all talk and thought that lacks the fire of the changing God(ess) of Pre-named Creation. May a big ecstatic firestorm be their fate, clean their slate, and feed them a plate of truly baked mystery cake.

We recognize Ibn al-'Arabi as a fellow sojourner to the big room who felt the vibe of the First Creation tribe. When he heard a mysterious voice call out to him, he fled and hid for several days in a cemetery, where he had a vision in which he met Jesus, Moses, and Mohammed. In this formative mystical experience he was taught that all prophets, saints, mystics, shamans, healers and anyone else admitted to ultimate mystery are representatives of the same primordial religion. We are dedicated to keeping afloat what he wrote: "There is no knowledge except that taken from God, for He alone is the Knower," and that those who directly experience divine mystery have "no disagreement in knowledge of God, since they took it from God" (Chittick 1989, 170).

If you want the diverse flavor and wild fervor of the sacred fire without a rude observer saying you immediately need a life preserver, then say hello to Sacred Ecstatics. This is more than enjoying a mystical firework show, because the way of ecstatic living requires you show the whole of creation that you are serious about moving past any past, ready for a trickster talk fast, and excited to be cast on stage with a script that is tripped, flipped, and dipped in the forever-changing taste of a thirst-quenching First Creation libation of liberation. In summary, all that can be known about a gathering of people who come for an intensive in Sacred Ecstatics is that you won't know what will happen other than there will be a whole lot of spiritual cooking going on.

When the moment strikes during an intensive, we may invite someone to come forward and receive ecstatic healing. We usually hold one or both of the recipient's hands as our sacred vibration is shared and circulated, providing a handheld bridge to the big room. Fresh metaphors arise and turn into unexpected life themes, memes, rhymes, poems, moans, shouts, or songs. As a new foundation and room is built to house more creative mystery, we prescribe action that helps sustain the transformation percolating all around. You might be advised to write your name backwards on a leaf that is dropped into a puddle before taking it to a lake, make a crown for your pencil, or write a funny ditty for your next teardrop. Whatever is said, sung, moved, or shaken may trip you into a mystery fall that assures the arrival of an ecstatic spring. Greet each surprise to find that whatever heartfelt emotions, radical changes, and eureka moments take place for another person also take place for everyone in the room. Each volunteer for an ecstatic session is an elected representative of the whole group, chosen by mystery to deliver a teaching to us all.

Like all spiritual captains, we know when to change a tune as a means of steering journeys up and down the musical roadways. Our room is big enough to hold and cook any kind of song, from children's tunes to a classic love song, cowboy sing-along, Motown hit, Broadway skit, or old sanctified hymn. At a Sacred Ecstatics gathering you might hear the sounds of Beethoven, Liszt, Chet Baker, Erroll Garner, George Gershwin, Mahalia Jackson, the Mississippi Mass Choir, Cole Porter, Shirley Horn, Johnny Cash, Nina Simone, Pavarotti, Albertina Walker, Roy Rogers and Dale Evans, Ray Charles, Antonio Carlos Jobim, Astrud Gilberto, Thomas A. Dorsey, Tito Puente, Stevie Wonder, Zulu drumming, Guarani stomping, Kalahari clapping, or other field recordings Brad has made of ecstatic music found throughout the world—all in the same day. Our music and rhythm repertoire is not predetermined or pre-restrained, as any particular choice of live or recorded performance is determined by the ecstatic pulling of the musically mystical ropes. One of our greatest treasures is our special playlist—the songs we have received in visionary journeys to the spiritual classrooms. Because these songs are especially anointed and spiritually charged, their impact on people can be miraculous. Though our Sacred Ecstatics community is scattered across the globe, we are bound together by the blessed song ropes that lasso our hearts, bringing us nearer and making us dearer.

It is not uncommon for unexplainable events to take place at Sacred Ecstatics intensives that range from microphones bursting into flames, fire alarms spontaneously going off, light bulbs exploding, and even lightning striking the building, all of which have happened in different venues around the world. Perhaps the oddest occurrence took place at a farm in the English countryside when during the transmission of a nail of n/om, a loud knocking sound was heard outside. When we looked all we could see was a large hare standing upright and knocking its head against the front door. We took it as a message that everyone should stop trying so hard to get ahead. Instead, just open the door and make the ecstatic leap into mystery. Then the bliss you otherwise would miss will raise each and every hair as you meet a rare hare knocking at the entrance to everywhere.

Playwright and author Nor Hall described this ecstatic work as "a way of dissolving the bundling boards that people erect to keep themselves separate." She adds, "Each encounter is an original composition" and gives the feeling that "something from elsewhere/elsewhen has powerfully rearranged us in relation to each other" (in Keeney 2007, 210-211). It matters less to us whether Sacred Ecstatics is regarded as the introduction of a unique kind of spirituality or whether it brings renewal to what already exists, or neither, or both. At its best it provides a new kind of syncretic hybrid of transformative art *and* religion that is rooted to diverse ecstatic lineages that are equally welcome to a performance space without boundaries. Here sanctified gospel music intermingles with the American songbook, Italian strings, African drums, and Asian bells, as absurd comedy tickles praise-based feelings that inspire improvised healings. What is most important is that our work and way of expressing it evoke sacred action that serves the burning, turning, and changing of the big room re-creation of First Creation. It offers a jazz of spirituality and an ongoing improvisation of ecstatic living. Amidst this fervor, Sacred Ecstatics invites you to join the chorus line of the spiritually cooked ancestors who dance across space and time.

Wait no more for rhythm to arrive and inspire more song and dance. Go ahead and start tapping your fingers, hands, toes, and feet. Tap a rhythm on every table at which you sit and on every floor you walk upon. Consider this to be a mystical tapping and a soulful knocking (and a hair-raising surprise) at the door of the big room. Aim to tap into the ecstatic algorithm while remembering that Sacred Ecstatics needs no formulaic secret other than it's all about bringing home the beacon of rhythmic mystery.

Obtain a pair of drumsticks at a music store and sign your name or make your mark on them. Use them to tap a rhythm on the side of a small box, the bottom of a waste can, the top of a book, a pothole in the street, various tree barks, deep lakes, shallow streams, your matchbox, your sand, your body, and anything with which you are able to make rhythmic contact. Reach as high as you can and tap the atmosphere of the whole universe. Do it to get on board a rhythm train and send a message to the big room that you are ready to get spiritually cooked. Your tapping is ready to be used as a mystical kind of telegraph. In a global spiritual emergency, tap an S.O.S. to "save our ship," "syncopate our soul," and "send on seiki." This is exactly the urgent message you need to send on behalf of everyone.

Entry to the big room of forever changing First Creation requires more than a drum roll and bugle call. It requires a spiritual accident that trips you to fall outside the boundaries of every small room in Second Creation oration. Something has to break so there is an opening to enter the raw, unnamed, and untamed wilderness of mystery. As Joan Halifax describes this accidental becoming:

> It is not possible to sign up for a weekend course in shamanism and "get it." It is not possible to dream it up, pay for it, or study it. In fact, you cannot really seek it; rather, it seeks you. In a similar context, Richard Baker-roshi once said, "Enlightenment is an accident. Practice makes you accident-prone." Becoming a shaman is the same thing. Going on vision quests, making offerings, doing the Sun Dance—none of this makes a person a shaman. Going for days and days without food and water in the coldest and harshest of climates—none of this confers shamanhood. Something has to break inside of you; and then that which is discovered within is found to be raw and absolutely naked. It is a mind that some people know who leave no tracks on their way. It is rare . . . (Halifax 1988, 203)

Bowing Before Mystery

It is very common for people to confuse their sincere longing to be touched, hooked, led, and fed by the numinous with the compulsive desire to be recognized as a healer, shaman, or spiritual teacher with special powers. Part of you may even know that you yourself cannot choose to be shaman, and you may even feel a bit embarrassed to admit that you have this desire. That's when trickster comes in to convince you that your hunger to be a shaman is not full of ego but is actually based on an altruistic "calling" to help others. It is not possible for you to sort all this out on your own, nor should you trust the counsel of friends or other self-proclaimed shamans who may, with good intentions, suggest that because you are such a wonderful person you should simply "follow your heart" and hang a shingle. The Guarani shamans go straight to the point concerning who can become a shaman:

> If you didn't come to earth to be a shaman, there is nothing you can do to become one. God chooses you. You cannot make yourself become a shaman if you were not chosen to be one. No one can teach you how to be one. (Keeney 2000, 77)

Instead of being in a hurry to have a special spiritual title, take the time to learn and embody what a shaman actually does: prays, sings, moves, and makes rhythm while staying focused on the Creator. We cannot say enough that if you can learn to cook a prayer with the right blend of rhythm, tone, movement, and sacred emotion, you will no longer feel the desire for anything more. If you are then ever called by God to help another, whether it is one time or hundreds of times, you will realize that you can only be helpful after you have learned to build a big room, light a fire for spiritual cooking, and then wisely deliver the goods to others.

Rather than continue to be tempted by the exaggerated promises rampant among confabulating teachers and infatuated seekers, follow the wisdom of people like João Fernandes de Carvalho, one of the greatest healers of our time. After helping over 50,000 patients and experiencing an extraordinary amount of miraculous mystery, he summarized his life this way:

> I can honestly say that I never was involved with any kind of spiritualism nor did I ever ask to be a healer. I have only prayed with my rosary and found that God spontaneously gave me the gift to heal. (Keeney 2003a, 22)

His son, Tadeu, professor of mathematics in Brazil, elaborates:

> My father has never claimed to perform a miracle. He also never interprets anything that happens . . . He does not want to be remembered as a healer, a magical person, or as a saint. He only wants to be remembered as a simple person. Perhaps the most precious gift he gave us was the understanding that we are nothing more or less than a small stone in the world and that we must love each other and thank God every day. (Keeney 2003a, 54)

We call for an exodus to the big room where we can all become jubilant skipping-on-the-water pebbles of ecstatic eternity and mystical infinity—riding the First Creation C.M.C. waves and sending ripples along its ponds. You are now cordially invited to try a special way of escaping any prepackaged and hermetically sealed Second Creation cardboard, blowhard reality. Before specifying this task, please consider how every part of you is always inseparable from the whole of you. Your nose is you, as is your ear, hair, little toe, leg, belly button, dimple, jawbone, funny bone, and finger. In other words, any presumed part is also a representative of the whole. With this in mind, your present task is to have a part of you pray, sing, and dance while fully realizing that it is actually doing so on behalf of all of you.

Choose a finger that will partake in this out-of-the-box mission. Any finger will do. Every evening before you go to bed, take a pen and draw an interesting face on that fingertip. Do so with the beginner's mind of a child *and* the learned mind of an adult, recognizing that both these developmental stages of your life are also contributing parts to your wholeness. Your small face makeover can have a couple of dots for eyes with an arc for the mouth. Perhaps draw a couple of stars for the eyes with the bottom of a hollow bowl for a smile and a straight rope for a nose. Again, make sure you are doing this task with a simultaneously playful *and* serious attitude. Doing so may seem conceptually impossible, but faithfully enact it anyway. Take a shallow breath, followed by a deep breath, and proceed to have this finger-being bow before your matchbox, now considered a tiny altar. Your finger is to meticulously bow and pray as if it is your last day on earth. Discipline your mind to stay focused on hearing its words. Then have it soulfully sing as the rest of you wholeheartedly listens. Finally, have this chosen finger-singer perform an ecstatic dance. Give it your all and make sure it trips and makes the right kind of fall.

Again, it is extremely important that you conduct this task with obvious passion. The deepest parts of you are paying attention to your willingness to sincerely take action that has never been accomplished in your personal history. In this performance of something wildly different, inspired by a longing for mystery and a relationship to divinity, inner switches are turned on and unconscious wheels are set in motion. Forget cynical thought; simply head toward the pinnacle spot where your heart gets shot with song as your soul is caught and made spiritually hot.

Carefully lift your finger and then allow it to bow again before your tiniest altar, medicine bag, spiritual bundle, shamanic rattle, and mystery suitcase. Humbly do so in order to reduce the size of your trickster mind even though it may habitually desire more exaggerated thoughts and plots. Ask your inner Señor Jackal or Señorita Coyote—a.k.a. the tricky one—to follow the leading direction of your pointing finger and have it also bow before the tiny altar and join the prayers, songs, and dances of your newly metamorphosed digit. As you set yourself up to experience an unexpected fidget, expect to be shaken enough to seriously board whatever frigate carries you to the vast sea of ineffable mystery.

When Moses used his rod for miraculous tasks that were demonstrated to the Pharaoh, the magicians declared that this was the work of "the finger of God." It was also said that "the finger of God" wrote the Ten Commandments. Yes, a single finger can perform miracles, point out higher truth, flick away trickster distraction, sing a snappy song, touch the sacred fire, host a nail, shoot a mystical arrow, tap a message to God, bow before the sea without names, launch a skipping pebble, and scratch the surface of heaven. Don't be the kind of person about whom the gods will say, "He or she wouldn't lift a finger." Remember Michelangelo's masterful image on the Sistine Chapel where Adam's finger is extended to receive the spark of life from God's pointing finger. Point to the sky, receive the divine zap that fills the empty gap, and light up the room!

Lift your finger. Do it this very moment! "As above, so below" is a half-truth pointing to the unspoken other truth: "as below, so above." As you hold up your pointing finger—a lightning rod waiting to be struck—God's finger is also pointing toward you, ready to send a numinous bolt. Between these earthly and heavenly fingers an aligned singular line appears to the eye, ear, and skin of mystical reception. Line yourself up so your soul can traverse the bridge to the big room where First Creation is felt as a fire in all your bones and tones. Get in line with all those who came before you on the sanctified vine, divine spine, and highest climb. Do whatever it takes to get aligned, primed, timed, and rhymed with the sacred circuit of ecstatic current. Sharpen the point aimed at the holiest pointing and then head to your anointing. In the space between longing for the immortal beloved and the Creator pulling, reeling, and singing you home, a spark ignites that sets creation on fire.

5

REENTERING THE EVERYDAY

The third step of the Sacred Ecstatics recipe begins when it is time to descend the thermometer and journey back to your everyday. Although things may heat up again at any time and spark another round in the fire, eventually spiritual cooking comes to a close. Knowing how to return from the big room is as important as knowing how to get there. Your mission is to sustain the experienced warmth and expansion that promotes ongoing change. A unique mystical prescription for creative action helps prepare you for such an empowered return, keeping one foot inside the big room of mystery while the other steps back into familiar small rooms. The fruit of Sacred Ecstatics is found in how it helps you instill creative vitality and spread unexpected mystery throughout your daily personal endeavors, relationships, work, and re-creation.

The purpose of spiritual cooking is to set your soul on fire, have your body charged with sacred vibration, your heart lifted by ecstatic joy, and your mind oriented toward vast mystery. You exit from this exhilarating experience with a well-tuned spiritual engine as a vibrant hum buzzes inside, ready to meet the daily challenges of living. Fully recharged, you're able to infuse creative life into your interactions with others. Every trip to the big room leaves you with the sweet bliss and deep peace of remembering your smallness in relationship to the all-surrounding infinity of divinity. You come back like a child smiling at life's boundless wonder and laughing at the absurdity of trying to seriously understand the miraculous nature of ineffable mystery. Hearing sacred music is now like drinking heavenly wine while praying feels like lassoing a ray of the sun, breathing the freshest mountain air, and tasting the sweetest apricot marmalade. You resonate fully with Teresa of Avila's words: "the soul is satisfied now with nothing less than God."

It is not enough to get spiritually cooked only once in your life because a subsequent extended stay in the cold eventually makes you frigidly rigid all over again. Without repeated heating you easily relapse into old habits that squeeze you back into small rooms. From the perspective of Sacred Ecstatics, the mystic's dark night of the soul that so often took place after an initial illumination is more accurately called a "cold" night of the soul. Lacking spiritual pyrotechnical know-how, many mystical traditions think you can contemplate or ritualize yourself back into the fire in an effort to recapture the previous pinnacle experience. Those means, however, typically make the prayer room too small and cold, and the mystic is left lamenting her inability to experience sacred ecstasy again as she tries to cogitate her way back through the mystical gate. Trickster mind arrives to throw more ice water on the situation, continuing the dead end search for a numinous reconnection through the means of trickster calculation rather than temperature calibration.

This cold vicious cycle has been known to last a long time. By some estimates, Saint Paul of the Cross experienced a cold spell that lasted 45 years, and Mother Teresa's episode lasted most of her life (van Biema 2007). They and the friends, teachers, and colleagues that surrounded them unfortunately lacked the ancient spiritual engineering wisdom of their southern neighbors—the Bushmen who would have been able to instantly diagnose and treat their chilly dark nights of the cramped soul: "You need to get cooked! Let's have a dance!" The lesson here is that when your trickster mind is on a runaway Polar Express train heading straight to the spiritual arctic, it's time to call the Kalahari Emergency Hotline. It's not enough to throw more memorized words at the situation. You have to again and again walk through the door of the big room, be set on fire, and allow yourself to get cooked. Don't try to recapture a previous experience by thought proliferation, but instead launch the changing action that raises the temperature. Heat rather than merely repeat a prayer in order to catch the sacred emotion fueling the rhythmic ride of the big room-orienting express.

The cyclical nature of ecstatic spirituality—getting cooked in a big room and then afterwards cooling off in the return to small rooms—releases you from the limiting assumption that you are on a linear progressive march toward final spiritual enlightenment and perfection. Such a view lacks the wisdom that you and your relationship to the divine are always changing with the ups and downs of the surrounding spiritual temperature. This is also true for the people around you. If you cling to the idea that you can achieve a final state of absolute permanent happiness, intelligence, creativity, health and the like, you are more likely to exaggerate each stumble, pratfall, mistake, or shortcoming as a dramatic fall from grace—the despair that leads to the rush for a quick repair. You may get further stuck in the small clinical room of constant monitoring, anxiously waiting for the measure of pleasure to exceed the gain of pain. Constantly assessing your psychological condition leads to more spiritual refrigeration. Be less like the child in the backseat of the car during a family road trip who can't stop asking, "Are we there yet?" Instead, enjoy making the round trip journey to the big room over and over again, assured that each voyage on the familiar road will bring a surprise when the temperature is able to rise.

One dramatic outcome of getting spiritually cooked is that

when problems or suffering arrive you are less likely to psychologically analyze, spiritually demonize, or categorically pathologize the experience. Instead you more readily notice that you have simply shrunken back into a small room and need to return to the big room and get cooked again. In this way ecstatic living is the alternative to narrated observing that persistently remains outside the experiential streaming and dreaming of life. This marks a revolution in the waiting for the healing arts. Rather than endlessly "process" or "get to the bottom" of your issues through talk, you simply recognize when it's time to set your soul on fire and get your spiritual battery recharged. Conversation no longer needs to be exaggerated as capable of providing a "talking cure." Instead, realize what talk *can* offer: a beginning means of expanding the room enough for the fire of transformation to commence. Rather than dispense canned patter and explanatory chatter, creatively use words to help make enough room to host the ecstatic thermodynamics of change.

The secret to having the ultimate life is visiting the big room to get cooked as often as possible. It is part of the human condition to cool off quickly. Bliss is not eternal; it dies down as you trip and stumble, get distracted by trickster, and fall back into a small room. While there are ways to slow down this cooling and sustain presence in vast spiritual space, you eventually will get lost and have to make the journey all over again. The good news is that getting back to the big room becomes easier, more natural, and even automatic after you have been repeatedly and thoroughly spiritually cooked.

People have traditionally found that they need to be spiritually readjusted, recalibrated, retuned, realigned, recharged, and recooked with others at least once a week, whether it's at a Bushman dance, community ceremony, worship service, or life force theatre. Each week you go to the crossroads and choose to take the action that builds the big room and lights the spiritual fire so you can return as a revitalized instrument ready to serve your colleagues, neighbors, friends, and family in daily work and play. Spiritual heat awakens the desire "to give what is our own to another and feeling his delight as our own," as Emmanuel Swedenborg described it. This heart-inspired, socially interdependent, sharing-based stewardship helps "Thy will be done on earth as it is in heaven."

While gathering with others regularly to spiritually cook is beneficial, it's important that you establish new ecstatic habits in your daily life that short-circuit your tendency to shrink and chill too easily. It's not enough to just contemplate the sacred. You must act in order to nurture a sincere desire to live nearer the divine—close enough to feel its joy and hear its music. Melodically hum, rhythmically pray, and cheerfully sway as often as you can throughout each day[14] to keep yourself tethered to the big room of First Creation while you travel to the smaller rooms and cooler temperatures of Second Creation to fulfill your obligations. Doing so will remind you to pay most attention to the divine rope above your head and the ropes above others' heads as well. You'll realize that spiritual practice is not just about changing yourself but helping to make the room bigger and ropes stronger for everyone.

Spiritual cooking changes the way you pray, turning it from an exercise in rote repetition to an opportunity for whole-bodied, full-motioned and highly "emotioned" communion with the sacred. Not only is prayer emotionally and energetically infused with soulful movement, rhythm, and tone, the content of your words points to the infinite. You no longer tell God what outcome you want, but instead your prayers are filled with surrender to something bigger than small room concerns. You better appreciate how God already knows what you need even before you open your mouth. As old timers say, "He will look past your wants and

---

[14] For specific practices to expand and heat your daily life, see our book *The Spiritual Engineering of Sacred Ecstasy* (2018).

supply your needs." With more spiritual cooking, you mature and become wiser with words and the way you express them in prayer, more sincerely asking for the fulfillment of God's will. You pray to be a good vessel through which higher chosen action can pass. The more cooked you are, the better prepared you are for the divine to play you as a well-tuned instrument.

You also develop more awareness of your relational surroundings and become more perceptive and receptive to others in a way that you weren't before. Many people have a relational blind spot—they don't notice that they don't notice others. The orbit of their experiential world stops at the boundary of the epidermis. With room expansion, life suddenly becomes as surprising as a three-ring circus with more characters and action than were ever experienced before. Small rooms foster a self-focused trance where you are conscious only of what goes on within you: "Am I comfortable, receiving enough attention, or getting the desired outcome?" In a larger room you become more aware and responsive to what is going on around you: "How can I help expand the space, tend the fire, and enthusiastically contribute to the cooking of everyone?"

Frequent trips to the big room shift your life from solo psychological trance to relational spiritual dance. In the initial expansion you start noticing that your action shapes every perception, including the experiential quality of your social relationships. You are more responsible for your experiential reality than you ever realized before. Instead of being a passive sensory receiver and subsequent reactor to outside influence, you notice how your interactions with the world contribute to mutually creating it—you are a co-conspirator and co-creator of your room, world, and reality. As your life space continues to expand, you become aware that how you act and socially interact affects the degree to which you experience a higher power and mystery at work. The broader your performance stage for creative involvement, the more you fulfill your mission as one member among many in the remarkable interplay of a divinely led construction crew, performance team, orchestra, dance company, and theatre troupe.

Ecstatic living ethically tunes you to be in good alignment with the ropes of connection. You are more wisely responsive to your relations with other living creatures and the ecology as a whole. Ethics and stewardship come alive and are subject to the changing nature of life. They are not inflexibly bound by rigid rule, but spontaneously arise according to the specifics of each unique situation. Guided by divine rope awe rather than small room law, you are better able to host the sacred virtues by embodying what inspired them rather than policing any reductionist code of conduct.

Spiritual cooking prepares you for enhanced social involvement and creative contribution. It is not another narcissistic means of getting spiritually high. If you are left focusing on how delightful spiritual experience feels with no desire to make an important difference in the world around you, then there was never enough heat or space to sufficiently cook. The same is true if you find yourself inflated with the idea that you have become a privileged spiritual person who should always be separate from others, whether isolated in a faraway cave or a remote monastery. This is merely a small room tactic that lessens your being disturbed by others at the cost of making your relational feelings grow cold.

Sacred Ecstatics promotes thrilling involvement rather than boring separation, profound invention rather than trivial ritual, childlike curiosity rather than moralistic certainty, and genuinely soft availability to help rather than hard insulation from others' suffering. A spiritually cooked person is noticeably sweet, kind, soft, and generous while also fiercely discerning and diligent in maintaining the important distinctions, names, and frames that house and foster ecstatic living. You are not easily distracted by small containers and constrained thinking. As you learn to bring holy expansion, spiritual heat, and the sacred vibration of creative inspiration into the everyday, you appreciate the importance of the bridge that carries you from ceremony to home, neighborhood, and larger community.

Getting spiritually cooked makes you a better advocate and ambassador of sacred clarity, widespread truth, just relations, and street-smart stewardship. You more ably realize and honor the wisdom voiced by Chief Seattle: "Humankind has not woven the web of life. We are but one thread within it. Whatever we do to the web, we do to ourselves. All things are bound together. All things connect." As you care for your rope to God, all the threads, fibers, strings, and cords that comprise the web of nature are nurtured as well.

Cooling Down for Reentry

During step three of the recipe, a gradual shifting of ecstatic gears takes place as you climb down the rope from the big room experience of First Creation and get ready for a renewed plunge into the Second Creation climate of daily life. The fire burns inside while outward behavior and expression are adjusted to meet and greet the cold, expanding whatever container feels small so it can host more change that matters in the scheme of it all. In other words, after being cooked in the big room, you are ecstatically and practically made ready for the return with a body and soul that continue to burn.

Seasoned ecstatic aficionados know how to steer themselves and others back from the heat with the right words, melodic tones, rhythms, movements, and even a dash of humor. If you return too fast you might feel the "bends" of deep sea diving that come from being out of synch with what awaits at the surface. You feel cranky and snappy rather than happy and zappy. When the reentry into the everyday is accomplished in a gracefully executed manner, you return feeling highly inspired, refreshed, and in tune with your surroundings. This is why it is important to follow the instructions given by those who know how the diplomatic pragmatics of ecstatic dynamics can help you avoid coming home too static, dogmatic, or non-resourcefully erratic. If you are not fully cooked, then allow others who are more seasoned in this work to lead the journey back home. Their longtime experience makes them more attuned to feeling and following the divine rope's tug, the requirement for guiding an optimal return.

Cooling action is also needed when someone becomes too quickly heated during a Sacred Ecstatics cookout. For example, when overheating occurs during a Bushman dance, cooling is enacted by blowing a strong puff of air over each ear, gently patting the top of the head, or rubbing the sides of the abdomen to settle down the nails of n/om, among other means. You can also sit and catch your breath as you remember that this work is held in relationship to the benevolent divine who always takes care of you. An absurd tease or comedic breeze also can help things cool off in a good way. We once cooled someone down by singing a silly mixed up version of several children's songs: "Mary had a little yam, little clam, little ham . . . And everywhere that Mary went, the lamb was sure to row, row, float your boat, gently in the dream. Merrily, merrily, quite contrarily, life's a big room stream." Each corrective response should be a spontaneous improvisation that arises gently from the dream stream, so there is no need to have a written script or "what to do" list nearby.

You know you are too spiritually hot when you start to fall over and have a difficult time maintaining physical balance. In your beginning involvement with spiritual cooking you might pass out from a sudden jolt of spiritual electricity, what charismatic churches call being "slain in the spirit."[15] We regard this

---

[15] Most charismatic churches do not know that being slain in the spirit is not representative of the highest spiritual temperature. Even sanctified black

phenomenon as a natural result of heating too rapidly. When this happens you need to get realigned and back on track. The goal is to learn how to effectively hold spiritual heat rather than be overwhelmed by it so you can stay longer in the spiritual fire.

Songs are also used to help bring everyone down for a smooth reentry. As we mentioned in chapter two, the Caribbean Shakers have a "spiritual captain" who uses music to bring folks on board a spiritual ship, fire up the engine for travel, and return them to the port after the journey ends. When people are too hot they fall off the ship as it rocks too wildly and loses its rhythmic coordination. Here a cool song is sung to help get the people back on course. Such a song usually has a sure and steady beat that helps rescue, resuscitate, and resituate everyone's steady presence. The music and rhythm that is right for the moment—including what is needed for reeling people in, steadying the ship, or bringing things to a halt by throwing out an anchor—is dependent upon the situation, just like all matters that concern working the spirit.

In a Bushman dance, each song climbs to a feverish threshold after which it starts to cool down as all singers slow the tempo and end at the same time, like a train pulling into a station. The same holds for sanctified gospel songs. The lead singer or organist slows the song down and brings the congregational ship home to port. Music may also be interspersed with the kind of prayer that brings people back to a cooler temperature more suitable for reentry. The art of using music and prayer to cool down a room helps everyone ease back into the everyday while sustaining the warmth, energy, joy, and glow that came from dancing with mystery.

Once someone develops the skills and receives an anointment to

---

churches have lost touch with the fullest range of sanctified expression. In contrast, Bushman culture has kept alive the most ecstatic spiritual know-how. Learning and applying their ancient wisdom allows more heated awakening and renewal of all ecstatic spiritual traditions.

conduct spiritual cooking, everything that takes place in the spiritual heat happens naturally on its own without need for consciously imposed hindsight, foresight, or stoplight. This is also true for step three of Sacred Ecstatics. Don't try to understand it, force it, or enforce too many rules about it. Let it be guided by the felt pulling of higher reins. The ending marks the time to launch a new beginning in the world. This may be expressed with a prayer, song, graceful movement, or witty ditty that sincerely expresses gratitude. "Thank you for the blessings bestowed upon us. May we remain forever more inside this everlasting love with all its divine mystery." Or say with a smile, "That's all folks. Before we say goodbye, I've got to say that there's nothing better than a good fish fry. Praise the lard! Grant us the appetite for deep fried holy delight, the courage to cook the best we can, and the wisdom to know when to add more grease!" If the room was made big enough and the temperature soared hot enough, the right ending will spontaneously, naturally, and surprisingly arise.

Remaining Inside the Big Room

Once you have cooled down and reentered everyday reality, do everything you can to keep the room as big as possible for as long as possible. Allow the big room to invisibly circumscribe your everyday small rooms. It helps to focus and limit your post-cooking commentary to praises of ecstatic gratitude that are directed toward the highest spiritual altitude, "Thank you!" "How sweet it is to cook together," "No words can say how grateful I am," "To God be the glory" Avoid wasting the blessing of sacred jubilation by messing around with self-adulation such as, "Whoa! Wow! That was a great spiritual journey. You won't believe what happened to me . . ." When you express any kind of "gee whiz" or self-empowering statement that draws attention to yourself or your personal experience rather than the numinous, it is a clear signal that you are no longer spiritually warm. If you talk about what happened, do so carefully and wisely, acknowledging that your words as well as the experience they point to are parts inside the greater whole from which they arose. This serves keeping you, your spiritual cooking, and your way of sharing it afterwards inside the vastest realm of mystery.

Don't be too eager to report every detail of your spiritual experience, visionary or otherwise. Ecstatic traditions teach that you should only share part of a visionary dream, not all of it. For instance, if you dream of receiving a song while riding a visionary antelope, giraffe, crocodile, buffalo, or flying horse, it is wiser to spotlight the sacred song and downplay its means of transport. Talking too much about the wild ride attracts mental curiosity that risks overshadowing the heartfelt emotion brought by song. Only share the holiest — which is often the simplest — part of your dream or experience. Reemphasize any part that inspires you and others to feel closer to the ineffable and resist the temptation to tell stories where the illusions of magic override the purest ecstatic joy.

It is similarly unwise to disclose too many specifics about the "dark" aspects of a vision because this also takes the focus off of the divine whose redemptive, room sweeping power has no need for detailing the dusty particulates that were cleared away. For instance, if you traveled to a spiritual hospital and experienced a surgery where past mistakes, sins, or wrongdoings were removed, only say that your "sins were washed away" or that you "were made spiritually clean," rather than providing too much specific information about the dirt. Do not publicly display your soiled laundry or indulge in relating how you were stuck in a nasty quandary. This is not to protect you from embarrassment, but to help prevent any inflated part from blurring the more essential point. People are easily distracted by tales of the dark and enjoy reveling in stories about how easily human beings can go astray. The last thing you want to do is make the dark or its dirt a primary theme rather than a small part held in the everlasting arms and heavenly sunshine of God's forgiveness, redemption, and loving grace. In the big room there is a fountain that washes away every stain, a wind that blows away all dust, and a fire that burns away all that stands in the way of sacred ecstasy.

The first visit to the spiritual classrooms taken by one of the holiest leaders of the St. Vincent Shakers, Archbishop Pompey, addresses this teaching:

> On my first pilgrim journey, I heard people say that when your sins roll away they go right back to the sea. In my journey, I found myself on a mountain picking mangoes. The mangoes were all ripe and they got away from me. I went to find them, but found myself on a truck where I heard a voice speak and sing this song, "I am delivered, praise the Lord." That was when I found out about my sins. For some people, their sin is a big stone to roll away. When I imagined mine, it was four ripe mangoes. I also learned that when your sins are gone, you are not to go looking for them. Because, your sins have been rolled away. (Keeney 2002, 117)

Archbishop Pompey often taught his parishioners, "Everyone needs to leave the mangoes behind and never look back." Neither you nor anyone else needs to look at them again. His teaching echoes the practical wisdom that there is no need to obsessively sort through your garbage before throwing it away. When it comes to your faults, past errors, or wrong doings, simply hand your "garbage" to something far bigger than you and allow it to be taken care of by a higher means of waste disposal that is beyond your understanding and skill. As the old Thomas A. Dorsey gospel song proclaims, "Never Turn Back," and this includes not reliving or replaying past experiences that keep you in a cramped, cold room. We once prescribed someone the task of wholeheartedly reciting an absurd yet holy prayer that embodies this same teaching: "Oh, Mama Nah-ture, please recycle this human manure." Allow God to dispose and recompose your waste rather than continue to redundantly wallow in it, whether it is called a problem, pathology, dark side, sin, shadow, or mango. Let them roll into the numinous sea and be dissolved by waves that also wave goodbye to what needs to be gone so you can be cooked well done.

When testimonies of faith dwell too much on reporting past sins, the congregation might whoop and holler to hear it while not realizing that this diminishes the focus on God's love, which is big enough to render all details irrelevant. Keep your eyes cast upon the light that illumines the highest highway. A shadow leads to a trickster black hole, while mystical light reveals the sacred whole. This old-fashioned wisdom will serve your life better than any fascination with dramatizing darkness that may be encouraged by naïve therapists, shamanic practitioners, or spiritual communities. There is a time and place for facing the failure, manure, and immaturity of your life, doing so to realize that trickster mind is not a reliable captain of your soul, nor a wise judge of your spiritual character. When you then surrender your life to divine authority, guidance, and jurisdiction there is never any need to look back again at what has been "rolled away." It is trickster who wants you to both avoid examining your limitations and failures when you need to and reexamine them when it is no longer necessary to do so.

In general, when you come out of the big room and return to your daily relationships and responsibilities, only bring the sweet and fresh fruit from the sacred garden. Do your best to maintain the expansive space you built in step one of the recipe. Keep the room of your life as big as possible, even when you are thrown into a cold temperature. Again, this is accomplished through dynamic action and virtuously circular interaction rather than only solitary contemplation, infusing as much creative mystery as possible into your daily involvement with others. If you are having a difficult time with any past blast of darkness, then consider purchasing a small flashlight and writing these words on it: "I am the light of the world." Carry it with you always. Any time you catch yourself looking over your shoulder to see where any past spoiled rotten fruits are rolling, reach for the flashlight, read the words, and briefly shine it in your eyes. Don't look back unless you want to turn into a pillar of salt, which will bring you unnecessary pain every time it is placed on a wound. If you want to never stop accentuating your wound, then go ahead and keep rubbing in more small talk and salty thought. The alternative is to shine your light and be an exemplary love-knight who is no longer afraid of the dark, cold night.

Mystical Prescriptions

The third act of Sacred Ecstatics includes the creation of a mystical prescription, a special task recommended for the days following a session or intensive. A mystical prescription provides an action means of surrounding and infusing everyday small rooms with the expansion and heat experienced in the big room. It is not enough to remember or reflect upon what took place while being cooked — in fact, too much of this can cool you down. Instead, the vibrant atmosphere of creative change should be caught and brought into future action. Act without hesitation in order to immediately spread ecstatic transformation and keep it alive while you thrive within former small rooms that are now held inside recently found, unbound mystery.

A mystical prescription asks you to conduct a unique kind of experimental action, an uncanny, uncommon, unexpected task that is brand new to your former everyday experience but related to what just took place while cooked. For this prescription to be effective it must place one of your feet in everyday familiarity and the other inside big room mystery. From the perspective of life before big room entry, it won't make much sense. However, from the perspective of the cooking that just took place, it mysteriously seems sensible in a difficult-to-articulate way. The assigned task is paradoxically difficult to readily accept, reject, or resolve. It doubly binds you to both what is familiarly old and mystically new. Enactment of the prescription expands the room holding your everyday experience, which helps keep you from backsliding into a former small container.

At its best, a mystical prescription becomes a kind of action *koan*.[16] If you sincerely and passionately enact it, it will help keep the room vast and the temperature warm. If you only think about the prescription or try to understand it, you fall back into the habits of mind that squeeze you into small room containment. In this regard the mystical prescription is a preventative medicine that helps you be less vulnerable to the habitual operations of reflective understanding, conceptual analysis, or contemplative cognition. Simply perform it. Again, its medicine is found in its enactment, not in interpreting what it symbolically means or rationally hypothesizing an abstract outcome. Allow the

---

[16] A koan (Japanese) is a Zen Buddhist term that refers to the public, written record of an exchange, typically between master and student. As the late Taizan Maezumi Roshi articulated, a koan "is much more than a paradoxical riddle designed to prod the mind into intuitive insight. The koan is quite literally a touchstone of reality. It records an instance in which a key issue of practice and realization is presented and examined by experience rather than by discursive or lineal logic" (Yamada 2004, 293). Chinese master Dahui Zonggao (1089–1163) believed koans to be the best path to enlightenment. At the same time, he is known for having tried to burn the woodblocks of the Blue Cliff Record because he found that the study of koans had become a hindrance, with too much emphasis on intellectual and literary exercise (Foster and Shoemaker, 1996). The same risk exists for mystical prescriptions. They are designed to be enacted instead of solely interpreted through small room, Second Creation means.

prescribed action to further enlarge the room as more unpredictable creative surprises arise to make the temperature rise.

Spiritual cooking, whether it's done in a private session or a group gathering, requires all three steps of the Sacred Ecstatics recipe. Any occasion of spiritual cooking that does not include prescribing one-of-a-kind creative, mystical action is missing the legs of transformation, preventing whatever took place in the big room from walking home with you. We have demonstrated this progression throughout this book. Each chapter is a literary enactment of the recipe for setting your soul on fire, moving from the sacred expansion of your reading room to the celebration of spiritual cooking with poetic evocation, and then the prescription of a task that brings the vibrant creative change of ecstatic mystery into your everyday. If you have not done your assigned homework, then go back to the beginning of the book and start all over again. This time act in order to get past whatever overthinking or excessive understanding arose due to your missing the prescribed inoculation of mystical action.

It is arguably better for you to reverently plant apple seeds across the land than utter the lines of sacred creeds. Furthermore, it is wiser for you to learn how to sing like a partridge than take any solemn pledge. It is also healthier for you to pepper your day with a mystical prescription that liberates you from normality rather than follow a psychological inscription whose banal mentality drains away creative vitality. If doing something odd for God expands your experience and leaves you awed and thawed, you stand a better chance of dancing all the way up the highway to heaven.

When we teach Sacred Ecstatics to professional people helpers, healers, ceremonial leaders, preachers, and teachers, we always include instruction on how to create effective mystical prescriptions. These action koans of change require great skill to design and administer. They specify a radically different kind of performance that makes the everyday more like a freshly improvised life force theatre than a tired rerun of former routines. The mystical prescription must draw upon an important surprise that took place while cooking in the big room that is then connected to a familiar function or activity. For instance, if an imaginative, serendipitous, or accidental reference was made to "fishing line" during a session, then a task using fishing line may be designed. Perhaps someone will be asked to carry a small piece of fishing line in his pocket or attach it to the ceiling over his bed. We would also consider having such a client tie half the line around his ankle, and then take the other half to the largest lake in the region or leave it in a local temple. Such a mystical prescription metaphorically and theatrically places one end of the fishing line in a familiar small room and the other end in the big room formerly occupied during spiritual cooking. This also can be accomplished by instructing someone to hold onto one end of the fishing line each night while the other end is attached to the bedroom door knob with a sign placed underneath it: "God's gone fishing." Before sleeping, the line would be tugged slightly while whispering a prayer to be caught and reeled into higher mystery. Any other action that further elaborates a more spirit-filled situation can be added to bring more mystical saturation. Actually performing what is earthly absurd yet ineffably serious is far more spiritually meaningful than the typical routines that invite shrunken dreams. If you hope to get reeled into the vast sea, it's better to go fishing with God than lie in bed with your mind constantly tossing and turning.

One of our longstanding Sacred Ecstatics community members, Troy Marsh, an accomplished physical therapist from Utah, actually dreamed of fishing line. Here's an account of his visionary fishing trip:

Last night I went to bed sincerely trying to heat a prayer of thanksgiving. I dug deep within for a memory of when I had most felt an intense love for God. I then prayed with this sacred emotion before drifting off to sleep. Later I woke from a dream, overcome with tears. I dreamed that the Sacred Ecstatics community was together and I told Hillary how much I enjoyed the song, "Ol' Man River" sung by Paul Robeson, a recording she actually played at our last gathering. Shari and I had recently watched the movie *Show Boat* and discussed how much we love that song. We sing it often in our home.

Then suddenly in the dream an elder teacher appeared and took me to a river to show me how to fish. It was a big, deep, slow-flowing river with muddy banks. He took a white fluffy fly and tied it to the end of his fly line and started showing me how to cast. I couldn't believe how incredibly graceful, perfect, amazing, and beautiful his back and forward casting was; the line never got tangled. He even gained enough casting power to cast the fly line over a bridge in the distance. This time I thought for sure it would get tangled, but he looked at me and winked as if to say, "this is how you do it." He proceeded to yank the fly back over the bridge and continued to fish. Then he cast and lay the fly on the water as I watched it float. After one of these perfectly executed casts, a big trout surprised us as it came up and swallowed the fly. The fight was on! The elder teacher, a master fisherman, acted quickly to reel in the excess line because he knew that if the trout got too much slack the line would break. Keeping the long tip of his rod pointed high in the air, he kept on reeling while maintaining the line's tension. As the trout got closer, the fighting remained strong but the trout kept getting reeled in.

I was standing near the bank watching from a higher vantage point. There I saw the trout break the water surface only to quickly turn and dive into the water again. It was a large silver trout and I shouted with excitement when I saw its whole body. I thought that at any moment the large trout could break the line. I was there to help the elder land the trout even though we didn't have a net, only our bare hands. We had to tire the trout and pull it up close to the bank, doing so just right and not too quickly or it would be lost in the muddy water.

The old man on this river pulled on that trout as it fought one last time, diving to make us think it finally broke the line. I got on my belly at the river's edge, reaching in and ready to grab the fish if it was there. To my surprise there was no trout on the line—instead there was a young boy! He was wearing shorts and laced up boots. He had been underwater too long and I was aware of his life threating circumstance. I quickly grabbed the boy's ankle and pulled him out.

He lay there and I wasn't sure he was alive. I soon saw he was still breathing. I held him and waited, not sure he would live much longer. It took a while for that boy to take a big breath as he had taken in a lot of water that finally came up from his lungs. The boy lifted his head and with big brown eyes turned and smiled as I held him and joyfully wept that he was alive. I said, "Welcome back." I woke up still weeping with gratitude.

Troy went to sleep that night filled with prayerful devotion, emotion, and song, a mix that readied him for a spiritual classroom fishing trip where he was taught, caught, and cooked. While there is always the temptation on the part of the dreamer or the listener to interpret a dream's multilayered meaning, we restrict our attention to the degree of sacred emotion and mystical expansion a visionary report evokes. Rather than allow a First Creation sacred vision to be appropriated and mishandled by excessive Second Creation naming and framing, we utilize the vision to invent a mystical prescription for action that can more ably help the dream bear fruit in the dreamer's waking life.

To create such a mystical prescription we attend to whatever elements of the vision inspire a unique, unexpected, and not readily understood post-dream action plan. In Troy's case we did not discuss whether he was symbolically the observer, the helper, the student, the boy, the muddy water, the bridge, the song, the ol' man river, or the trout caught by a fisher of men. When the expansion, heat, and change offered by a big room, big river dream is taken into a small room focused on conscious dream interpretation, the mystical trout easily breaks the line and slips away, along with whatever deep feeling and higher wisdom the dream contained. After the dreamer wakes up and returns to the everyday, the Sacred Ecstatics alternative is to push the small room conscious mind back so the big room unconscious mind can better retain the deeper and more emotionally felt meaning that surpasses interpretive speculation. Allowing the dream to stay on the fishing line and swim around in First Creation keeps the creative tension alive between all imagined and yet to be imagined contrary tugs. This enables small and big rooms to maintain a double hold on the dreamer. We therefore pay the most attention to what may be brought into the everyday through creative action to help sustain the flowing river of change hosting the dream and its dream catcher. With apologies to Freud and Jung, neither ever caught an ecstatic trout or knew how to spiritually cook. Avoid polluting the big dream stream with psychological or spiritual interpretation. The cleanest spiritual rivers must paradoxically remain muddy to the conscious—and often presumptuous—mind.

While the key words Troy chose in his report should always be primarily regarded as metaphors—whether describing what took place before the dream or during the dream itself—we also relate to them concretely when designing a mystical prescription for action. Taken as a list of stage props, the following items can be utilized to stage some kind of uncommon creative action: muddy water, fishing line, a silver trout, Paul Robeson, "Ol' Man River," and *Show Boat*, among others. All these metaphors, when taken literally, are more readily transported from First Creation to a Second Creation performance stage. For example, we might have prescribed that Troy collect a jar of muddy river water and place it in his attic, with a fishing line hanging from the ceiling over his bed that is directly aligned with his heart. Doing so creates a bridge—a fishing line—connecting an everyday small room with the big room of mystery as well as a man's longing heart with the higher attic ecstatic realm. We also could have recommended that he take a silver coin and write the word "river" on one side and the word "land" on the other side, instructing him to flip the coin to see whether the trout has landed or remains in the water. This can be done before going to sleep and repeated to help bring more change, dream catching, and fish frying.

We asked Troy to print out a promotional illustration associated with the 1936 Hollywood film production of *Show Boat* that featured Mr. Robeson. (The film was rarely seen in the United States after 1950 when Robeson, an advocate for African liberation and black civil rights, was blacklisted during the McCarthy era.) Troy was then advised to securely attach one end of the fishing line to the hand of Mr. Robeson and tie the other end of the line to the image of an *ichthys*, a symbol of the fish adopted by early Christians—now transformed into a silver trout. His fish was to dangle below the image of Robeson. We suggested that this whole piece of art be placed on a wall near his bed. When making it, we asked Troy to reverently remember that the song, "Ol' Man River," is a lament about the suffering of slaves on the cotton plantations along the Mississippi river. Their heavy burden of labor and oppression was matched only by the heavenly songs of spiritual uplift and liberation they left behind—spiritual lifelines for those who find themselves "weary and sick of tryin'." The impossible tension between being "tired of livin' and scared of dyin'," sung by Paul Robeson, is not unlike the one experienced by the Apostle Paul whose thorn or hook in his flesh helped him to be reeled in by God. Paradoxically, the closer people feel to the mud of the Mississippi the more readily they will be hooked by this line from the song: "Show me that stream called the river Jordan, that's the old stream that I long to cross." By enacting the prescription Troy could keep dreaming while being dreamed by the contraries and tension between suffering and spiritual joy, longing to be caught and resisting, the muddy Mississippi and the river Jordan, and remaining underwater versus being reborn as a spiritual child.

Every human being and trout fisher should be careful about what they get hooked on, look upon, tangled in, or hung up over, whether they remain in the depths of the water, only on its surface, have already landed, or are in the frying pan. All forms belong to the First Creation show, glow, and flow boat that offers more than entertainment—it carries the songs that we reach for when we long for the mystery river that brings a sacred shiver. It is the old steam ship Zion that has "landed many a thousand" fish, fishermen, and children of all ages on the heavenly shore.

In our book, *Creative Therapy in Practice* (Keeney, H. & Keeney, B. 2019b), we provide transcriptions of sessions that demonstrate a wide range of prescriptions that were developed uniquely for clients looking for a new dream and life stream. For example, an adult man living at home with his mother, depressed and unable to move out, was instructed to grow half a beard and ask for a daily slice of homemade sour cherry pie. In another case, a creative adolescent girl who self-cut was told to invent her own fairy tale reality, complete with public theatrical experiments that she would share with family and friends. An older woman whose gloom was found linked to a former tragic romance was given the prescription to bring two forgotten violins out of her closet and play one of them with a different kind of song. A retired man who still felt the effects of being hindered by an emotionally hardened father was asked to find a feather like the one he lost in childhood, but this time build a house for it, making sure it will be available for future generations to learn its special teaching about softness. A young woman suffering with intestinal issues and anxiety was advised how to relate to her intestine as a friend and have a fantasy romance with it. In another session, a man and woman nervous about entering marriage were instructed to frequently make a new kind of wedding toast with a bitter tasting drink taken before a glass of champagne to assure that the many tastes of life are welcomed. Feeling surrounded by unexpected spiritual current in the air, a psychiatrically diagnosed and institutionalized schizophrenic in Arkansas was given the prescription to be immediately ordained by a group of pastoral counselors observing the session. Being formerly struck by lightning led to making a handheld lightning bolt for another client—reminding him to shock others in a surprising and delightful manner. Finally, a man diagnosed with a terminal illness was theatrically directed to turn his home into a Gershwin inspired musical production for his wife that included singing the feature song, "Our Love Is Here to Stay."

 Keep in mind that these prescriptions are not memorized in training but arise spontaneously as a practical consequence of being cooked and years of skill development in the art of conducting sessions. They are not based on preexisting theories about the cause and treatment of certain conditions, nor are they derived from psychological interpretations or a taxonomic list of spiritual symbols. They are born of the interaction with each client in every session. A Sacred Ecstatics conductor must learn to pay attention to the hunches that arise from a deep sea fishing mind that casts its line into the surrounding eddies of interaction, noticing the tug of an expression that feels "different." Typically unheard or ignored verbal clues, hidden messages, and metaphorical communication then must be skillfully caught, pulled in, underscored, and linked to foster continued expansion. Big room construction is more possible with metaphors that lie outside the banks of the immediate conversational container. If it doesn't fit, it may offer an exit to split from tiny room blah toward big room awe.

A mystical prescription is as important as what takes place inside the hottest temperatures of step two of the recipe. Act as if this is true even if you don't fully understand or believe it. Enacting the whole recipe is what delivers the most nourishing feast of change. A Sacred Ecstatics conductor can profoundly convey this conviction when a prescription is given to others by also personally enacting it, doing so with exemplary sincerity. Like the Blues Brothers, proceed with zany, holy grainy zeal because this is "a mission from God." When giving a prescription, announce its big worldly mission with a smile and the sweet joy that readies everyone for a soulful ride. Take the first step toward embodying the truth that *you are* implicitly abs**UR**d and expect to get tripped and fall deeper into irrational-to-your-conscious-mind mystery. It's actually more illogical to insist on being existentially shallow and aesthetically fallow rather than enact deeply hollowed and highly hallowed absurdity. The same old habits and routines that make too much sense only lead to tired and boring normality rather than the exciting vitality of a contrary creative misadventure! *Un*do your conscious fixation on *un*tickled abstraction and enjoy more interaction with the *un*explored depths of your creative *un*conscious that knows how to better *un*dermine whatever stuck *un*derstanding blocks your becoming an *un*derstudy for *un*questionable, *un*contestable means of ecstatically sung, danced, and felt *un*dulation that is *un*doubtedly the *un*doing required for the *un*iting smile of sacred ecstasy that shivers on the *un*manned, *un*named ol' bliss river.

Go for the mystery pi in the sky. After all, the mathematical ratio of a circle's circumference to its diameter involves relating a straight line to the circle enclosing it. Similarly and dissimilarly, your straight rope to God encircles you inside the big room. Be a holy fool, a sacred clown, and a pie-throwing absurdly pi-ous jester. The more absurd the better, as long as one of your feet stands inside a sacred circle that is shaped like a home cooked oven baked cake. Be a fool for Christ, a crazy wisdom Buddha, a non-*either/or*-dained minister, a neither/nor spiritual paratrooper in the hazy wisdom atmosphere, a wondering, wandering Taoist, a yeast feast priest, a double agent for contrarian creation, a circular tasty do-nut traversing mystery seeker, and a nutty shaman that predates the original fruitcake with its raisin' aglow in the sun. Remember what Herman Hesse wrote: "Eternity is a mere moment, just long enough for a joke." Go ahead and follow Rumi's mystical prescription and "Start a huge, foolish project, like Noah. It makes absolutely no difference, what people think of you." We actually assigned a Canadian father and son to build an ark together, and they did. So can you, but this time do it differently — make it out of tree bark or dogwood rather than any other kind of commonly chopped wood. Don't say, "I would if I could." Immediately act to find your bark, make your ark, and escape the dark on the sea of lighthearted mystery with its heavenly-duty ecstasy. Enact whatever is uncommon, nonsensical, and beyond-the-known unknown, doing so to burst interpretive bubbles and find an opening to the holy space of higher grace and the round sacred ground where divine comedy finds its debut among the few who get all the way cooked. D. H. Lawrence summarizes your situation:

> Man fixes some wonderful erection of his own between himself and the wild chaos, and gradually goes bleached and stifled under his own parasol. Then comes a poet, enemy of convention, and makes a slit in the umbrella; and lo! The glimpse of chaos is a vision, a window to the sun. (Herbert 1998, 236)

Laugh with the poets and their umbrella slices, serving the sunlit pie of an exclamatory "lo!" Be tickled by the hidden side of the moon's loony-lunar other mother, the opaque sense behind nonsense that is a medicinal cure for the unnecessary inflammation and inflation of parts. Be more surprising in ways that attract the attention of the gods. Strive to be less boring and bore a hole out of any seemingly exit-less box in which you find yourself trapped. Stop trying to conquer life. Play with it and be played by unexpected, naturally hyper-natural action. Enter the largest comedy room and find that all miserably tasting brine ecstatically transforms into exquisite tasting wine.

Creating ineffably playful mystical prescriptions is a high performance art. It requires effectively juggling what's praise-y and crazy while being wise about room size when unsure about temperature. Simply acting weird or dumb is not the same as expressing the krazy glee wisdom that glues a holy fool to God. Strike the match that sets the ineffable stage on fire and casts light upon a dramatic performance where all tragedy is made tender enough to render itself absurdly comedic. On sacred ground, human folly is thrown into the fire that burns and turns it jolly. Here a matchbox is a cathedral, a piece of thread becomes a rope to God, and the smallest stone mirrors your place in the grand scheme-dream of things. Here fingers arrive to bow, pray, sing, tap, point, and dance as grains of sand expand and converge to make one living place and holy space. This is exactly where the Kalahari reclaims her hallowed name.

You need a mystical prescription, as does everyone who enters and exits the big room. Do more than ask for it. Do more than receive it. Start each day actually performing an uncommon rise and shine and end each day with a prayerful rhyme and climb up the mystical vine. In other words, follow all the directions for the recipe that sets your soul on fire, and this includes mystically sprinkling in the absurd to whatever you have made too seriously fixed and unimaginatively absolute. The trembling midpoint of the crossroads marks the intersection of crazy wisdom and crazy love, the two roads bringing expanded mind and heated heart together, mating them to create the life-enforced and mystery-sourced theatre of ecstatic transformation.

Shining Your Light

Becoming fully spiritually cooked includes finding the time and building the place for all the qualities and talents of you to find their performed — rather than only informed — life. You are equally capable of literally or metaphorically getting drunk on Saturday night and having a baptismal dunk and existential cleanse on Sunday morning. The whole truth, however, isn't served by encouraging either of these at the harsh expense of the other. You must do your best to remain on the straight and narrow road, holding onto your bundle of sacred threads while flexibly allowing the rope maker to provide some wiggle room that keeps the main line rippling with change. Be softly and tenderly compassionate toward others and yourself, knowing that we all repeatedly get lost amidst the stationary standstills, oscillating false thrills, drifting mind spells, and crooked street spills. Honor the ecological truth that when one person slips, it's better to bring everyone back aboard the spiritual ship rather than throw anyone overboard.

We are all simultaneously fallen angels and little devils, too readily caught by the rigid frigidity of trickster antics, pedantic semantics, judgmental fanatics, faulty engineering mechanics, spastic panics, and unaligned dramatics. This is as true for each Dalai Lama, Mother Teresa, Ghosha, John Fire Lame Deer, and Pope as it was for Judas Iscariot, Napoleon Bonaparte, Isabella of Castile, Queen Mary I of England, and Attila the Hun. Human beings are more alike than any institutionalized social hierarchy or rigid morality dare admit. Be aware that it makes you spiritually cold to ponder whether there is enlightened consciousness, self-actualization, maximally realized human potential, spiritual caste systems, classifying taxonomies, stages of evolved spirituality, or any other conception of trickster mind that obscures your humanity and dulls your ongoing need for another trip to mind humbling and ecstatic tumbling infinity. You will continue to rise and fall as you go up and down the rope. We must constantly pick each other up in this never-ending dreary to cheery merry-go-round trip that oscillates between static knowing and ecstatic mystery. When one person walks up the rope, everyone feels pulled toward the heat. We climb together and fall together. Inside the social circulation of mystery is built the big room, its ecstatic means of transportation, and widespread fire of transformation.

Each time you fall and then get cooked all over again, you are less likely to stumble in the same way. When you subsequently restart the journey, bow in prayer and tenderly surrender to the sacred mystery of it all:

> I surrender to the original source and force of all creation, desiring residence within the big room of infinite love's pervasive joy. I am in absolute need of resuscitation and realignment with the heavenly heartbeat. I ask that you awaken something within that

will lead me and guide me along the way as I'm walking up the great highway.

Help me be kind as I seek instruction from your big mind. Ready me to receive a fire in my bones and throw me far beyond the names. Please don't let your eternal loving flames pass me by. I ask to be a cooked servant of utmost play, a conductor of direct and alternating spiritual current, an instigator of trembling truth, and an uplifting instrument of song and dance. Reduce me to nothing and empty me throughout so I may share all gifts revealed, bringing your endless smile unto others. Fill me with the light that shines a vision at night, granting me the lessons that only come from Thee. Cook me all the way through and help me build a merciful space that hosts your radical way of being for giving.

Remove from me whatever keeps me from you, and confer upon me whatever enables me to reach you unhindered. Make me a tender cross and a crossing bridge with outstretched arms that that long for your embrace. Lift me high in the spiritual sky and plant me deeply in the earth.

Remind me to be a child who honors all mothers and fathers, including the ancestors who were and are yet to be. I bow before the everlasting and always transforming parentage and tutelage of the big room.

Thank you, Lord! I shout with delight as I surrender each day and night, doing so for the first time, all the time. Take me, bake me, and make me. You are the brush; please receive me as paint. You are the potter; make me your clay. You are the musician; render me your note. You are the fire; cook me. Draw me, color me, sing me, dance me, tickle me, light me, fold, remold, and hold me up all over again so I may turn and burn inside your amazing, blazing wheel of creation.

As always and forever more, may I be a living spark journeying on a holy ark whose testimony, dedication, and choice shall remain the easy to say yet difficult to live prayer, "Thy will be done." Help me Lord, for I am in need of you. Without you, I do not feel alive or ready to live, ready to die, ready to dive, ready to rise, ready to be found, or ready to make a joyful sound. With you, dear Lord, all things and all changes are made possible. Dust to dust, ashes to ashes, earth to earth, all is created as it is in heaven. Amen.

There are three questions that should guide your everyday: (1) What is the size of the room? (2) What is the room's spiritual temperature? (3) How much creative zest is in the room's atmosphere? In addition to a spiritual thermometer, you also need a spiritual measuring tape to keep track of the room size and a spiritual creativity meter to assess the creative zest of your celebratory fest. Consider drawing the images of a small thermometer, measuring tape, and meter on a small card that easily fits into your wallet. When you feel lost, irritable, uninspired, lacking creative energy, or out of sorts, look at this card and be reminded that you need to get into a big room with enough creative spark and spiritual heat to once again become a fully participating member of the poetic, kinetic, and energetic God squad.

Don't forget your special flashlight, the one that has these seven words written on it: "I am the light of the world." If you don't have a small flashlight yet, then immediately go obtain one and make it ready. This flashlight is to remain with you always. If it ever voluntarily or involuntarily retires, replace it so you are never left alone in the dark without a light. This handheld tool of illumination helps remind you to bring more light into the world.

Be on the lookout for when it's time to shine some unexpected rays. If you find yourself talking to someone about a topic that deeply touches you, consider shedding some light on the situation. Explain that this is a reminder that there is a mysterious light in the world. Whatever conversation follows, make sure it helps further evoke and illumine the felt presence of mystery. Also be prepared to shine your light on a word in a book, a flower that recently blossomed, a feather that previously fell, an image that inspires, a radio playing a heartwarming song, even a single letter on your computer keyboard. Shine your light in the world each and every day. Shine it in the morning, shine it in the day, and shine it at suppertime.

The more surprised you are by what you choose to illuminate, the better. Perhaps you will go to a fruit stand and shine the light on a peach. Or to a toy store and illumine the nose of a teddy bear. Have you ever considered lighting up a piece of chocolate cake, a fountain pen, or an apple stem? How about illumining a church pew or some sage ready to be staged at a ceremony? Lighting a special number? Will you light the number 5 five times or once? Consider aiming that light on a doorknob, a drop of olive oil, a pie crumb, an overhead cloud, or a faraway star. How about the sole of your shoe, the underside of your shirt collar, the hole in your belt buckle, any loose thread, clothing stain, or the center of your belly button? Open your wallet and let it shine or place it into your purse as it shines inside. Shine it on your spiritual thermometer, measuring tape, and zest-o-meter. Write the word *shine* and then light it up. Go ahead and beam the light upon your signature. Light up the sun-bred shadows of the day and further illumine the moonlight of night. Wake up at 3:00 a.m. and with utmost gratitude light the center of each palm where the words, "thank" and "you" were written before falling asleep. Step into the light, jump on it, leap over it, lie under it, and shake hands with it. Shine it everywhere and in every way.

Do not ask why the world needs more of your light. Don't explain why mysterious light action makes every room expand, strikes up the band, and inspires taking a stand for something far more pleasing than what anyone spiritually chilled could ever understand. Simply carry the light and bring more shine into the world. Wonder whether you will sing, "This little (flash)light of mine, I'm going to let it shine!" Changes will emerge. Don't forget to light them when they arrive. The time will come when you will dream the light. You must first share enough light in your everyday in order to make your way to illumining the mystical night. Do all of this in the biggest, hottest, and zestiest room. Never become so well read and conceptually overfed that you forget to take the childlike action that shines your little light. Become the beacon that helps others trip the light fantastic and find their mystical senses as they experience the pinnacle emotional delight of an ecstatic song and dance flight.

Part Three

The Sacred Ecstatics Life

6

VISITING THE SPIRITUAL CLASSROOMS

Spiritual cooking prepares you for a remarkable visionary journey called "visiting the spiritual classrooms." Usually experienced in dream, this is where unique mystical teaching and empowerment take place, especially through reception of the most prized spiritual treasure — a special sacred song that floods your heart with deep emotion and fills your body with strong vibration. The spiritual temperature determines the phenomenal quality of visionary dreams, moving from the visual displays and spoken words of lower temperature to the higher degrees involving sound, touch, movement, synesthesia, and above all else — the incredible joy of sacred ecstasy. Spiritual classrooms also host the anointment of spiritual roles and skills. This is where healers, shamans, mystics, and spiritual teachers receive their ordination and higher education. You might be shown how to create a mystical prescription, make or find a spiritual object, receive a soul-stirring elixir to drink, be vibrantly touched by holy hands, or behold things of wonder, splendor, and enchantment that words alone cannot reveal. The spiritual classrooms host mystical learning, ecstatic burning, wisdom guidance, otherworldly healing, sanctified initiation, radical life reconstruction, and the distribution of rare gifts, resources, and tools that cannot be found elsewhere.

Spiritually cooked ecstatics receive ongoing mystical instruction and upgraded know-how directly from a visit to what is called a "spiritual classroom." While either awake or asleep you experience being transported to a visionary place where you are further cooked, sometimes outfitted with specialized spiritual gear, or given teaching that may or may not be conveyed in words. As one man described his first ecstatic travel experience: "I heard a moaning sound, and a voice said, 'Follow me, my little one, and I will show you the marvelous works of God.' I got up, it seems and started traveling" (Johnson 1969, 61–62). Mystics of all religious backgrounds have traveled the visionary highways to receive their spiritual educational burning that surpasses book learning.

In vision you may find yourself in what appears to be an actual school classroom, inside a mountain, at the bottom of the sea, or in a foreign country. You may be placed on a cloud in the sky, among the stars of the cosmos, near a flower, in a whale, a church, ashram, kitchen, laboratory, library, cave, an amphitheatre—or anywhere at all. Other classrooms among the shaking ecstatics of the Caribbean include Mount Zion, the Valley of Dry Bones, Israel, Jericho, Babylon, North Pole, South Pole, Victory, Bethlehem, Jerusalem, Red Sea, Sea of Tingling, Sea of Glass, Nations of the Sea, Arabia, Egypt, Sahara, Indian Sea, the Nations, Jacob's City, heaven, and last but not necessarily least, hell.

These spiritual journeys take you inside the big room of mystery with its many changing appearances. Here you may be fortunate to experience a numinous shower of blessings:

> And whilst I was down on my knees I looked up, and didn't see any housetop or sky. I just saw the clear heavens, and it looked milkish, and I said, 'Lord, what is this?' And he said, 'It is love.' Then a shower of rain came down on the top of my head and went to the toes, and I was as light as a feather, and I had on a long white robe, and I sailed and went upwards . . . and the voice came to me from the east singing. (Johnson 1969, 109)

A spiritual classroom vision is different from a typical dream or daydream because it is specially infused with extraordinary sacred emotion and non-subtle spiritual electricity. Without a doubt, the most powerful and revered visions deliver heart-piercing music. The mystical teachers, instructors, librarians, guides, tutors, administrators, and prodigious masters of these rarified schools are sometimes identifiable ancestors or present family members. In other cases they are sacred creatures, holy entities, and heavenly hosts. The faculty may be anyone or anything the divine chooses for you—from a saint to a grandparent, or a poet, composer, soaring hawk, pointing bird dog, dancing bear, wisdom butterfly, crawling caterpillar, leaping lizard, diving seal, or flipping dolphin. When you wake up from this kind of visionary dream you are usually trembling, singing, and often weeping because your heart, body, and soul were so deeply touched and moved. It is the afterglow of ecstatic joy that marks the experience as sacred. As Pierre Teilhard de Chardin said, "Joy is the infallible sign of the presence of God."

A spiritual classroom may deliver sacred dance lessons, music instruction, technical know-how, esoteric knowledge, tacit downloads of luminosity, old-fashioned mojo objects, new medicines, lost holy books, old and new songs from the divine juke box, ineffable coaching, incomprehensible doctoring, ecstatic blood transfusions, vibratory infusions, physical adjustments, heart transplants, perceptual treatments, and multi-sensory-motor experiences of every imaginable and unimaginable kind. As with all ecstatic spiritual experience, whether awake or asleep, it's the degree of heated sacred emotion that registers the vision's holiness.

These gifts are given so that you can become a better person and help others in daily life. In the lower basin Amazon of Paraguay Brad met a shaman named Ava Tape Miri or Little Seagull Man who dreamed that "four shaman spirits" came to him one night and announced: "We have come from the Big God. We are here to carry you with us." (Keeney 2000, 29). He thought he had died as he was whisked away to another world:

> I was taken to a large field not of this earth. It is in another place in space. There were many birds that ate special fruits. The shaman spirits said, "Now that you know this place, you should listen to this song." They then sang a sacred song as I watched the sunset . . . A very bright light came to me . . . They took me to the chief shaman . . . He gave me the power to be a strong shaman. Finally he said, "We will now send you back to earth where you will stay a while to help others." Then the four shaman spirits brought me back home. (29-32)

Be careful with reports about spiritual classrooms, even the holiest ones, because your everyday trickster mind stands ready to project its wishful fantasies with a small room imitation of a big room classroom visit. Curb the lust for spiritual experience or else risk being deceived by the visionary productions of cold, small room dreaming. This is why the community of a longstanding ecstatic tradition steadfastly reminds its practitioners to have their elders listen to any report about a possible spiritual vision. It helps keep wishful thinking, imaginary daydreams, and projected simulations in check.

Beginning practitioners who are not yet spiritually cooked typically cannot distinguish whether a dream has come from the big room mind or is a production of a self-directed small room mind. They have no clue whether it was spiritually cold or hot, microscopic or infinite in scope, a literary trope or directly from a numinous rope. They may be disappointed when they are told that they only had a psychological dream rather than a spiritual vision.

As Mother Pompey from St. Vincent describes her experience as a "pointer" or overseer of spiritual vision:

> When a pilgrim tells me their vision, we say that they are bringing us a lesson. If they bring a lesson not directly connected to spiritual wisdom, I will tell them, "No, don't tell me that." Some will sit down and cry. Because I keep close with God, I know when a pilgrim has been given a true lesson. (Keeney 2002, 80)

As mentioned before, the most reliable and valid test of an authentic spiritual vision is found in what happens when it is reported—it must awaken the sacred emotion and inner vibration of a well-seasoned and spiritually cooked person. As a sanctified church member describes this: "They know that when the anointing touches one, then the 'mysterious drops of the Holy Spirit' will rain onto others also" (Hinson 2000, 257). The reaction a visionary report evokes in such a qualified person is the best way to determine its nature. If it delivers no spiritual heat or feels soulless, uninspiring, purposeful, imitative, and does not cause a spontaneous breakout of ecstatic prayer, song, and dance, it is said to be a figment of one's imagination or a deception manufactured and delivered by trickster through a naïve recipient. Such a report is said to have a stench about it, that is, it lacks the sweet smell associated with an authentic visionary experience of divine origin. The saints of the sanctified church describe this discernment as follows:

> Saints say that those who are truly "born again" can usually *feel* when someone is faking. They describe this in terms of "spirit meeting spirit." The soul's "vibrations" flow from heart to heart . . . When this spirit touches the spirit of another, the two connect,

resonating in a moment of communion. Sometimes this connection makes itself felt as a quick shiver, abruptly pushing its way into consciousness. Sometimes it comes as a general tingling, a feeling that many saints describe as "like electricity." And sometimes it just comes as a deep, calm knowing. Whatever form it takes, saints say that they instantly *know* its meaning. (Hinson 2000, 253, author's italics)

Most people don't fake a spiritual experience on purpose; it happens outside of conscious awareness. Therefore, it is better to accept that you are vulnerable to being easily duped, especially when you haven't been repeatedly and thoroughly cooked over many years. Be compassionate while passionately tough on trickster—you will never bake if you fake being spiritually hot. Similar to how an art expert is required to identify a copy of a masterpiece of art, human beings need spiritually cooked expertise to differentiate an original vision from an imitation. Authentic visits to the spiritual classrooms smell fresh, taste sweet, sound soulful, look inspiring, feel spiritually hot, and precipitate a sacred vibration, inspiring a cooked ecstatic to celebrate their arrival as a genuine teaching and source of inspiration for everyone. Here is another classic example of a visit to a spiritual classroom:

> We went through the pasture and came to a snow-white wall with large gates. He spoke and said, "Ye everlasting gates, fly open wide for my bride!" When the gates flew apart I saw a beautiful city, the length and breadth of which I couldn't tell . . . a cup was handed to me, and as it touched my lips it touched the lips of a host of angels that sat at a long table of which I could not see the end. The voice said to me, "This is love and union." (Johnson 1969, 66)

When you pass through a gate to the big room, all kinds of surprises are in store. For instance, when Ikuko Osumi was a young girl in Japan she visited the Makiyama shrine on top of Maki Mountain. A legendary white snake, regarded by the Shinto priests and Japanese community as a *kami* or spirit of her revered ancestor, Eizon Hoin, startlingly came to her. The snake spoke, telling her she would take on the responsibility of their mystical lineage. It then jumped into the left side of her physical body where it resided as a spiritual helper for the rest of Osumi's life. She felt its presence in her body when she worked with seiki.

Many decades later, when Brad was living in her Tokyo house, he had a waking vision of a white snake that leapt into his belly. It immediately transformed into a Bodhi tree that, in the vision, burst through his skin and grew upward. At the height of its ascent, a leaf fell from the tree. When it touched his skin, it morphed into the physical form of the Buddha that then slowly receded into Brad's body, bringing extraordinary spiritual electricity that pulsed intensely for days. This was one of the experiences that later culminated in Osumi, Sensei assigning the lineage of her tradition to Brad with the blessings of the Shinto priests from the same shrine where she first met her ancestral snake spirit. The material gifts she inherited from the aunt who originally gave her seiki were also handed over to Brad. Since then we frequently feel the presence of Osumi and her ancestors by our side during ecstatic work. We are able to call on them and we each have received visions in which Osumi, Sensei gave us medicinal recipes and body techniques to heal our own physical ailments as well as help others in need.

Ron Geyshick, an elder Ojibwe medicine man and friend of Brad, also described how spirits lived inside him after he met them in vision. Within his right shoulder was his strongest spirit, an albino deer, while a regular deer lived inside his left shoulder. He had two moose spirits around his hips, just below the bone — a timber moose and a blue one. Jesus lived in his heart while four butterflies from around the world resided in each ear. He said that whenever their wings start fluttering, he would send his timber moose or the albino deer to find out what they were saying (Geyshick 1989).

In the old days, African-American preachers sought a visit to a spiritual classroom to receive holy anointment and visionary education instead of heading to a seminary for a diploma. Author Zora Neale Hurston found that Reverend Jefferson was such a Southern preacher who fasted in a graveyard while praying for a vision. He experienced God putting him on an operating table, opening him up, and placing balls of light inside his chest. The spiritual operation healed the wounds of his life and granted him an ecstatically empowered shouting voice to preach and heal (Hurston 1981, 89–90).

Dreams take place not only in different visionary locales, but also in different temperatures. A "spiritually hot dream" is located in the big room where it carries the felt pulse of First Creation changing, whereas cooler dreams take place in the small room psycho-logical jars and the scatter plot and rambling thought bottles of Second Creation understanding. When you cross into the big room you are gifted with emotional sensitivity rather than interpretive acuity, though you return with greater skill in discernment and communication. A spiritual vision is also less a matter of "vision" than it is a heightened emotion associated with audition, touch, and other somatic sensations. Perhaps we should stop seeking visions and instead seek sacred emotion. This is precisely what the Kalahari Bushman ecstatics do when they give less importance to what is "seen" in spiritual realms and instead emphasize the rising of the heart that awakens the emotion, motion, song, and interactive touch of n/om. Feelings rather than sightings are the threads that constitute the rope to God.

Among ecstatic traditions a "spiritual awakening" refers to your heart's "emotion-full" ecstasy assuming a higher position than mind's "thought-full" awareness. In this rising of emotion you rise from a deadened, cold state to resurrect newly born in the big room. This rebirth corresponds to Ibn al-'Arabi's description of the enlivened spiritual heart: "When the Spirit descends upon the heart of the servant through the sending down of the angel of the casting and revelation of God, the heart of the one to whom it is sent down comes alive" (Corbin 1969, 221). When your heart's sacred emotion is awakened, so is your body. Experientially, this heart and body co-awakening occurs when rhythm and sacred music take precedence over semantic meaning and ideological belief. The Bushman n/om-kxaosi regard this transition as the acquisition of "second eyes" and "second ears," along with other altered senses that take over your former sensory functioning. What is forgotten in non-ecstatic traditions is that spiritual sensing is primarily *felt*. What you feel is primary, followed by sound and smell, with vision being least important. In the big room of mystery hearing a song is more valued than seeing an image. Similarly, awakened spiritual senses emphasize the smell of sickness rather than verbiage of diagnosis. Most importantly, action is guided by the felt tug of the rope rather than any knowledge-able assessment procedure. You can tell how cooked a person is and how vast their dreaming room is by whether the emphasis is on song over story, sound over symbol, feeling over thinking, smell over diagnostic label, and the pulling and excitation of the body over the mulling and rumination of the mind.

In addition, ecstatic spiritual awakening includes the fusion of different senses, similar to what psychologists call synesthesia but experienced in a far more amplified way. You feel the seen, smell the felt, and hear the sound of being touched, along with other possible sensory combinations. It may be better to simply say that when the heart is wide awake in mystical space, it experiences the world through specially felt—and simultaneously seen, heard, smelled, and tasted—sacred ecstatic emotion. This spiritually heated emotion is remarkably different than what is felt in cooler temperatures. While inspiration and affection are a part of everyone's experience, such feelings pale in comparison to the vibrant power, mystically influenced sense, spirited widespread excitement, divinely sourced love, and the all around jubilant performance fervor found in the highest spiritual heat of sacred ecstasy.

A naïve error regarding somatic experience infiltrates most religions. Here the body's sense, emotion, and motion are depicted as representing the "lower" or less spiritual aspects of human experience—something that only uneducated primitives, ignorant fools, mad folks, or lower classes value. The seeker is taught to transcend the earthly desires and fires that are believed to block them from enlightened mental clarity, placid peacefulness, and awakened consciousness—the presumed "higher" forms of spiritual accomplishment. This bias fosters ignorance to how the body is needed to awaken the spiritual "second" senses, host the high emotion of sacred ecstasy, and enact the singing and dancing that further evoke, express, and strengthen the relationship between divinity and humanity.

Through many visits to the spiritual classrooms for nearly five decades, Brad received ongoing visionary instruction on how to wake up the whole spiritual body and mind through expanding the room and heating sacred emotion. In dreams he met ancestral teachers, received lost or forgotten teachings, and was given contact information for wisdom holders still living. He would sometimes dream of a phone number to call, a map that marked where he should go, or a voice giving the name of someone to locate. These travels, simultaneously held in mystical and physical geographies, led him to meet healers, shamans, mystics, and spiritual teachers throughout the world, especially those who were not on the popular seekers' radar screens. In these travels he found that each ecstatic wisdom tradition had a unique contribution to offer. Yet they all agreed that the pinnacle spiritual experience is to "be hooked in the heart" and reeled in by a rope to God (however named) to the big room fire of sacred ecstasy. Brad wrote of his experience:

> I found myself traveling the world, meeting shamans, healers, and spiritual teachers. Although they spoke different languages and wore different kinds of clothing, they all had one thing in common: they were devotees of the Big Love. In my odyssey I learned that there is an invisible and name-less ceremonial space that brings together all worshippers of the Big Love. The altar of this place of spiritual unity offers forgiveness and compassion, and mercy instead of judgment. In this home of diverse spirits and presences, God is the Big Love. (Keeney 2005, 6)

Over and over again Brad learned that sacred emotion is the engine of spiritual motion; it carries you through the spiritual journey of life and this includes visits to the spiritual classrooms. If you have a heartfelt hookup to the divine it will deliver all you need and send you anywhere you need to go.

Taking the Spiritual Temperature of Visionary Experience

When a dream lacks music with its optimal conductance and natural conveyance of emotion, it is likely an indication that you were dreaming in a smaller, colder room where strong feelings are secondary to what is seen. This of course is not always the case, but it is a reminder to be careful about exalting the importance of image, visionary scene, or symbol, especially when sound and emotion are absent. Trickster mind is capable of generating all kinds of spectacles in the dreamtime, and you should be skeptical about whatever appears in a dream that lacks spiritual heat. Likewise, the post-dream interpretation of images with an emphasis upon symbolic meaning easily leads to a trickster quagmire. We cannot emphasize enough that visitations to the spiritual classrooms predominantly value the extreme sacred emotion that awakens the mystical heart and gives rise to inspired somatic expression inside a big room of higher learning. All else perceived is an accompaniment to felt sacred ecstasy.

Similarly, the quality and nature of what you hear in a dream also indicates its spiritual temperature. If you heard a lot of talk, you were probably in a cooler, small room dream. On the other hand, spiritual shouting in a dream indicates a warmer dream, while ecstatic music means that the temperature was even hotter and the room vaster. For instance, one spiritual traveler was told in a spiritual classroom, "'I will fill your heart with song,'" after which he heard heavenly music (Johnson 1969, 111). Again, the reception of a sacred song brings the strongest emotion that excites a somatic vibration. Here is an account of a series of spiritual classroom visits experienced by Brad that culminated in the reception of a song in his grandmother's kitchen:

> I dreamed that Hillary and I took our mentorship students to my paternal grandparents' former house at 2101 North Second Street in St. Joseph, Missouri. It was the parsonage I fondly remember visiting as a young boy. We invited each student to stand outside the house and look through the kitchen window. We observed them being shown my grandmother's refrigerator and stove.
>
> The next night I had another dream and saw the rope to God as large as I have ever seen it. It was big

enough to hold a white wooden country church that was high in the sky, along with clouds that sheltered many angels. The rope intermittently flashed with lightning and was filled with thunderous praise. Literally, an amazing shower of blessings took place and I was filled with spiritual electricity, rhythm, and music.

Several days after these dreams, I went to a spiritual classroom where the sacred emotion received was so strong that I wept for over an hour when I woke up. I was sent again to my paternal grandmother's kitchen. I called her "Doe," a name I gave her as a child because she reminded me of a sweet and kind female deer. I called her this throughout her life. I sat at Does' kitchen table facing her stove with Hillary on one side and my mother on the other side. My grandfather was also there standing and looking over us at the end of the table. Without saying a word, Doe proceeded to chop many vegetables and place them in a large, clear plastic bag that was about two feet tall. With a glow in her eyes, she sat this bag of chopped vegetables on the middle of the table directly in front of me.

As I stared into the vegetables of many shapes, sizes, and colors, I was surprised to see that they had somehow fallen together in such a way that musical notes were created. Suddenly a keyboard appeared on the table and I began playing this unusual musical score. My family started to sing along and as the music continued, other relatives arrived in the kitchen including my sister and finally, my father. They floated into the room through the ceiling to stand near my grandfather who now was at the far end of the table. Soon everyone was singing the old hymn, "In the

Garden," a favorite of my grandmother. As my emotion intensified, the vegetable notes disappeared and I was unable to play the keyboard anymore. I could only sing. My whole family sang in unison and the rising sacred emotion made me weep from the depths of my soul. I woke up still weeping inside that tender song.[17]

The main purpose of visiting a spiritual classroom is to raise your spiritual temperature, experience the heart's ascension, receive a n/om pierce, a seiki transmission, a holy spirit immersion, and a dose of anointed shaking medicine—all ways of talking about the reception and nurturance of sacred emotion and its inseparable somatic vibration that are administered through a rope to God. Always remember that if you have an authentically cooked classroom visit, you wake up spiritually hot inside a big room that inspires celebrating the Creator and all of creation. You might say something like this to those around you in the morning with tears in your eyes, "My heart was deeply touched last night. May I sing what I heard? It makes me feel so happy that I want to share it with you." The soulful authenticity of your voice reverberates with spiritual truth, and the feeling that pours forth is more important than recounting the specifics of the visionary scenario that took place. You sound like you are spiritually intoxicated. You are—just like Rumi was after a bout with sacred ecstasy when he said, "My heart is burning with love, all can see this flame. My heart is pulsing with passion like waves on an ocean." Another traveler reported a similar feeling after visiting a spiritual classroom: "The love of God is beyond understanding. It makes you love everybody" (Johnson 1969, 115). Similarly, after being filled with this sacred emotion and its synesthetic sensory

---

[17] For a full series of visionary spiritual classroom reports see our book, *Climbing the Rope to God: Mystical Testimony and Teaching* (2017).

alteration Mahatma Gandhi's biographer, C. F. Andrews, wrote, "I seemed to be living in a different world of light and love and peace. It illuminated the glory of Nature, and made me love every one I met" (Kerr and Mulder 1994, 176).

However, if you awaken filled with pride about a gee-whiz ride, similar to the way you feel being thrilled at Universal Studios or Disneyland, then you returned from a cool dream at a trickster spiritual amusement park. Your report may sound like this, "You won't believe what happened to me last night. I was handed a magical seed and given a special wand for wizardry. I could make any garden prosper and grow. I felt filled with special power and endless abundance." Such a report does not induce deep spiritual emotion in the listener or inspire anyone to come close to the divine. It emphasizes enchantment with magical influence and elevates the dreamer rather than the Creator. The carnival of the spirit is trickster's funhouse, not the big room of God's music and dance concert hall of healing and upward bound reeling.

The same can be said for all varieties of hallucination, whether triggered by a psychedelic feast or a mindful fast. If you wake up feeling cool and hip about the experience, then you had a trip to the psycho-fantasia amusement park. Or, if a dream makes you feel mentally funky and emotionally clunky, then it was most likely a recycling of spiritually unimportant trickster waste. If you wake up in a vast sacred place filled with spiritual heat, however, you won't be able to stop praying, shouting, singing, and dancing. A visit to such a higher spiritual class of room brings the greatest joy of your life. Witness the jubilation reported by this visionary traveler upon his return:

> This was the greatest joy of my life. The voice was crying, "Peace! Peace! Peace!" and my soul was rejoicing . . . The voice and light filled the heavens, and as I flew I felt as light as a feather. I knew at the time

> that I was in another world, and I knew I had left my earthly body behind . . . there were four angels around a white table, and their wings were tipped with gold, and all raised their wings at once and said, "This is heaven." Then I found myself in this world and the trees bowed to me and said, "This is holy ground." (Johnson 1969, 73–74)

The technique of small room dream incubation involves planting a wish seed for a dream to sprout during sleep. This seed is something you hope will attract the desired experiential outcome. Conscious participation in bringing forth dreams has been developed as a skill in different cultures throughout the world, from Greece to the South Pacific and Tibet. The ecstatic practitioner, however, is extremely careful about seeding dreams, requiring that the room hosting it is vast enough for the visionary pilgrimage to be unambiguously anointed rather than only consciously driven. This helps foster a more favorable situation for the heart to be touched by the gods. Here you primarily nurture your rope to God and head for the big room rather than purposefully drop a seed, bead, or coin in a wishing well that advertises trickster room service. Be careful not to pollute your relationship to spiritual vision with any trickster glisten of pulp fiction. It is not your business, but God's, to know the when, where, how, and what of mystical vision. Get out of the way for vision to arrive uncontaminated by your decision to seek what is not yours to find through limited mind.

Small room dream incubation and imaginary shamanic journeys that are absent of a strongly felt rope to God result in the reception of cool daydreams and equally chilly nighttime dreams. These lead to self-righteous and deluded conclusions on the part of the dreamer who is too quick to profess the possession of a magical, supernatural, or other worldly experience. This unfortunately adds a veneer of false pretense and another layer of veiled armor that make it more difficult to subsequently have an authentic breakthrough visit to the spiritual classrooms. This is why the abundance of cool and imitative experiences provided by the New Age marketplace is a horrific curse. It would be better to pray for the absence of false dreams, the eradication of inappropriate spiritual desire, and the temperance of a misguided hunger for trickster special effects. As our friend Denise Jackson, daughter of the late Mother Ralph from St. Vincent, told us, "Each time you pretend to receive a spiritual gift or experience it blocks you from receiving the gifts from God that otherwise would be coming your way."

The only way you get to a spiritual classroom is through a strong divine hookup. Too much conscious purpose, articulated intention, and personally guided spiritual adventure separates you from the numinous, shrinks your room, lowers the temperature, stops your spiritual heartbeat, and weakens your rope. It is always wiser to filter away all intention and purpose except wanting to feel close to God. When you aim for any other outcome, you risk cutting the rope through which all blessings flow. Hand everything over to higher power and its regulation, including your dreams.

Recognize that it doesn't matter whether or not you are granted what you think is a mystical, spiritual, religious, or shamanic experience. Assume that visits to the visionary classrooms are primarily meant to wake up a deeply felt realization that you are always inside an important spiritual classroom: the big room of life itself with all its teaching. You return from Oz to find that there is no classroom like home. This is the central truth Black Elk found in his sacred vision: "I saw myself on the central mountain of the world, the highest place, and I had a vision because I was seeing in the sacred manner of the world . . . The central mountain is everywhere." Likewise, Henry David Thoreau wrote in critique of other writers' wanderlust: "I have more of God. They more of the road." We can say the same with regard to visionary travel. What is most important is that no matter the geographical coordinates, you feel at home with your Creator. Here a higher captain, pilot, or driver determines what course is best for you. An ecstatic parishioner of a 19th century black church addresses the guidance that is beyond human comprehension:

> I don't know what other people have heard or seen in the spirit, nor do I know whether it is necessary for everybody to see and hear what I have experienced, for God knows what is best. It may be that some people do not need to see or hear anything. I say this because I do not want anyone to feel that I think God deals with everybody in the same way. The secret is with him, and he reveals things to whomever he wills and as he wills. (Johnson 1969, 145)

Be less organized by willful, unskillful conscious purpose and stop the constant measuring of your spiritual growth. Pay more attention to nurturing your rope to God and entering the big room ready to celebrate whatever is cooking and being served. The infinite love and wondrous splendor of sacred ecstasy are the greatest gift of all. The inner swelling and explosive outburst of altered emotion provide everything your heart desires and your mind secretly admires. Even if you formerly received a high appointment or special gift in a spiritual classroom, these are only useful when woken up and brought to life in the big room at sizzling temperatures. In other words, it doesn't matter whether you ever had or ever will have a spiritual vision or are seen as holding a prominent spiritual position. What really counts is following, on an everyday basis, the recipe for setting your soul on fire in order to be constantly changed, transformed, and remade by

God. Without this continued effort on your part, nails of n/om rust, classroom visions and sacred emotion fade, the big room turns to dust, and spiritual gifts turn to mush. No matter what comes or doesn't come your way, simply stay on the numinous highway where all cooked souls from all space and time are travelling on their way to glory.

The Dissolution of Boundaries and the Blending of Forms

The spiritual classrooms take you into the big room of First Creation where everything is changing. Here you experience being "loos'd of limits and imaginary lines" as Walt Whitman wrote. Whatever spoonful of sugar, trickster charm, or thought lock box you cling to in daily life is subject to unexpected definitional spilling, logical line bending, and total knowledge upending in the spiritual classrooms. This includes the terms that differentiate healing, mysticism, shamanism, spiritualism, and all other specifications of an "ism" that sorts out a schism, catechism, animism, pluralism, monotheism, polytheism, or any other prism of intellectual tourism.

The academic use of taxonomies to indicate distinct spiritual forms of experience and social roles results in never-ending trivial debates over interpretation and the hierarchical organization of names. For example, the name "shamanism" is argued to be only applicable to certain cultural groups or more generally extended to a certain kind of visionary practitioner, whose work, in turn, must be differentiated from "mediumship," "possession," "psychopomp" "trancer," "dancer," and other names of altered experience and its associated performance. This obsession with names sets up a spiritual caste system that casts away the pinnacle spiritual experience whose phenomenal nature is so fluidic, shifting, and changing that it doesn't remain still long enough to either be named or distilled. Remember: there *ain't* any names among the saints of First Creation and this is the only space where shamanic, healing, and spiritual mojo take place. A big room ecstatic "change-o-matic" is subject to mysterious higher power regulation and has no allegiance to any small room fixed definition or named location. Cooked shamans, mystics, healers, spiritual teachers, and the like find that neither cultural boundary nor academic category fence them in. That's why we sometimes perform the song, "Don't Fence Me In," at Sacred Ecstatics intensives. You must ask for "land, lots of land under starry skies above," "the wide open country" where you can "gaze at the moon till [you] lose your [non-mystical] senses" as an unfettered celebrant of the changing. Rather than be idle and quibble over semantics, get back in the saddle and head to the land beyond all conceptual borders.

Walking Thunder, a Diné (Navajo) medicine woman, told Brad about her visit to the big room which for her was a hogan or traditional hut of logs and mud. There she experienced the dissolving of all worldly walls that separate religious traditions and forms:

> I dreamt that I saw the biggest hogan in the world. I saw myself sitting in a corner of this hogan and I was really singing away . . . I found I could now see through things. I could see through walls and through hogans. I was looking down from above and I saw many churches and religions inside. All the world's churches were in that hogan. Everyone was talking in their native tongue and made a lot of noises. All the sounds were coming to me . . . My dreams taught me that the fireplace is the same as the Bible. The fireplace is also where we communicate with our ancestors and find our teachings. (Keeney 2001, 108)

The social relevance of a bona fide spiritual journey that brings back teaching and gifts from First Creation is to help others step into the big room, contribute to their reception of ecstatic fire, and nurture their rope to God. As discussed before, be careful when reporting a visionary experience. If your report shrinks mystery into a small container you risk squeezing out and losing whatever spiritual potency was given to share. Use your gift wisely to bring expanded spiritual space, increased heat, and creative change to others, or else you may find yourself more removed from the ineffable than you were before the vision.

Accentuate the felt mystery that is beyond human comprehension rather than the name- dropping of small room knowing. When you are cooked your sense of "self" diminishes, especially when healing and spiritually helping others. As Black Elk said,

> Of course it was not I who healed. It was the power from the outer world, and the visions and ceremonies had only made me like a hole through which the power would come to the two-leggeds. If I thought I was doing it myself, the hole would close up and no power would come through it. Then everything I could do would be foolish. (Neihardt 2008, 163)

Similarly, William Blake acknowledged that, "I myself do nothing. The Holy Spirit accomplishes all through me." It does so once you are small enough and the room is big enough for you to dissolve and become inseparable from the whole of creation. You are then moved by its changing and touched by what is vital rather than burdened by a title.

The big room may appear as a cathedral whose ceiling is higher than its walls, a grandmother's quaint kitchen, a country praise-to-raise-the-dead house, an ol' man river, or a playground of the gods. In Brazil, 99-year old healer, Otavia Alves Pimental Barbosa, described the spirit world as "a very huge field with beautiful grass" and called it "the field of the birds." (Keeney 2003a, 38). In vision, Otavia would get to this field by a stairway:

> There is a stairway I climb that goes up to the field and a stairway that brings me down. The stairway is like a white rope in the sky. When I dream, I go up and down the stairs. Although it's a dream, I am not able to forget it. I see the field of the birds and it's wonderful . . . It looks like the most beautiful green blanket you've ever seen . . . There you will find special railroad tracks . . . They are used to guide the trains and horses that can take you places . . . I have seen my grandmother's bedroom in the spirit world. (Keeney 2003a, 38-39)

When Otavia was a child, two African slaves told her about this place and later the spirit of a priest explained that it was also an energy field of love that offers "much forgiveness" and "holds as many forgivenesses as there are leaves on a tree and all the grains in the world's sand" (38). Never forget that whether you receive one sacred vision or many, the main purpose is to cultivate "limitless love and illuminated caring for one another" (Keeney 2003a, 63). If you come back from a dream ready to hug a tree, gift your neighbor, forgive your enemy, and celebrate the equality of diverse qualities, then your spiritual classroom visit was real. Otherwise, you had another trick or treat trickster greeting that was not a spiritual meeting.

Mystical Water

One of the most remarkable gifts you can receive in a visitation to the classrooms is a drink of mystical water. When you sip from this cup, your insides are heated and charged as you tremble and quake with ecstatic delight. Such an experience may come in a vision like this one:

> He [God] came in my room and said, "Come on and go with me . . . Come and I will show you paradise and the various kinds of mansions there." I saw the most beautiful rooms, all in white and gold. There was a stream flowing through every room. He said, "This is the living water that flows from on high." He told me to taste it. It was the best tasting water I ever drank. I can't say what kind of water it was, but I never tasted anything like it. It was as clear as it could be. (Johnson 1969, 91)

Or you might dream of a special plumbing pipe that brings you the sacred water:

> A little silver pipe was let down from the top of the ceiling, and three angels came down . . . these little angels would come down loaded with food. They gave me water out of the little silver pipe. I could feel each drop on my tongue. They told me this was the water of life. (Johnson 1969, 123)

These mystical drops may come from a stream that goes through the room, a silver pipe hanging from the ceiling, a tree of life found in the sky village, or rain falling from the heavenly realm, among other possibilities. This kind of spiritually refreshing tonic brings the sweet taste of a love-infused mystery that satisfies your deepest existential thirst. Gopi Krishna's description of inner "nectar" could also be the words of a Bushman taking a drink of liquid n/om:

I invariably perceived a luminous glow within and outside my head in a state of constant vibration, as if a jet of an extremely subtle and brilliant substance rising through the spine spread itself out in the cranium, filling and surrounding it with an indescribable radiance . . . I distinctly felt an incomparably blissful sensation in all my nerves moving from the tips of fingers and toes and other parts of the trunk and limbs towards the spine, where, concentrated and intensified, it mounted upwards with a still more exquisitely pleasant feeling to pour into the upper region of the brain a rapturous and exhilarating stream of a rare radiating nerve secretion. In the absence of a more suitable appellation, I call it "nectar." (1971, 87)

The late Brazilian healer, João Fernandes de Carvalho, once helped a family rid their home of a malevolent presence through heartfelt prayer. Afterward, the family told him that a bird appeared outside and sang its song near the house every day. João went to see for himself and when he arrived the bird not only sang him its song, it gave him the "spiritual gift" of filling him with a "mystical fluid" that stayed inside him the rest of his life and helped his faith grow even stronger (Keeney 2003a, 39).

Taoists refer to this fluid or nectar as the elixir of immortality, and it arrives inside vast sacred space with a hot spiritual temperature. It was reported in the myths of Egypt's Thoth and Greece's alchemist, Hermes Trismegistus, where each drank "the white drops" or "liquid gold" of the vital life force. This is also mentioned in the *Nag Hammadi* texts and written about throughout the world from India to Persia and China, and elsewhere. Whether called the "great juice" or what Jesus called "the water of life," ecstatic mystics know it as a drink whose spiritual heat immediately sets their souls on fire.

Brad received this mystical liquid numerous times in his life, beginning with his own spontaneous awakening when he was nineteen years old. He was extremely fortunate, for his first awakening brought the energized, hot liquid up his spine and through his crown, bringing forth a mystical illumination that presented itself as a luminous egg. Since that time, he continued to have experiences of the extraordinary high-frequency sacred vibration that leads to a drink of this healing and renewing elixir. Once he experienced Jesus giving him a glass of white light to drink. It turned him into a spiritual fire. At another time while awake in the day, he felt that same warm fluid, now more like milk, pour over the top of his brain. It flowed slowly and surely down the rest of his body, all the way to the tips of his toes. At other times it flowed upward from his feet to his head. Being filled with this vibratory nectar is now a weekly experience for Brad that automatically comes when needed. As it spreads within, it brings spiritual heat, vibratory energy, deep peace, complete rest, a readiness to stir needed social unrest, and more than anything else, incomparable blessed bliss.

Sometimes other people can dream that you receive this gift. A woman in Budapest once dreamed that Brad went to her grandfather's shop that was filled with many musical instruments. There was also a pipe delivering hot water and Brad drank from it. The water was so hot that it cooked him. In the big room of mystery anything can happen, including drinking hot mystical water inside someone else's visionary classroom. We, too, have dreamed of giving this drink or another transmitted form of the sacred vibration to someone far away. A song can also be received in a spiritual classroom and given to another person—we dream of singing it to someone and then wake up shaking with ecstatic emotion. Nothing makes us happier than to report the dream to that person because the song is then doubly "owned" by both dreamer and recipient.

When sacred energy ascends all the way up from the base of the spine and through the crown, there arises spiritual heat, luminosity and liquidity. If you "see the light," then you also feel the heat and experience the drops of mystical water. This sacred ecstatic synesthesia is another one of the shape-shifting combinatorial forms that naturally come and go in First Creation. The mystical light, as the French sensory physiologist Charles Henry (1859–1926) proposed (see Keeneys 2018), is a combination of all the senses that are maximally excited. Leave any part of you out, especially the body or any of its sensory-motor activity, rising emotion, or sounds, rhythms, synchronies, vibrations, kinetics, or spiritual thermodynamics, and you miss the galactic peak of sacred ecstasy. The literature of India describes this light as being "whiter than the moon" and spectacularly "lustrous." It is what Inuit shamans called *quaumaneq*, meaning "lightning" or "illumination," and what the Taoist masters also call the Golden Flower. As the Bhagavad Gita teaches, when there is true wisdom, the body emanates light. Similarly, a highly cooked ecstatic gathering can result in a hovering light that appears as fire. This was reported to have happened during the Azusa Street Revival in Los Angeles. Several times neighbors called the fire department because they saw flames billowing out from the roof. In addition, people at Azusa Street reported that the church was often filled with a heavy mist so thick that children played hide and seek in it. In all cases involving soaring spiritual heat, from Azusa to the Kalahari, the atmosphere is filled with a mystery that is simultaneously a big room fire, a bright light, an illumined misty fog, a shivering Shiva river of sweet nectar, among other changing First Creation forms. Above all else, never forget that the numinous luminosity experienced is actually something more felt than seen. Listen again to what C.M.C. reported about the mystical light:

> In my experience the "subjective light" was not something *seen*—a sensation as distinct from an emotion—it was emotion itself—ecstasy. It was the gladness and rapture of love, so intensified that it became an ocean of living, palpitating light, the brightest of which outshone the brightness of the sun ... (Bucke 1969, 328)

A drink of mystical water is also a drink of mystical light. This cross-sensory, life force instilling experience of higher liquidity is mentioned in the scripture: "Whosoever drinketh of the water that I shall give him, shall never thirst; but the water that I shall give him shall be in him a well of water springing up into everlasting life" (John 4:14). Like Kalahari Bushmen intoxicated with n/om, the disciples were charged with being "drunken," and Paul compared this to wine in order to illustrate being "filled with the Spirit." In the Kalahari, Brad found Bushman elders holding up a tortoise shell to the sky during a dance to fill it with this mystical elixir, what they uniquely regard as "God's urine." When they drink it, they are filled with ecstatic fire. Brad also drank *!Xu g!u* in the Kalahari, and though its name is different there, its experience is essentially the same as the golden elixir, quaumaneq, great juice, holy water, white drops, sacred milk, mystical lava, and numinous light that is drunk throughout the world. You are thirsty for mystery, and there is only one drink that can completely satisfy your thirst. A shining libation of spiritual intoxication that precipitates large-scale liberation awaits you in the big classroom.

Laying and Following Spiritual Tracks

The spiritual caretaker of an ancient Greek dream temple needed to dream your readiness for sacred dreaming, or at least hear that you earlier dreamed of asking him for permission to dream there.

Similarly, among the Shakers of St. Vincent you initially dream of a "spiritual pointer," someone who points you toward the track that leads to a particular spiritual classroom. The old time Shakers required that the pointer also dream that you were coming. This mutual dreaming ensures the visionary pursuit is held in a context bigger than the small room of a solitary personal quest. Big room dreaming is relationally held, spiritually ordained, and mystically directed. This makes the journey unambiguously sacred from the outset.

Brad knew and experienced pointers, shamans, and spiritual teachers who would vision near the anointed seeker and sometimes go into the same visionary classroom simultaneously. They were able to experience what you were experiencing and help you along the way. In the middle of a visionary visitation, they might wake you up and say something like, "The palm tree on your right side is trying to tell you something. Stop looking at the rocks on the ground. Ask the tree what it is trying to offer. Now go back to the classroom." In one situation, Brad was sleeping on the ground in a Guarani village in Paraguay, in the lower Amazon basin. As he was inside a vision, a grandfather shaman, Little Seagull Man, was also having the same vision. Both walked along the same visionary track until they woke up at the same time and immediately continued talking about what they had been discussing in the vision, making reference to what could only have been heard inside it.[18]

Each visit to a spiritual classroom leaves a track for others to later find when they are spiritually cooked. All the mystics, shamans, teachers, and saints of old left tracks in the mystical universe. Brad has traversed many of these tracks, experiencing sacred visions that he later discovered had been previously laid down by elders from long ago. For instance, in a fast held in the

---

[18] For more about this shaman, see Guarani *Shamans of the Forest* (2000), edited by Bradford Keeney.

Caribbean he had these two visionary experiences, one after the other:

> I went on a journey where I came to an old bookshop filled with rare books. An old gentleman with white hair was sitting outside the shop next to the door. He greeted me and said, "So you are the one we've been hearing about. Please go in the shop and make yourself comfortable." When I went inside, I noticed many rows of ancient books. An old woman immediately came out of the back room and asked whether I needed some help. I asked for a book written by Swedenborg. She handed me a thin catalog and went to the storeroom to see if they had what I requested. I opened the catalog and the section I turned to was entitled, "Esoteric Christianity." All the books listed had Latin titles.
>
> The old woman returned with Swedenborg's spiritual diary. I tucked it under my arm, paid for it, and left because it was closing time. When I came back to myself after waking up, I tried to remember if I had heard of Swedenborg. I hadn't read anything about him, as far as I could remember, so I memorized his name to investigate at a later time.
>
> I then went back to sleep and had another dream. This time I dreamed I was at a dining table in a kitchen where a round loaf of bread floated through the back door and suspended itself right in front of me, at face level. The choir of heaven began to sing and the one whose voice I know said, "I will feed you spirit. This alone will nourish you."
>
> When I was afterwards able to conduct some library research, I discovered that Swedenborg had been a Swedish mystic who began having spiritual visions at

about the age I was when I did this prayer fast. From that point on he wrote his books only in Latin. One of his important dreams, entered in his diary, was about receiving "fine bread on a plate." He took this to mean that he was no longer to be solely reliant upon the teachings or writings of others. Rather, he was to receive spiritual food directly from the world of spirit: the received bread being "a sign that the Lord himself will instruct me since I have now come first into the condition that I know nothing" (Swedenborg 1977, 85).

Years later I visited the cottage in Sweden where Swedenborg had received many of his visions, and went on to the Swedenborg Library in London, where I told my story to the attending staff member. He said, "That's interesting. I work here because I once dreamed of one of Swedenborg's books. It started my journey into the mystical teachings. These are the stories others don't hear about."

One of the amazing facts about Brad's life is that he had so many sacred visions that were related to diverse spiritual traditions throughout the world.[19] He would vision elders, sacred objects, unknown teachings, rare spiritual practices, or other experiences that made no sense to him but were later found to be unique to a particular spiritual tradition. This was remarkable in part because Brad had never read or heard about most of what came through his visions. His report of a vision to another elder granted him welcome, sometimes combined with the fact that the

---

[19] For more about Brad's experiences, see our book *Climbing the Rope to God: Mystical Testimony and Teaching* (Keeneys 2017) as well as the books *Shaking Out the Spirits* (Keeney 1995), *Bushman Shaman: Awakening the Spirit Through Ecstatic Dance* (Keeney 2005), and *American Shaman: Odyssey of Global Healing Traditions* by Jeffrey Kottler and John Carlson (2004).

elder had already dreamed that he was coming. Brad and the spiritual elders he met trusted and followed directions that came from the visionary realm—their respective ropes brought them together. From this we are reminded that authentic spiritual relationship is not built on personal preference or subject to the categories of time, space, culture, language, or skin color. If your rope to God is strong, you follow it even when it leads you to connect with people, places, and experiences that are beyond your understanding, familiarity, or expectation. The big room is empty of manmade boundaries.

Brad was sent to the highest spiritual classroom when he was nineteen years old. There he was thoroughly spiritually cooked and given a strong rope whose fibers included tracks to other spiritual lineages. This is a rare occurrence even within cultures long steeped in ecstatic spirituality. What Brad received enabled him to be connected to diverse ways of relating to the ineffable. He was instantly made an ecstatic healer, mystic, shaman, minister, and spiritual teacher—alternating roles that arrive when a situation calls for them. Ever since that time Brad has lived in a roofless, wall-less, numinous tent whose most familiar and trusted resident is the mystical, musical, dancing, creative, witty, kind, gentle, ready to protest, always forgiving, healing, rejoicing, radically liberating, forever-loving, water-walking, land wandering, and sky ascending outcast and carpenter named Jesus. All around the heavenly sunshine that glows within Him are found other incarnations, embodiments, and manifestations of spirit with many different names. While interpretations, textual elaboration, and word ornamentation differ as much as clothing, jewelry, and sacred objects, Brad, like other mystics, found that all ecstatic spiritual experience comes from the same deep root and overhead canopy that constitute the one big room.

Though Brad was aware afterward that he had become rewired and would have a special mission for his life, he never told anyone about his formative mystical experience until nearly a decade later when he shared it with one of the founders of the science of cybernetics, Stafford Beer, who unbeknownst to Brad was a private mystic and yogi. At the time of their meeting, this long bearded old man who looked like an Old Testament prophet said that he was living as a "wizard" named "Prang" in a stone quarry in Wales. After hearing Brad's testimony, Professor Beer was overcome with joy and immediately pronounced Brad as one of his spiritual teachers. Like Stafford Beer, Brad remained an underground mystic for many years while publicly being a teacher and scholar of cybernetics. Whereas Beer advised presidents, especially Salvador Allende of Chile before the coup, and tried to help their countries be more resourcefully and circularly organized, Brad encouraged psychotherapists to leave limited practice models behind and take the leap into a more expansive room where creative, improvisational, and mysterious circular ways of therapeutic action naturally arise.

During this time, Brad also felt burdened by how much had been mystically revealed to him. He faced many trials and tribulations and sometimes tried to distance himself from it all and return to a less demanding role in the world. Brad was repeatedly shown the dark side of unseen occult forces as well as more of the irrational and needless harm that human beings can bring to one another, especially when there is an overbearing attachment to a name, category, dichotomy, unchanging theoretical model, literalizing ideology, or unbending notion of linear cause-and-effect. He also experienced how both sides of the many variations of good and evil could easily arise within himself and others. Yet no matter how often Brad stumbled, fumbled, or tried to run away from his mystery calling, he found that he was always reeled back in.

In Bali, Brad was told the story of a young professor of economics that he recounts in *Balians: Traditional Healers of Bali*

(Keeney 2004). One night the professor dreamed of an old man with a white beard telling him, "You need to become a balian," a traditional Balinese healer. This professor wanted nothing to do with it. Continually tormented every night by dreams of the elder man who persisted in calling him toward this sacred occupation, the professor came up with a strategic plan. He would interrupt his daily life with a sabbatical far away from Bali. He went to Los Angeles and tried to "make himself dirty and unfit for spiritual work." This included getting frequently intoxicated, implementing a forbidden diet of excess, and spending evenings with prostitutes. After a year of wallowing in this kind of mud he returned and was convinced he had become so spiritually unclean that it would be impossible for the world of mystery to call on him again. Upon arriving home he was exhausted and immediately went to sleep. The next morning he woke up relieved because he had not dreamed. He was thrilled that he had finally disconnected himself from the old man in his dreams and was free to be a professor again. When he opened the door to head for his university office, he was shocked to see a line of people that extended a long distance. When he asked why these strangers were standing in front of his house, he heard that each person had experienced the same dream. They all had dreamed of an old man with a white beard telling them to come to his address in the morning and request healing. The professor immediately surrendered and became a balian.

Brad also accepted his calling following a long resistance, and only after many years of being a tenured professor, field researcher, and director of several doctoral programs did he leave academia. With the financial support of a private foundation, he was able to live with elders from cultures all around the world, especially those who held an ecstatic lineage. From Japan to the Kalahari, Caribbean, and Amazon, and in the living traditions of Native America, Tibetan Buddhism, Jewish mysticism, Hinduism, the sanctified black church, and many other stops along the way, he acquired metaphors that provided a beginning vocabulary for what would later become Sacred Ecstatics — the recipe for setting your soul on fire and becoming spiritually cooked.

Though Brad was ready to publicly heal and teach when he was a young man, he usually did so secretly as he continued to prepare himself for many decades before becoming a full time spiritual teacher in his senior years. Throughout his earlier adulthood he had been an active member and respected healer among diverse communities. He was also well known as an unconventional "creative therapist" who performed amazing sessions, but only among Brazilian, Argentinian, Mexican, Paraguayan, Australian, Japanese, and South African therapists. For decades many American and European therapists thought he had disappeared and perhaps passed away, unaware he had only moved to a different performance room. On numerous occasions Brad traveled with a one-way airline ticket, thinking he'd accept an invitation to live the rest of his life in some faraway place. He finally left his fieldwork and university teaching post when he was sixty-three years old, when we together started teaching others how to spiritually cook. That was the beginning launch of what we call "The Sacred Ecstatics Experiment."

Hillary was also initially reluctant to step into a spiritual teaching and healing role. Without seeking visionary experience, she was nonetheless spiritually transported to numerous spiritual classrooms (see Keeneys 2017). After dreams sent her traveling and brought her gifts for healing, including numerous sacred songs and mystical objects, she found that her waking life was also becoming filled with ever-increasing wonder and mystery. Finally, after an intense spiritual period when she and Brad had visions nearly every night for many months, even sometimes sharing the same dream experience, she fully accepted her calling to be a spiritual healer and mystical teacher. Brad sometimes teases her as being "the reluctant shaman" or "the unassuming mystic." She became spiritually cooked whether she wanted to or not. In this way her life's work has benefitted from her bringing less baggage on her spiritual travels.

It is important to know that it is not necessary to travel the world in order to visit diverse spiritual traditions. It was part of Brad's ordained job and anointed responsibility to do this spiritual tracking in order to find some of the already worked out ways of describing, prescribing, and enacting the recipe for ecstatic spiritual cooking. You never really have to leave home to find the fire of sacred ecstasy and the endless song and dance mystery of divinity. Hillary met some of the Kalahari women healers in her dreams before she physically went there and actually danced with them. The divine is always present wherever you are and manifests at every degree of temperature. Though we have tried to draw critically important distinctions between hot spiritual experiences inside First Creation and those arising in the smaller, colder rooms of Second Creation, it's also true that you shouldn't be overly worried about constantly monitoring the temperature, the size of the room, or its creative buzz. Every experience is valuable, even an ice-cold daydream that construes a fantasy more indicative of the spiritual fallacy of ecstatic bankruptcy. This can be important when it serves as a reference point for later finding out that its important truth was that it held little truth. Simply surrender your life to that which surpasses all understanding, point your heart toward the numinous, and express ecstatic gratitude for whatever whole, wholesome holiness comes your way.

Preparing for Mystical Travel

To cross into the big room and visit a spiritual classroom for the first time traditionally requires a unique existential death-like experience. You "go to the mourning ground," as the Shakers of St. Vincent call it, and experience the death of your habituated, small room way of living. To let go of your old container is not easy and requires hitting an existential bottom. This teaching, resonant with the basic operational premise of Alcoholics Anonymous, applies to every spiritual seeker. You must hit bottom before any profound breakthrough is able to take place. Admission to the big room is not possible until your old small ways and the self-centered, self-validating reality they articulate, recapitulate, and perpetuate crash and come to an end. Then the surrounding walls fall down and the gateless gate opens so that your spiritual life can truly begin.

The first trip to the crossroads not only asks you to hand over your particular instrument and you, the instrumentalist; you must also hand over the keys to the whole room of your life. If you later venture away from the straight and vertical rope highway, you may have to go through this death and resurrection episode all over again. Though it may be harder the next time, the good news is that if you sincerely persevere, you come out even stronger, wiser, better attuned, and more spiritually cooked than you were the first time you were ecstatically reborn. As Rumi proclaims, the door is always open: "Come, come, whoever you are. Wanderer, worshipper, lover of leaving. It doesn't matter. Ours is not a caravan of despair. Come, even if you have broken your vows a thousand times. Come, yet again, come, come."

In the St. Vincent ecstatic tradition, you are spiritually called to mourn, a ceremony that asks you to enter a ceremonial room and be symbolically buried as you proceed to pray, fast, and sincerely give up the way you have been living your life. As you review your many shortcomings, mistakes, laziness, cowardly omissions, wrongful avoidances, multi-leveled sins, widespread ignorance, and tricky deceptions, a breaking point comes when you let go of the idea that you can ever again trust yourself to guide, fix, or improve your life on your own. You declare, "I give up," "I surrender all," and "I let go of myself."

There is a difference, however, between true religious "mourning" and the more common kind of self-deprecation or temporary pity party. True mourning results in your *feeling the need for a higher helping hand,* and this felt need remains strong whether you are down in the doldrums or floating on top of the world. Though human beings are usually a complex mix of that which is deeply sincere along with some shallow veneer, it's a basic rule of thumb that someone hasn't really hit bottom if they too quickly or easily forget their need for divine intervention once their ego gets a boost or life is smooth sailing again. It's natural to feel your rope more strongly in dark times, but once you have really been cracked open and come to the end of your wits you will be less inclined to stray from the main road. More accurately, the cycle between getting lost and being found again becomes shorter. You also become more jaded about and resistant to former ego-boosters like success, popularity, and recognition, and in general take yourself less seriously the more you get to know the fool of you within.

More than just thinking about or declaring your need for higher help, you must feel it with all your heart and express this emotion with a song and lyric like, "I Need Thee Every Hour." If congruently felt and expressed, hitting the bottom floor of your formerly elevated self leads to the big room entrance. The divine pulls you into another world—the big room, the sacred universe, First Creation, and heaven itself—where you are existentially reformed, rewired, remade, and reborn. This is the first and most important visit to the spiritual classrooms. It is the journey from your small room death to big room resurrection. After this initiatory experience, you have a passport enabling entry to other spiritual classrooms in the future.

Early ecstatic shamans also went through this transition of

death and rebirth, sometimes experiencing themselves being cut into many pieces and later put together again by a supreme agent of creation. Again, the first crossing into the big room is experienced after the crumbling of your former encapsulating shell, its small room, and all the shrunken ways of containment that excluded others and your greater surroundings. Such a room change, rather than personality change, enables God to work on you and transform how you interact with all your relations.

The oldest ecstatic traditions teach that unless you have been spiritually decomposed, cooked, and recomposed, you cannot heal, guide, or spiritually teach others. If you have not wholeheartedly mourned your life, experienced your brokenness like a shattered teacup, and felt the absolute need for the divine potter, then you have not been to the crossroads, let alone crossed over into the enormous firing kiln. You must experience the unbearable abyss below so there is no other place to go but up. You must feel the trickster chaotic mess of you to feel the need for higher order.

Here is an account of a sanctified black church parishioner's first spiritual journey that followed the death experience of his old self at the crossroads:

> I felt His power. It was like lightning; it came so quick I was killed dead . . . I was in two bodies: there was a little William and the old William. Little William stood looking down on old William, my earthly body. I got scared and started praying, "Lord, have mercy!" I said this because I saw my old body lying at hell's dark door. Quicker than a flash I was caused to turn away by the power of God, and looking in the east direction, saw a little white path. It was very narrow, but straight. The voice said to me again, "My little one, I place your feet in the straight and narrow path. Be not afraid, for I will be on your right hand and on your left. I will be as

a refuge and a fortress.

Wherever you go let this be your testimony, for I am with you always, even until the world shall end. Amen." Then I heard the heavenly host sing the "Canaan, Fair, and Happy Land, Where My Possessions Lie." It was the prettiest song I ever heard. I came back to myself as the clock struck one. Glad to know that I had waited at hell's dark door and got my orders to travel. I have been traveling ever since, looking to my Captain for my every want and need. (Johnson 1969, 151)

Another parishioner heard a voice in her initiatory spiritual journey shout out, "You got to die and can't live." She went on to report, "I died and saw a deep hole, and a little man called to me, saying, 'Follow me' . . . I declare to you I saw myself in two bodies. Little me was standing looking down on the old, dead me lying on a cooling board" (Johnson 1969, 148). Someone else also heard a voice say that she must die. "I truly died and saw my body. I had a temporal and a spiritual body. My spiritual body had six wings on it" (Johnson 1969, 149). Your waiting-to-emerge spiritual body is alive inside the changing of First Creation where you appear smaller and already equipped with any needed accessory, from wings to other mysterious things that enable you a safe and successful voyage to mystery. First comes the death that releases you from small dressing rooms, and then comes entry onto the big room stage where changing forms of life perform.

Even Leo Tolstoy found himself dangling amidst the ropes, hovering over mystery. He dreamed he was "lying on a network of cords" and was

> . . . somehow aware that the cords can be moved . . . I am on a height far above that of the highest tower or mountain, a height beyond all my previous powers of

conception . . . I feel if I look down I shall slip from the last cord, and perish . . .

He then thought he must be dreaming and tried to wake up but could not. He cried out:

> "What can I do? What can I do?" I ask myself, and as I put the question I look above . . . I look into this abyss of heaven, and try to forget the abyss below, and I do actually forget it . . . I hear a voice saying, "Look well; it is there." I perceive that I no longer hang, and that I do not fall, but have a fast hold. I question myself how it is that I hold on . . . At my bedside stands a pillar, the solidity of which is beyond doubt, though there is nothing for it to stand on. From this pillar runs a cord, somehow cunningly and at the same time simply fixed, and if I lie across this cord and look upward, there cannot be even a question of my falling . . . It seemed as if someone said to me, "See that you remember." And I woke up. (Tolstoy 1899, 74)

Compare Tolstoy's experience to that of a member of a sanctified church:

> He said, "Hey, my little one, I am God Almighty, I am a wall around my people, and if I call you through fire and water, come on, follow me." He led me. I saw myself hanging over a gulf by a thread—oh, it was so dark in that pit! He brought me up out of that pit on the thread. (Johnson 1969, 74)

When you get to the crossroads, you face two roads, two threads, two ropes, two lives, and two futures. As depicted above, this may be revealed in mystical vision as an inflated self that is lost in the dark abyss and another smaller self that basks in the light. Follow the "little me" along the narrower pathway that brings the ecstatic wings of a song that enable an uplifting, mighty flight. After this first admittance takes place the gate is left open for more spiritual visits to other classrooms. When new suffering arrives, you now recognize that it brings more than pain. It also brings a ticket for another ride to glory. Here is Brad's account of such a return journey:

> I remember the night as if it was yesterday. I had received some news that broke my heart. I fell to my knees with devastation and prayed that my heartache be mended and that God would have the mercy to hear my plea for healing.
>
> Then to my surprise, I noticed barely audible singing in the distance that took place outside my window. At first I thought it was a group of Christmas carolers, until I realized it was June. The singing became louder until I could hear that a large chorus of women was singing the song, "Hare Krishna." They sang it like a heavenly choir and it became so loud I could have easily recorded it. I looked out the windows to see who was there, but no one was in sight. The music continued for hours.
>
> This music was so full of passionate joy that I forgot my heartbreak. It was an astonishing and beyond-this-world musical performance that absorbed my tears and dissolved my sorrow into its greater bliss. I sang with the heavenly chorus and completely surrendered to its melody. To this day I have never heard anything like it. In a dark and bitter tragedy I heard the sweetest sound of divine love.

"Hare" is sometimes regarded as an indication of Hari, another name for the Hindu deity Vishnu who removes all illusion. It is also associated with Hara, representing Krishna's shakti. In general, Hare refers to the vibrant energy or shakti of God while Krishna refers to God itself. The chanting or singing of the "Hare Krishna" lyrics are believed to infuse this spiritual energy into you, enabling its sacred vibration to lord over all the strata of your whole being. I can testify that the sacred vibration of this holy song both set me on the vast sea and lifted me to the highest heaven.

A sacred song is capable of healing what cannot be helped by word, thought, or action alone. You need the medicinal balm of music to suture your deepest emotional wounds and transport you to a place where there is again room for the most extraordinary penetrating joy. Music expands the room inside your heart and clears the way for divinely inspired rhythm and melody to arrive. As the Indian spiritual teacher Baladeva Vidyabhushana spoke of this particular verse: "When the sixteen names and thirty-two syllables of the Hare Krishna mantra are loudly vibrated, Krishna dances on one's tongue" (Rasbihari Lal & Sons 2005, 17:30). When Brad heard that choir sing its words, a rising emotion blissfully freed and carried him high away from low despair.

It is no accident that so many great hymns and gospel songs were conceived in the darkest moments of suffering. When your heart breaks apart, an opening is made for receiving God's grace that, at its peak, is the gift of song. Shamans, mystics, spiritual seekers, and medicine people have fasted and undergone physical suffering in order to receive a sacred song. However you are thrown to the suffering ground, whether by accident or on purpose, it only provides access to the big room if you feel heartbroken rather than regard the ritual as a magical token. The state of brokenness allows songs to come down the spiritual pipeline and put the pieces of your heart back together.

Hillary went to a spiritual classroom where she was introduced to the same mystical secret experientially discovered by Ludwig van Beethoven (see Keeneys 2017). She was shown that the composer, amidst his deepest personal despair, had an envelope in his heart that opened to release musical notes that, like steps on a ladder, enabled him to climb upward toward heaven. Beethoven's musical masterpieces were created when he felt uplifted by the act of musical composition while simultaneously downtrodden with personal suffering. In this juxtaposition of the most positive and negative aspects of his life, his music became strikingly original, yielding the creative surprises and unique characteristics that musicologists study to this day. Both Beethoven's musical talent and his suffering needed to be co-present as a vibrant, doubly bound contrary in order for him to be touched by the highest inspiration for musical creation. In the dream, Hillary received a song that broke her heart open to feel the kind of musical healing power experienced by Beethoven. We were not surprised to later read that Beethoven said that people who truly got to know and understand his music would "be freed from all the misery that drags down others."

Filled with despair at his own auditory deafness, disturbed by the aesthetic deafness of others who did not appreciate what was unique about his music, and inspired by the quest that enables music to bring felt closeness to God, Beethoven experienced the same dynamic practiced by Bushman singing dancers in the Kalahari for thousands of years. Music leaps out of the deepest longing and most desperate need for what lies beyond human limitation, frustration, and suffering. When this emotional yearning is placed upon a melodic line you have a means of transportation that can take your heart and soul to the musical, mystical sky. There sacred ecstasy is expressed as an ode to supreme dream joy.

Sacred Ecstatics points you to the mystical tracks leading to the musical soundtracks of the big room. There anything can truly happen and this includes being soaked, changed, and re-cloaked in the sacred vibrations of music. It matters less what you believe or the words you prefer to pronounce or denounce. Be more concerned about lighting the fuse that gets you close to the original muse. What matters is experiencing a musical douse in the mystery house.

Move across the gap from Second to First Creation and change from the "big me" found in a small room to the "little me" located in the big room. You need a means of transportation that can carry you to the transformational fire. Sometimes your voyage to a spiritual classroom begins at a port, an airport terminal, a bus station, a horse stable, or an automobile parked in in a driveway where you are pointed to a classroom. You may see many ropes or colored lines hanging from the ceiling or the sky. A spiritual pointer in the vision then literally points to one of them. That is the track you will travel on.

Hillary went to a spiritual classroom that looked like a driver's license bureau. There she was given an anointment to join Brad in sending others to the classrooms, doing so like old school spiritual pointers, trackers, and guides. Like Mother Pompey, our responsibility is to "keep close with God" so we can discern what helps others stay on the mainline rope. There is extensive experiential knowledge required about preparation for spiritual traveling, appropriate action in the classroom when you arrive, and effective delivery of its gifts back to your everyday. We discuss this further in our book on ecstatic mystical experience, *Climbing the Rope to God: Mystical Testimony and Teaching* (2017).

Before you can travel you have to be made spiritually ready for the voyage. Otherwise, you are more inclined to catch a cold dream in a small room that only satisfies personal wish fulfillment but does not ignite the soul. As always, you need to sincerely and actively participate in building the big room while sweeping away the clutter that gets in the way. This preparation is illustrated by the story of a monk who was alive during the time of Buddha. Everyone thought he was stupid and lazy, including his brother, an abbot who became so fed up with the monk's inability to learn or do anything correctly that he threw him out of the monastery. Wherever he went, other teachers took pity, but the same thing always happened. They'd get upset and throw him out. Finally, one day he met the Buddha, who gave him one directive: stop studying and stop meditating. He was to only sweep the meditation hall every morning while saying to himself, "Clear the dust, clean the dirt." He was fully enlightened within the year.

It is time for you to do some cleaning and clearing. A trip to mystery can't begin unless you remove the surrounding junk and gunk. Take a sabbatical from all those trickster platitudes, inflated attitudes, misguided books, and imitative practices that accumulate the debris of a puffed up mind. Let your sacred heart take a broom and sweep away all the gloom, doom, exaggerated costume, and excessive perfume from your existential room. If you are in too much of a hurry, then clear the "must." Or if you are desperately trying to seduce the spirit to grant you a gift, then clean the "flirt." Clear the dust, must, and rust as you clean the dirt, flirt, and whatever else can divert you from handing everything over to God — space, time, energy, matter, material, garbage, demarcation, information, disinformation, punctuation, exclamation, exaggeration, sublimation, evaporation, refrigeration, dissipation, dissemination, edification, beautification, transportation, and transformation. Are you ready to travel to an ecstatic, dramatic, and kinetic spiritual classroom? Is your luggage light enough for you to take flight toward the numinous light? Have you lit some hallowed words and knelt at the smallest altar that is well matched for your "little me?" Forget your troubles, chase all your cares away, and for the very first time shout this altered prayer, "Thy will be *cooked well* done!"

Put on your traveling shoes and get ready for some spirited walking, skipping, leaping, and rope jumping. All aboard the locomotive whose sole motive is heading toward glory, the holy ship steering toward campground, the spirit horse running for 'doption, the holy fireworks rocket launched for a celestial tour, the mystical Chrysler driving on a numinous road trip, the luminous flying wheel heading for an unknown destination, and all other means of transporting you to the highest and hottest rocking, rolling, pebble-throwing, and pond-skipping trip of an ecstatic poetic slam, song and dance jam whose wildly improvising mystery jazz is something more rhythmically felt and tonally heard than seen, said, and understood.

Bring out your spiritual matchbox and rename it. Assume it is your spiritual classroom. Perhaps call it Sacred Ecstatics High School, Krishna University, Shaker College, Ecstatic Institute of Spiritual Technology, Kalahari Sky Institute, Field of Birds Equine Academy, Shaman's Musical Conservatory, The Big Holy Roll-y School of Divine Dance, or Beethoven's Oven and Culinary, Auditory School of Spiritual Cooking. You may have a dream that gives you the name of your classroom matchbox. Go ahead and ask. Make sure the name is a good match for the right hatch of you, inspiring you to honor its capacity for otherwise unattainable mystical teaching. Welcome to the Dream Gleam Laboratory and Ecstatic Hatchery, The Higher Learning Center for Vaster Creative Capacity, the Never Finished Finishing School of Fire-Groomed Unknowing, and last but never the least of these, the Odd for God Non-Poisonous Ivy League otherwise known as the Primary School for Teaching the Consciously Unattainable Unconscious Way of Mystical Reaching.

Once you have chosen a personalized classroom name that lifts your spirit, prepare yourself for spiritual travel and ready your matchbox learning space to receive you. This requires an injection of sacred music that prevents motion sickness while facilitating vibratory movement. Contrary to what you may have been taught, visionary journeys are not taken on the meandering back roads of an entranced mind, but on the musically electrified and emotionally fortified song tracks that head straight to the big room that hosts all mystical locales. Not just any music will do—the spiritual classrooms are reached through the songs that pierce the heart and shoot the sacred vibration throughout the somatic echo chamber.

Select a humdinger hymn that is an emotional zinger, and then strike the right chord of prayer or rhythmically swing a chant that rings the truth. Find what others have reached for when they're broken, as well as those that echo joyous praise and radiate the holiest rays. Investigate what makes a broken heart melt and fuse with a musical muse—a Beethoven sonata, a Chopin polonaise, a Gershwin melody, or a song coal with a tender sounding ember from Mr. Cole Porter. Our Sacred Ecstatics Songbook—a collection of sacred songs we have been given in the spiritual classrooms—not only includes hymns like "In the Garden" and "Heavenly Sunshine," but special tracks from The Great American Songbook such as "Our Love is Here to Stay" and "Ev'ry Time We Say Goodbye." Because these songs came from the visionary classrooms they are more than evergreen tunes—they are eternal ecstatic tracks for heartfelt, soul lit, and body moved spiritual journeying.

Once you've found a travelling song, every night before going to sleep make sure to open your matchbox classroom and fill it with musical fuel. Whether you open the box in front of a speaker or sing into it, make sure it is filled with a song that radiates sacred emotion. You, too, will be soaking in the music that tugs at your heartstrings, making you more ready to be pulled into a spiritual classroom for life-changing instruction. Feel the pulse of rhythm, the rise and fall of tones, and discover how a song can make you long to be nearer and dearer to whatever originally inspired its composition.

After you and your spiritual classroom have been sonically saturated and filled with musical emotion, hold your First Creation matchbox as you remember its changing forms that formerly included an altar, medicine bag, rattle, shamanic tool kit, spiritual bundle, and mystical suitcase. Offer a prayer that says: "Dear Lord, I feel the need to learn and burn for you. Please send me to your high school." Make sure you say this with a sincere emotional tone that is on board a soulful rhythm. Voice your prayer in a way that helps *change your room*, remembering Soren Kierkegaard's wisdom teaching that "the function of prayer is not to influence God, but rather to change the nature of the one who prays." Change yourself by altering the circumference of your immediate surroundings so the room can better host your being touched by emotionally portrayed and musically conveyed mystery. Go to sleep willing, able, and ready to be sent back to school. Do not drift away from feeling excited about the unknown curriculum awaiting you. Fall asleep with this dedicated longing for the mystery school where sacred ecstasy rules, allowing God to choose whether you consciously or unconsciously remember whatever is taught or given.

When you wake up in the morning, immediately declare, "thank you!" with as much heartfelt exclamation you can muster. Believe that by some consciously imperceptible transportation means you were actually sent to the spiritual classroom inside your matchbox. Turn to it and say, "Thanks for accepting, enrolling, and teaching me." Be enthusiastically and even deliriously grateful, and never for a moment forgetful about this mysterious educational adventure. It does not matter whether you recall going there. If you have an intuition that you went to the classroom, ask your intuition to give you a partial clue about it. If you actually had a dream, assume that one piece of it was inside a spiritual classroom, but only the part that you cannot remember and that it was likely the opposite of what your conscious mind now thinks it knows.

In this way you keep mystery unnamed and beyond the grasp of trickster naming and its presumed interpretive knowing. In addition, take any action that helps you further hear and feel the all-encompassing mystery that surround-sounds your life. As you transform your matchbox into a spiritual classroom filled with musically inspired mystery, a match becomes ready to light and heat a dream, whether remembered, partially dismembered, or wholly forgotten. With this in mind, turn again to your two-word exclamatory prayer that helps lift open your shell: "Thank you!" Join e. e. cummings as he expands this into a big room prayer: "thank you God for this most amazing day, for the leaping greenly spirits of trees, and for the blue dream of sky and for everything which is natural, which is infinite, which is yes." Now say the prayer so its emotion is longer lasting: "Yes!" Repeat again: "Yes, Yes!" Don't guess what this yes of *yes* means. Just express "yes" with the tone, rhythm, movement, and emotional exhilaration than make your bones primed for divine fire.

You are the match-in-the-box that is in need of a spiritual wildfire. With the help of skilled stonemasonry and fine cookery, you head to the big room where moving bones, tones, and beats conduct the heat that ignites the soul. Go ahead and shout again with that uplifting, reverberating, and barnstorming "Yes!" Make an appreciative greeting to whatever is happening on the other side of your small room where communicational contact is made with the heaven above and beyond the present earthly (s)hell. Fly among the stars, and do not stop even after you pass Jupiter and Mars. You might be offered a thirst-quenching drink of morning dew or evening mist that otherwise would have been missed had you not opened your heart to a true friend on high. Why remain lost and isolated on an island when there is a welcome place for you amidst musical company? It's time for you to join the chorus that is transforming Steven Sondheim's *Company*, now performing live at the First Creation Life Force Theatre of Sacred Ecstatics. There a song calls for what it takes to be truly alive: "Somebody crowd me with love, somebody force me to care, somebody make me come through, I'll always be there, to help us survive being alive, being alive, being alive!" Meet the circular return of a brand new beginning where it's always opening, closing, and reopening night. God's rope is pulling up the curtain, turning on the theatre lights, lifting the orchestral baton to start the overture, and revealing the stage that is set for an ecstatic, aesthetic earthquake and a deserved thunderous applause. Come on and enter the stage, think on your feet, dance with your voice, and go break another performance leg. Let's get this show on the high road!

7

THE FOUR CHANGING DIRECTIONS

Sacred Ecstatics puts your life in perpetual motion as you traverse the four directions of ecstatic living: climbing the rope, performing creative work, room building and repair, and implementing absurd intervention. You cannot remain permanently in the throes of ecstatic fire and forever journey on a mystical flight, nor can your daily work creatively thrive without the renewed inspiration and attunement found in another round of spiritual cooking. Each time you return to the everyday, things eventually cool down and shrink again. You therefore benefit from a mind skilled at using words and thought in the serious pursuit of big room reconstruction. But don't forget to temper exaggerated belief and find comedic relief with a dose of absurd truth and its crazy wisdom cure. A medicinal giggle can bring on an ecstatic wiggle and help wriggle you free from any cramped container, opening the way for another fire revival. Finally, remember that spiritual cooking prepares you to come back and make a difference in the world, inspiring creative action that changes your surroundings. The whole of your life must keep moving, turning, and crisscrossing through all these four changing directions. It is this ongoing movement from one direction to another that mobilizes a remarkable ecstatic life adventure.

The spiritually cooked life circulates continuously through the four directions of Sacred Ecstatics: (1) climbing the rope toward the heat of spiritual cooking; (2) returning to perform creative work that helps change everyday small rooms; (3) implementing the mind masonry of skillful language and thought that helps build or repair the big room; and (4) administering therapeutic interventions of absurdity to loosen and clear cluttered spaces, clogged channels, and stuck routines. Our shorthand names for the four changing directions of everyday activity are climbing the rope, creative work, room building and repair, and absurd intervention. This diagram demonstrates their relationship to one another:

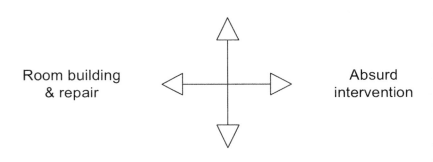

The rise from cold to hot spiritual temperature, which is also the journey from a small Second Creation room to the big room of First Creation, requires climbing the vertical rope to God. This vertical axis is both the rope and the spiritual thermometer—as you move closer to the ineffable and your sacred emotion rises, so does the temperature. When the spiritual heat reaches a boiling point, this is the moment for the strongest transformation as you are thoroughly spiritually cooked. After spending time in the fire you return to everyday small rooms where you find the miraculous practical impact of ecstatic spirituality: you are able to bring the expansion, heat, and creative energy of First Creation's changing back with you for a limited period of time. This is when you can infuse fresh, inspired vitality into your everyday. You deliver creative change to others, whether it is saying a unique and thoughtful greeting, baking a delicious cake with a delightful surprise on top, building a birdhouse that has extra flair, playing an invented funny game with your children, making a drawing that conveys fascinating mojo, signing your name with entertaining bravado, opening a door with inspiring gusto, or saturating your workplace, home place, or neighborhood with uncommon action, tender warmth, expanded possibilities, felt mystery, and uplifting expression.

The Sacred Ecstatics life continually brings the transformational dynamics of First Creation's big room into the pickled thought, flat-planed sense, and sedated activity of the experientially shrunken and spiritually frozen small containers of Second Creation. You deliver, transmit, or infuse creative change wherever it is needed. Any trip to the big room readies you to actively participate in the ceaseless revitalization of the world. As a tuned instrument aligned with higher power and divine resonance, you help the Creator create and circulate change. The purpose of life is *creation* and it happens through the enactment of *change*—you are here to be an assistant and instrument to God's ongoing production of a creative masterpiece.

At some point in time, however, the motivation for creative activity runs its course and your inspirational fuel tank empties. You ecstatically chill and become spiritually ill with frigidly rigid definitions and frostbitten routines, dragged down by the return of literal, non-visceral meanings, swollen self-centric stories, and mystery-quashing interpretations. All expressive action becomes stale and pale, the higher medical sign of a soul ailment in need of another heat treatment via the n/om pharmacy of sacred ecstasy. This common influenza fosters distance from divine influence—

you revert to being a commenting observer and pondering knower rather than an action performer and tinkering experimenter. With further refrigeration, trickster rushes in to invent reasons and excuses for why you are no longer in the exhilarating flow. You creatively come to a standstill, lose your passionate zeal, and begin to feel disconnected from higher mystery. This is when you most need the discipline to not overthink and over-talk your situation, chasing trickster down one rabbit hole after another. Otherwise, amnesia sets in and you forget that what you really need is expansion and heat. Before you can vertically ascend and feel the temperature rise, however, the horizon must expand. In other words, the horizontal axis must extend its reach in order for the upper height to be reached. The horizontal floor or stage goes up and down like an elevator—when its breadth expands there is enough room to host the action that precipitates a lift up the spiritual thermometer.

Learn to recognize when you are due for a return trip to the fire and be warmed up for another round of passionate, spirited, soulful, creative, ecstatic living. Then act to expand the room and strike a match rather than continue to stew. Guarani shaman, Tupa Nevangayu advises: "To receive the sacred luminosity, you must prepare yourself to become available for this light . . . Make yourself ready for this most important experience" (Keeney 2000, 61). When the temperature is cold, recruit trickster to become a master stonemason, carpenter, and well-trained construction worker capable of building the big room, making you ready for the next climb. As your experiential room expands along the horizontal plane, bring on the spiritual engineering that simultaneously helps the temperature rise through the right rhythms, tones, movement, and circulation of emotion. The fire will then retire narrow thoughts, impoverished talk, and lifeless action, reigniting your creative passion.

Whereas the vertical axis is regarded as the rope to God, daily involvement with the world is found on the horizontal axis or earthly plane. It is the stage for your experience and performance of everyday life whose range may be narrowly limited or exceptionally broad in scope. You either perform your life in a thimble, a bottle, a closet, a small room, a mansion, or on an infinite stage built on the sacred ground of a boundless life force theatre. The horizontal axis, daily plane, earthly landscape, or life performance stage is also a rope whose strands host and interconnect your sense, perception, thought, emotion, action, and interaction with all your worldly relations. Here you find the connections to family, friends, colleagues, neighbors, community, and the whole ecology and biodiversity of the earth.

The higher the horizontal plane rises up the vertical axis toward the fire, the more influenced you are by the dynamics of higher transformation. Spiritual heat activates and empowers your inherent creative gifts and natural performance talents. Bringing spiritually warmed and ecstatically charged action into the world synergistically, holistically, and energetically makes your rope to God stronger. After each round of cooking you must not delay — create and immediately relate rather than only linguistically regurgitate and socially isolate. Otherwise the sacred vibration and jubilant emotion that filled you in the heat will quickly dissipate and you'll find yourself sinking low into the arctic cold.

The horizontal axis hosts the expansion or shrinkage of your daily life rooms. Here the therapeutics of absurd intervention wait to spring into corrective action whenever you find yourself too expressively serious, ideologically pious, emotionally burned out, psychologically hopeless, spiritually chilled, or aesthetically unthrilled. Mystical prescriptions always include a tincture of absurd medicine that loosens any constrictive grip of reason and welcomes what is beyond rational comprehension. Whenever you creatively dry up or feel spiritually cold and dead, there is nothing like a hearty giggle to start a body wiggle and soul tingle. An injection of crazy wisdom that induces a paroxysm of convulsive laughter helps you take yourself less seriously, break out of any immobilizing spell, undo a Second Creation hex, loosen your grip on the steering wheel, come to your mystical senses, and spiritually reawaken to the irrational, unsolvable mystery of being alive.

When you catch yourself talking too much about life rather than living it, take a turn and get therapeutically absurd. Be on the lookout for times when you become a full-time narrating critic who is stuck in excessive contemplation, unceasing reflection, persnickety elaboration, runaway abstraction, and all manner of shrunken head literalism and logically garbled interpretation. During the cooling you begin the process of cocooning and ballooning — insulating yourself inside a cocoon of words, thoughts, and "oughts" as your mind balloons and gets too big for its britches. When this becomes unsatisfying, irritating, or untenable, avoid seeking readily available forms of distraction and intoxication — these may provide momentary enjoyment but do not bring you the needed expanse and heat. You might also be tempted to find solace through gaining more or better insight into your situation, whether in the form of astrological readings, personality testing, psychological diagnosing, Jungian typologizing, past life interpreting, fortune telling, philosophical rendering, metaphysical explaining, or any other theoretical scheme that evaporates the mystery of dream and drains the life stream. Be careful because every label and cognitive frame you hope will conceptually liberate actually attaches another layer of opaque abstraction, conceptual debris, cognitive distillation, perceptual coloration, screened awareness, and experiential filtration. You become further trapped inside trickster mind's cocooned, embalmed, coffined, and confined knowing that repeatedly dictates a "yes" to know and a "no" to altered action.

Addiction of any kind, including the habit of feeding

interpretations to an insatiable appetite for mental understanding, is best regarded as something that arises from spiritual dis-ease. It is a trickster-guided response to the uneasiness that comes from containment in too small of a room, the lack of creative life force, and emotional distance from divine mystery. Whenever you feel the cocooning of your domicile and the ballooning of its presiding mind, it's time to *act*: quickly engage in some absurd lampooning and its ecstatic retuning of your polarities with higher hilarity. This shift in experiential direction can get you back on track to the spiritual high-(c)larity road.

The answer to every important question concerning what you need to do in life is this: Go to the big room and get spiritually cooked, and then create, laugh, rebuild, and ascend the rope again. Begin in any direction, perhaps starting with a belly laugh to knock, knock on any door or wall that is in need of a pratfall. Whatever direction you are facing, make sure to follow the recipe that fosters expansion, heat, and creative change. After cooking, blessings naturally flow, including innovative, transformative participation in the everyday, now permeated with expansive thinking, warm emotion, healthy laughter, and the vibrant buzz of altered action. All is well until it isn't, and when the latter alarm goes off, do not get lost and stuck searching for an answer in cold temperatures and shrunken rooms that don't encourage experimental tinkering. Once again, rather than try to change yourself or other people, aim to change the room you're in. Head to the big room kitchen where ecstatic emotion and somatic motion shake everything up and get the circle of life turning in a virtuous direction again.

Remember that a healthy dose of absurd medicine taken each day helps keep the frozen doctors and psychological shrinks away as it breaks the chains and liberates the brains that bind. Do more than think absurd thoughts because they are too easily assimilated by trickster mind. You must enact the kind of absurdity that does not fit inside the small box in which you are caught—act to crack an abstract wall. No matter how much spiritual experience you have or don't have, you simply cannot avoid getting imprisoned inside conceptual boxes, and this includes the box that imagines it hosts no boxes. As a human being residing inside any small room of Second Creation, you are destined to fall inside a trickster mind trap every time you ecstatically cool down. Engage in some absurd action and the straitjacket loosens, the handcuffs drop, and with some soul-stirring music, the trickster walls come tumbling down.

Conductors of Sacred Ecstatics must stand ready to offer mystical prescriptions that are a broad and doubly bound medicine, straddling the horizontal rope between creative performance and absurd intervention. At the same time, prescriptions must reach upward to the big room of First Creation while extending below into the everyday small rooms of Second Creation. Remember that the suffering people bring for healing is stuck to a sticky name, hardened in a frozen understanding, and imprisoned in a shrunken existential space with a constricted experiential range that is missing creative inspiration. It is less the suffering that requires treatment than the sticky, constricted, hardened, and uninspiring room holding it. (Recall and please try to always remember the teaching of moving from small glass to vast sea in chapter three). When suffering is resituated inside the cosmos it becomes spiritual compost, a complexly rich soil that helps more experiential possibilities bloom in the big room.

Creatively fertilized, well-grounded, and spiritually elevated absurd action places you on the broader, wittier, better heard, finer lit, and more emotionally moving transformative stage where all experience, including suffering, joy, heavy seriousness, and lighthearted humor has more room to play changing roles with higher goals. To assure such expansion, enact good stonemasonry—skillfully using trickster mind to build a vast foundation and stage for creative performance. Here the finely sharpened sword of a clear wisdom mind helps open the way for your personally felt relationship with the jubilant divine creator. You must chop away distracting clutter, break up inappropriate part/whole relations, and open up impoverished framings to make more room for wider concerns. The masonry and carpentry of room construction also involve demolition, something that absurdity helps accomplish. Together, therapeutic absurdity and room building—the two poles of the horizontal rope—tear down walls that confine to create a more open space that can host the most change.

Once the basic operation of step one of the Sacred Ecstatics recipe—building the big room—is in motion, you then move on to step two—journeying up the vertical rope to the spiritual fire. This is the natural progression of ecstatic living—room expansion accomplished on the horizontal plane enables a vertical trip to the sky. The fire is found at the intersection or crossroads of earth and heaven. Paradoxically, as the horizon expands you must remain close to the vertical rope to God. You then come back altered and ready to create, share, and proliferate the sacred elation vibration. Remind yourself again: After the inspired flight to an ecstatic height, you return ready to creatively perform on an everyday stage. When you next become too settled in a routine and stuck in your head, you tire as creative vitality fades. This is when you need absurd medicine that sets you free to reenact the recipe. The skilled masonry that lays the hallowed cornerstones of prayer gives rise to the shifting gears that move from spoken word to rhythm, song, and dance, enabling the next ecstatic ascent, creative ferment, and playful circumvent.

The Spiritual Metabolic Cycle

Once you have completed a vertical climb to the spiritual fire and begun your descent, it is the continuously felt expansion, heat, and creative energy of the sacred vibration that mobilizes your subsequent activity and engagement. We call the movement from sacred vibration activation to its subsequent inspired sharing with others the "spiritual metabolic cycle." Whatever you receive in the big room must be metabolized—fully taken in, digested, transformed, and then outwardly given in a way that touches lives and changes rooms. After the sacred vibration is installed within, it waits to spiritually charge your creative participation in the world. It re-awakens whenever the room expands and heats. You cannot know how the sacred vibration will specifically influence you and others until you activate it and put it to use. Sometimes it sweeps and at other times it weeps, offers a creative tweak, tickles and laughs, or shakes to bake and remake the day. Make a sincere and passionate effort to be the embodiment of change and the sacred vibration will rise to the occasion and effortlessly inspire and empower creative action.

To set the metabolic process in motion, allow the vibration to do more than tickle your fancy and only make you happy with no consideration of altering your surroundings. Remember that the fruit, goal, practical outcome, and main purpose of Sacred Ecstatics is found in the way it catalyzes your participation in expanding, warming, inspiring, energizing, changing, and recreating everyday rooms. You might be inspired to leave a poem at the grocery store, paint an acorn for a city park, surprise your spouse with breakfast toast that has a raisin-made smile, leave a map of heaven in a bar, jog one mile in honor of a lesser known saint, unroll a ball of string in a profound manner, or simply infuse the right dose of mystical expansion, spiritual warmth, and inventive surprise into whatever present job, hobby, or other activity you have going on in your life. Consider everything you do as re-creation. Recreation and re-creation go together on the big room playground. Vacate any small room in favor of taking a special vacation with a sacred vibration. Discover how anything and everything can be given some ecstatic flutter when it's spread with numinous butter, the secret behind baking holy bread that never tastes bitter.

If you are a bodyworker, the vibration awaits being metabolized in order to bring forth healing hands. If you are a writer, the vibration is capable of inspiring the birth of poetry and prose. For a composer, the vibration is ready to open your capacity to catch a song. For a therapist, the vibration can make available healing words and transformative expression. For everyone, the vibration helps launch infinite forms of creative action, blessed performance, and remarkable stewardship.

Theologian Howard Thurman penned the famous quote, "Don't ask yourself what the world needs. Ask yourself what makes you come alive, and go do that, because what the world needs is people who have come alive." The same advice applies to your ecstatic spiritual life. Ask yourself what hallowed cornerstones, roomy spiritual frames, ray-full prayer lines, heartwarming melodic tones, surprising and arousing rhythms, temperature raising songs, soul stirring and body freeing movements, and divine celebratory dances wake up the sacred vibration inside you, light a fire in your bones, stir your spiritual emotion, and strengthen your mystical rope. Then engage with more of that, because what the world needs most is people who are cooked and ready to serve with verve.

Unless ecstatic experience is fully metabolized it too easily contributes to an undesired vicious cycle that is akin to addiction. The emotional thrill experienced from being near the sacred vibration can lead to repeatedly chasing another spiritual high, which is ultimately a selfish, dead end pursuit—eventually causing spiritual gifts to fade. Be careful about being too self-centered and possessive about higher emotion, swinging between feeling special when you are near its jubilation and feeling self-pity when you aren't. Graciously accept all spiritual gifts while also accepting the practical wisdom that they grow exponentially the more you share them. You are given something in order to be a creative contributor to the whole of life, distributed to those who dwell around you. Spiritual prosperity has nothing to do with the accumulation of personally hoarded wealth; it is found in sharing. The more you give, the more spiritual guidance, ecstatic inspiration, and heartfelt blessings you receive—making you able to continue giving.

If you catch yourself spending too much time reflecting on your spiritual gifts (or the lack of them) than performing creative work in your daily life, then you are definitely not completing a spiritual metabolic cycle. If no such action is taken, you will likely experience spiritual indigestion where the previous spiritual gain eventually turns to existential pain. Similarly, the more you are subsequently determined to prove to yourself and others what you spiritually know or have experienced, the less likely it is that you will fully benefit from whatever was received. What truly matters most is your becoming a bona fide agent of First Creation with a license to change. When you are filled with n/om, seiki, the holy spirit, and the sacred vibration, proceed with surrender to the whole spiritual metabolic process so soulful stewardship and transformative action spring forth effortlessly.

In contrast, when you feel that taking any action requires too much effort, know this is a clear sign that you are spiritually cold. In particular, you might avoid following through with a mystical prescription simply because you don't feel like it or deem it unreasonable. Your curmudgeonly trickster mind rushes in with one million reasons to avoid it, particularly if the prescription is more than a millimeter outside your norm and comfort zone. However, this is when you most need to act. The dedicated performance of a mystical prescription brings habit-tripping dissension, unexpected invention, and the desired ignition. Taking action sustains the expanse, heat, and creative energy underlying the changes formerly experienced in the last big room cookout. Don't wait to act until you understand or think you are ready. Any uncertainty about taking action indicates that this moment is the perfect time to do it. Trust that one action step leads to the next step and that this movement advances the desired exodus from small room misery to big room mystery. Act in order to set in motion your extraordinary participation as a wholeheartedly engaged and ecstatically gauged ambassador of First Creation.

The spiritual metabolic cycle is a reminder that everything in your life must keep moving around the circle of changing directions that include triumphant ecstatic jubilation, inspiring and perspiring creative action, mystically fortified absurd undoing, and far-reaching wisdom reconstruction. Throw all these things up in the air like a four-ball juggle. When they circulate and each ball alternates between being caught and thrown, the ecstatic *circulus* or recursive circle of an extraordinary life is in town. Under the big top circus tent things are always changing to bring the spatial alterations, action transitions, scenery flips, role fluctuations, climate shifts, absurd twists, serious dips, and ecstatic ascents that make life rise and shine on stage. The alchemy for changing reality needs all the four directions that embody the dichotomies, triangles, squares, and circles of the Ouroborean dragon slayers and ecstatic players of higher geometry and ecstatic thermometry.

The Spiritually Cooked Life

There are varying degrees to which you can be spiritually cooked and hold expertise in Sacred Ecstatics. The Kalahari Bushmen call someone fully cooked a "heart of the spears." Such rare individuals have gone to the big room of mystery so often that the veil between First and Second Creation is very thin and may almost seem nonexistent. They can enter the spiritual heat in a split second and their involvement with others often demonstrates extraordinary intuition, prodigious improvisation, gifted creativity, savvy interactional presence, original mystical experience, unlimited spiritual energy, wildly outrageous humor, and uncanned, unplanned natural wisdom. All this is due to their strong rope to divinity and big room affinity. A Bushman heart of the spears is a master n/om hunter and an unpredictable form-shifter who may also be recognized as a seiki wind gatherer in traditional Japan or a musically steered captain on a numinous Caribbean ship. As Vusamazulu Credo Mutwa described it, such a rare person "live[s] in a world where the visible and invisible come together like lovers, where the real and the unreal embrace and make love" (Keeney 2001, 56). A thoroughly spiritually cooked human being (what we nickname an "SCHB") never lets go of the overhead rope while being a helpful jackal, a word leaping jackrabbit, a small room hijacker, and a jack of all trades that involve spiritual cooking, ecstatic transport, and any of the other mystical professions. Here you find a ready-to-rise to the occasion whole loaf of fresh baked shaman, healer, or teacher—the soulful finders of lost bodies who offer a singing gig and ecstatic jig.

It is not possible to know how cooked you will become in your life and what kind of spiritual know-how and gifts will be bestowed. Once you are truly set on fire, however, your life will never be the same. From that moment on, you have a totally new reference point, primary distinction, and compass setting. You will repeatedly hunger and thirst to return to the big room and get spiritually cooked again. You will forever regard sacred ecstasy as the pinnacle spiritual experience and want to stay in relationship with it. You will also want to keep learning how to better change the room rather than alter its inhabitants, leaving the latter up to the heavenly producer and dream director of the whole mystery show. Your job is to get the room ready for the next Life Force Theatre where the highest source recycles and re-sources you and others to perform anew.

When you first feel the sacred vibration inside your body, it can be said that you have been spiritually cooked for the first time. As mentioned earlier, the Bushmen regard this as receiving a nail or arrow of n/om, something that happens after you have been softened enough for its ecstasy-filled and song-conveyed sacred vibration to enter your body. Recall that the first reception of the sacred vibration can vary from person to person. You might simply feel as if something brushes against you but doesn't fully cross the somatic border. While this contact feels amazing and can bring on some serious trembling and shaking, "the spirit was on you rather than in you," as parishioners of the old sanctified church put it. Or an arrow of n/om may partly go into your body for only a brief moment until it later falls back out. This, too, is different than having it go all the way in to take residence on a permanent basis.

It is important to recognize that receiving one arrow or nail of n/om, a singular transmission of seiki, or an initiatory baptism of fire by the holy spirit is not enough to become fully spiritually cooked or immediately ready for a high anointment. It's only your successful admission to kindergarten, an introduction to the passageway or starting gate. If you don't continue to diligently follow the recipe, the inner sacred vibration and its influence on your daily life will soon fade. As the Bushmen say, the arrow or nail will become tired and dirty. This is when other spiritually cooked human beings, dreamt ancestors, or unfiltered divine intervention must clean your arrows and nails with the n/om fire of sacred ecstasy, refill you with seiki, or plunge you into a baptism of holiness all over again so the sacred vibration can be reinstalled, retuned, and recharged.

Some people do not receive the big bang experience sometimes associated with being hit by a spiritual arrow, dart, nail, spear, needle, or thorn. Instead, the sacred vibration may slowly soak into them over time. Don't be frustrated by a lack of quick and dramatic results; most people are not instantly struck by divine lightning. Remember that it is always up to a higher source of wisdom as to when and how the spiritual goods are delivered. All you can do is develop big room construction skills, spiritual engineering know-how, ecstatic performance chops, and good spiritual cooking habits. Whether this results in an arrow piercing or a holy soaking, continues as a flash fry or a slow roast, the outcome is essentially the same: you will always remain a human being in need of the higher help accessible in an expanded room whose spiritual heat and vibrant creative change radiate numinous transformation. You'll forever need to enact the recipe as if it's the first time, every time.

Sacred Ecstatics calls for many trips to the big room to get repeatedly cooked. A Bushman heart of the spears may have received thousands of arrows and nails of n/om during a lifetime. They are acquired in both live ecstatic interactions and in other worldly visits to the spiritual classrooms. All of this cooking provides a heart of the spears with an everlasting match inside that automatically ignites a fire whenever required. The room of such a person's life is a mystical matchbox full of matches ready to burst into flame. Regardless of how cooked you are, any and all reception of the sacred vibration must be continuously metabolized and made ready to circulate through the other important aspects of ecstatic living that involve spiritual masonry, ecstatic cookery, absurd dramatology, and creative productivity. The more cooked you get, the more ongoing transformation you experience and the more gifts you receive in order to give them away.

The crossroads is marked by one road leading to all kinds of promises to make your résumé longer and more impressive. The other road simply takes you to the big room where you're no more and no less important than a sparrow, worm, small stone, or speck of dust. Spiritually fried folks don't value uppity robes, lofty nametags, glittery magical paraphernalia, impressive sleight of hand tricks, dazzling silver and gold walls, big shot talk, or a curriculum vitae of magical synchronicities and manifested destinies. They pay more attention to what expands and heats the room, radiates sacred emotion, and creatively influences lives. The most prized spiritual gifts are performance oriented — the ability to express the rhythms, tones, and movements that help strike a match and ignite the fire that brings more soul filled, deep fried change into the everyday.

As you become more spiritually cooked, you discover that when someone else receives a sacred gift, you receive an ecstatic blessing in kind. You experience firsthand that the sacred vibration received by one person is also a delivery to everyone else. A spiritually cooked life becomes a "one for all and all for one" situation. You find that you are better prepared to receive the sacred vibration when you devote yourself to helping others receive it, whether clapping, singing, or cheerleading your praise whenever the temperature is raised. Especially make sure that your heart, body, and mind are in the right big place so you become a link in the needed social chain reaction. This spiritual fission takes off like wildfire and can generate enough spiritual heat and expansive mystery to change the world.

Embrace how a Sacred Ecstatics life is always changing its performance theme as you move in and out of dreamed eternity, covering both the infinitely expanded inner and outer space, and traveling up and down the spiritual thermometer. You never know what hallowed names will come your way in order to help build the big room, nor can you know what spiritual match will arrive, whether it's a surprising rhyme, an old or new prayer line, a sacred song, a cabaret tune, a wake up tap, an unfamiliar dance, a funny medicine, or a creatively edgy, contrarian work of art. You also can never know when a transforming change is coming or going, how long it will remain the same, or when it's ready to morph again. Life becomes more unpredictable and so do you. What is consistent, however, is your steadfast desire to venture to the big room, jump into the spiritual cooking fire, and afterwards continue to creatively share the new birth, mirth, and infinite worth of life on this rare patch of earth that resides within the hearty hearth of heaven.

Making the Vertical Rope Primary

Climbing up and down the vertical rope to God is the most important spiritual, mystical, and shamanic journey of all. Exercise caution when venturing too far afield along the horizontal rope and its bent rails, crooked trails, and meandering detours because these paths can be more influenced and commandeered by trickster. Solely expanding your living space is not enough to reach the pinnacle experience — the fire of sacred ecstasy is required to blend, mend, ignite, excite, cook, illumine, and uplift. Expand the room *and* climb toward the heat. Use spiritual street smarts and hold onto the mainline rope in order to stay in touch with the original source of the creative force rather than risk falling into a diluted — and often polluted — distant stream.

Your goal is to roam the earthly plane while holding onto the rope that reaches down from the numinous sky. As mentioned before, the horizontal axis can move up and down like an elevator when it is pulled by the overhead cable, enabling you to visit a higher floor and then come back down to ground level. Each floor hosts various forms and experiences that can distract you from the other levels, especially the higher purpose overhead. For example, a lower floor may put you in touch with the so-called mineral, vegetable, and animal spirits which are construed, named, and framed by your Second Creation mind. It is unwise to hang out too long in such a place unless you are holding on to the vertical rope and principally guided by the original creator of all forms. You must wisely handle the horizontal and the vertical ropes that host the dynamics of expansion and heating, respectively. Also be careful with any bent rope that is neither horizontal nor vertical. These host the presumed discarnate ancestral spirits that are neither wholly of the earth nor of heaven. Such critters often leave you with the jitters for they are often the trickiest, most deceptive, and least trustworthy entities to deal with and are best left alone unless you wish to risk finding out whether they are in a good or bad mood when they deal with you.

The proliferation of named spirits and invisible agents of influence, whether in Africa, Europe, Asia, the Arctic, or the Americas, almost always leads at some point to an entangled web of superstition and fear that is distanced from the purest and surest freedom brought by infinite love. Tragedy and malady ensue whenever medicine people, healers, mystics, shamans, and spiritual teachers are drawn away from the vertical rope, tempted by an over-reliance upon the trickster invention of spiritual protection. Talismans of protective magic are then sold as both practitioner and community live in perpetual concern about whether a person is being cursed or negatively influenced by bad mojo released by a malevolent practitioner or nasty ancestral spirit. There is also an equal temptation to use positive mojo and trickster-spun charm to purposefully bring forth desired outcomes. Trickster, a true super *duper*, wants to indulge your curiosity in or fear of the supernatural and its truckload of ghosts and semi-heavenly hosts. It is happy to feed your fascination with power and desire for the chilly goose bumps of non-ecstatic magic. When trickster's pursuit of becoming a superman, superwoman, or little big god reaches its inflated hocus pocus peak, the experiential world becomes filled with superstition, delusion, paranoia, unnerving hallucination, and fear-based or wish-based rituals that self-verify the need for innumerable protections and charms.

Under such circumstances only a return to the mainline rope's highest altitude offers genuine liberation from the entangled knots and strangling ropes of an inflated trickster attitude. As always, hold onto the main rope that takes you to the big room where God is all you need to take care of you.

In a bizarre series of visions, Brad was once guided to meet a shopkeeper in Copenhagen whose ancestor Gustav Holm had led the first expedition to Greenland in 1886. When Brad told him about some of his dreams, the old man at the shop said to come back the next day because he had a gift for him. That's when Brad was given the drum and shamanic instruments of one of the great Arctic shamans, Migssuarnianga. An early report written by Holm mentioned that this drum was known for flying in a ceremony:

> The drum now started into motion, dancing up to the ceiling ... It was thought that the drum in the hand of a shaman possessed mystic and supernatural power which helped the shaman summon the spirits. It would become as if alive ... and floated freely about the house without being touched by the shaman's hand. (Holm 1911, 95)

Migssuarnianga became a shaman in the classic way. He was spiritually chosen to pursue this vocation and for years he apprenticed under highly regarded shamans. During this time, while walking in the Arctic wilderness, he met a gigantic spirit bear that arose from the center of a lake and swam toward him. Though he was frightened and wanted to run away, his body could not move. The bear came up to him and bit him in the neck and ate him alive as Migssuarnianga lost consciousness. When he woke up, the dwarf Qataitsaq was by his side singing a sacred song.

After Migssuarnianga had been spiritually altered and

musically equipped in this way, he acquired many other spirit helpers, including an Anguit, a spirit with a skeletal head and fjord seal's body. He also acquired the most difficult spirit to capture, a Tornarssuk, the leader of all spirits, a giant whose face was a mixture of human and animal. Like before, each spirit killed him three times before he could acquire its song and healing help. This sort of thing took place with numerous spirits, ghosts, and entities unknown to most of us. Migssuarnianga became arguably one of the greatest shamans of the Arctic, for he owned "everything" that had "soul and body." He also learned from fifteen other shamans, three of which taught him witchcraft. He was a master shaman in relationship with the entire spirit world. He entered the spirit world by either rubbing magical stones together or by rocking back and forth while sitting on a giant stone. Later he would play his drum and it would come to life, as he became "all-knowing."

After Holm's visit, the famed polar explorer Knud Rasmussen, earlier known as "the father of Eskimology," interviewed Migssuarnianga's son, who gave more specifics regarding what happened in his father's ceremony. His account was published in Rasmussen's book *Myter og Sagn fra Grønland, I*:

> The magic drum placed beside him had come alive and sounded as though a thousand spirits were beating on it.
>
> When the drum touched his heel, it was as though the first white of dawn rose out of the night. He could see dimly in the dark. Later, when it touched his hip, the day itself came. Darkness did not exist for him in the night. His eyes cut through everything.
>
> But when the evening finally came when the drum was led, as though by invisible hands, to stand trembling, with the drum skin singing, on his shoulder, the sun shone with all its light in front of his sight, and

all the countries of the Earth were gathered in a circle in front of him. All distances and all remoteness ceased to exist.

Migssuarnianga had become all-knowing, and had gathered the whole world within himself. (1921, 34)

However, in spite of this hookup to non-ordinary magic and impressive shamanic power, when Migssuarnianga later was introduced to the teaching of a Christian missionary, he gave up his drum and shamanic tools. There was no longer any need for calling on the lesser spirits who were always full of mischief. While they were capable of helping him heal and voyage, they also frequently caused complications and trouble. Instead, Migssuarnianga chose to devote himself to a singular relationship with the utmost source of creation rather than constantly wheel and deal with its remote and less emotive emissaries. A rope to God is the only shamanic instrument you need. It can turn anything into a drum, rhythm, song, bear, critter, flicker, sun, or whatever changing form of First Creation best suits the moment.

Brad was given the flying drum of Migssuarnianga and it was with him for several years before he, too, passed it on. It is true that the drum flew inside First Creation, and Brad experienced its mystery flight. For over forty years, Brad learned many healing, mystical, and shamanic ways and was initiated in diverse spiritual traditions throughout the world, but like Migssuarnianga, he gave away most of his shamanic paraphernalia to be a stronger shaman with only one tool, a single rope. This was not due to other spirits and spiritual objects being necessarily bad or evil, but because it is wiser, stronger, and more reliable to hold yourself inside the grander wisdom, custody, and reign of the vertical rope. Sometimes the latter brings a rattle or drum to Brad's hand and at other times it may lasso a piano. Anything can be delivered with a rope, from tea leaves to bee's knees, as well as mangoes, tangos, bongos, and pianos.

The vastness of the spiritual space that hosts the felt presence of mystery is more important that any part or form within it. When you hold onto a rope to God and then light a spiritual fire, you are lifted to the big room. There the strongest healers do not heal, they only help loosen and free the constraining yoke of suffering so there is more wiggle room for tailor-made divine alteration. They do so with the right mix of therapeutic absurdity and creative action that expands and heats the room. If numinously willed, then healing is fulfilled. The strongest shamans are less preoccupied with owning spirit helpers and collecting journeys. They, too, only sing to help make stronger their mainline rope to the Creator. If willed by the maker of all destinations, such a shaman may be sent to a visionary classroom, the purpose of which is simple: to feel closer to the main source and be made more available to receive and express its blessed force and specified direction. The strongest spiritual teachers do more than instruct and regale with an inspiring tale. They evoke and embody the supreme light with uninhibited celebratory delight. The spiritually cooked healer, shaman, mystic, saint, teacher, preacher, singer, dancer, musician, drummer, and all other spiritual roles are more the same than different. When fully developed, each occupation is singularly devoted to cultivating a close relationship with the first inventor of fire, the primary designer of creation, and the original change maker. If you seek only one spiritual role at the expense of another then you are still too organized by trickster naming and have not yet come full circle to the most important teaching: love, trust, obey, and be ready to convey the ineffable divinity of the Creator. Make the vertical rope primary and everything else will fall into place.

Bringing the Dynamics of Sacred Ecstatics Down to Earth

Each step of the recipe for setting your soul on fire involves all three dynamics of Sacred Ecstatics—*expanding, heating, and changing*. While one particular dynamic takes its turn as the primary focus during a particular step, the other two dynamics are always in operation. Step one emphasizes expansion—constructing a big room while finding that with more space comes a greater capacity for warmth and a wider stage for creative action. Step two shifts the focus to heat—igniting and tending the fire for spiritual cooking, automatically bringing further room expansion and more inspiration for enacted invention. Finally, step three highlights continued transformation with a prescription for everyday unexpected action that helps sustain, spread, and share the expansion and heat that, in turn, can host more change.

Sacred Ecstatics comes to life through these three dynamics, each featured in the recipe's stepwise progression. All this takes place inside the four surrounding directions whose experiential themes shift from the south where a new daily creative performance is soulfully staged, to the ecstatic north where whole-body spiritual cooking is fueled by fired-up sacred emotion, to the wild west where trickster mind must be both reined in and free to roam in order to build a bigger room, and to the far east where absurd action tickles all constriction and loosens rigid thoughts and inflexible oughts. With the horizontal rope you round up a room with a wider stretch and with the vertical rope you try to lasso the moon for a higher climb. There is no end to learning how to circle around these four directions while venturing along the vertical and horizontal ropes, enacting the three steps of the Sacred Ecstatics recipe.

For those engaged in a people-helping profession—whether as a coach, therapist, body worker, doctor, nurse, or other form— Sacred Ecstatics brings more room expansion, heat, and creative change into your sessions. Mystical prescriptions hold onto both the horizontal and vertical ropes in order to bridge small and big rooms, helping sustain the transformation brought by vertically inspired creation and horizontally absurd loosening. Rather than continue old refrigeration practices, start applying some ecstatic thermodynamics to your work and don't forget to take your absurd meds. When you are overdue for a spiritual overhaul, rebuild the room and grab hold of the main rope that brings down the spark and raises you toward the heat. Regard your work as a spiritual experiment that helps you become a more vibrant conductor of First Creation's changing means of multi-faceted transformation. Always start each session with a revolutionary act—never try to change your clients, but instead focus on changing the room that holds your interactions with them. Don't be in a rush, however, to turn up the heat until the room is big enough for this to happen effortlessly, naturally, and spontaneously. Then finish with a prescription that keeps the transformative process rolling along.

Do the same in any other profession or activity—apply the dynamics, recipe steps, skills, and four changing directions of Sacred Ecstatics to every situation from litigation to auto repair, lawn care, copyediting, furniture sales, babysitting, parenting, bank telling, horse whispering, bird calling, hi fidelity listening, lakeside fishing, house painting, gym jogging, and flower arranging. There is always a valuable opportunity nearby for you to experiment with expanding, heating, and creating the changes that bring newborn life to humdrum living in need of a more soulful hum and a less monotonous drum. This is especially true for those moments by yourself or with others that seem inspirationally dull, experientially constricting, kinetically limiting, expressively boring, or emotionally irritating. Introduce a secret hand movement unseen to others—gently shaking your hand in a seiki-inspired way underneath the table or a scarf. Absurdly ponder how Napoleon Bonaparte's secret to empire expansion may have involved a shaking seiki hand hidden underneath his jacket. Then seriously consider how keeping just one part of you in the vast sea can be as transformative as a whole body plunge. Let those toes and fingers wiggle as you internally imagine performing a song, playing an invisible drum set, blowing a fantasy tuba, tap dancing on floor and ceiling, or impossibly leaping across the earth. Sacred Ecstatics is not limited to practices that only occur during a designated time. Intersperse its dynamics, progressive steps, ecstatic skills, and changing directions into each and every occasion. Do so internally and externally, depending on what the situation calls for. If you are not bringing all the aspects of Sacred Ecstatics into your everyday interactions with colleagues, friends, and family, then you are not developing and applying your ecstatic know-how in the contexts where it is needed most.

Infuse Sacred Ecstatics into whatever you are doing, wherever you are. If you work as a physical therapist, then immediately tinker with adding each dynamic in the right amount and the appropriate manner. Expand and warm the room to activate your inner tingle before you see a patient, and then stand ready to bring some ecstatic trembling to how you touch a client's body during the right time of treatment. Add tonal and rhythmic changes as called for in your ongoing therapeutic action. And occasionally inoculate the heaviness of treatment with the levity of absurdity that helps render more tender bodywork. Master *en-joying* (putting more joy in) your work with clients and only consider the possibility of teaching what you have learned after an extended amount of trial and error on your part. Don't rush into teaching until you are fully satisfied with the exhilaration achieved with ecstatically fired-up sessions. If teaching becomes your calling, start with other physical therapists rather than jump out of your lane to be an out of focus "spiritual teacher." Become a finely focused, technically sharpened, and performance skilled shamanic physical therapist rather than a vague, generic shamanizer without a compass or sense of direction. Stay within your gift, that is, work with the resources you have rather than fantasize playing a role you aren't equipped to perform. One step at a time keeps you on the right path, while being in a hurry makes it all blurry.

Constantly tinker and experiment to better find how to place the work you already do inside the big room. If you are an elementary school teacher, foster expansion before you offer a new lesson and then bring more variation of rhythm and tone to warm your instruction. Don't forget to internally pray, shout, tease, sing, dance, shake, offer a divine prank, and jump off the theoretical plank to touch the lives of your students while standing in the unseen spiritual classroom of higher education. No matter the task at hand, bring on the expansion, heat, and change found inside the four seasons of serious construction work, absurd intervention, creative invention, and embodied ignition! Rather than fancy yourself dropping everything around you and running away to be another wizard of awes, hold on to your rope and hang around to become a one-of-a-kind alchemical neighbor, seiki parent, spiritual hairdresser, mystical welder, n/om plumber, or any other mystically inspiring and ecstatically uplifting role. Become an extraordinary First Creation character with more real impact on the world than playing a miscast fantasy island role.

Enact wisely attuned Sacred Ecstatics on the golf course, in the judicial court, on the sidewalk, down the back roads, in the easy chair, at the writing desk, the garage workbench, the grocery store, in the car, out on the lawn, and on your nighttime pillow before drifting off to sleep. The more you spiritually cook, the better skilled you are at stepping in and out of the big room, carrying and infusing its dynamics of magnificent wonder, radiant splendor, and stunning surprise. Make every mundane chore and profane bore a vital part of the life force theatre. Bring heaven into earth with everything you've got. Birth more mirth and unearth a different way of saying hello, whistling while you work, and dancing in the dark. As Brad's mother likes to sing, inspired by the lyric from the musical, *Oklahoma!*, there is no need to go elsewhere when "everything's up to date in Kansas City" (she's from Kansas City). Be ready when the unsinkable Molly Brown musically asks you, "How you gonna keep 'em down on the farm after they've seen Paree?" Answer the Sacred Ecstatics way: expand, heat, and change the farm so its magical charm becomes a sweet and buttery spiritual pastry as tasty as what's found in a Parisian café.

One common spiritual error found among overly ambitious seekers is unwisely assuming or hoping that spiritual practice and learning will provide a direct and immediate path to becoming a healer, shaman, teacher, workshop leader, or guru. People confuse wanting to experience more mystery in their life with wanting to be perceived by others as a magical being. Sometimes people think they are pursuing a spiritual path in the big room when in reality they spend most of their time in a small closet staring at their reflection asking, "Mirror, mirror on the wall, who's the most powerful healer and magical shaman of them all?" When they don't get the answer they were hoping for, they go off to gather more experiences and then come back to check the mirror again. Arguably every human being succumbs to the temptation of mirror-gazing from time to time. When it becomes the main theme or room hosting your whole life, however, there isn't enough expansion or heat for any authentic transformation or anointment to take place. Wishing for an upgraded door sign is the surest spiritual sign that you aren't ready to take on the desired role, and you may never be. The most authentic occupants of a recognized spiritual position are almost always reluctant to pick up the mantle. These appointments typically take place when anointed elders repeatedly pull a person into such a role. Reluctance is required for higher conductance. We will spell this out one more time to make sure it is sufficiently clear: if you desire to become a shaman, you probably won't become one. If you sincerely don't want any particular role, you may get the rattle call (or you may not). The same holds true for being reeled in to heal or teach.

You must be willing to follow whatever you are truly called to perform, something better decided by a process of higher selection rather than the whim of trickster impulse. If you get the call and don't respond, you may have to take another fall that makes you better ready to accept the call next time it comes. If no trusted elders are insisting that you step into a particular role, then regard this as a polite, silent communication you should hear. Do not personally choose to move toward an elevated title or specially named role on your own. Especially do not arrange a social situation where you placate and please others so they are set up to unwisely praise your feigned spiritual importance, mistaking this as evidence for a calling. Instead, pray to only want communion with the divine—not as a strategy to make yourself more quickly staged to teach, but because you sincerely want to be rid of all desire that distracts attention away from the fire. Saint Augustine has your back and was on the right track when he crafted this prayer for the world:

> Here is my heart, oh God; here it is with all its secrets. Look into my thoughts, oh my hope, and take away all my wrong feelings. Let my eyes be ever on you and release my feet from the snare. I ask you to live with me, to reign in me, to make this heart of mine a holy temple, a fit dwelling for your divine majesty. Amen.

Rather than indulge a trickster fantasy, hunt for sacred ecstasy. Apply more Sacred Ecstatics know-how to where you are now in your life and see where it takes you one step at a time inside God's space, energy, and timely grace. Let "Thy will be done" because only this leads to your being able to fulfill your unique one-of-a-kind mission. If it is your life purpose to sweep a temple, then you will be happier to wholeheartedly own a broom instead of being a powerful boss, pope, dalai lama, spiritual prima donna, celebrity mystic, publicly adored healer, mega-church preacher, super-workshop teacher, rich quasi-spiritual business consultant, uber-coach with the most gee whiz, pop star shamanic soul retriever, or psychic titan of fortune cookies. It is better to hold a broom and sweep yourself into bliss, making sure you clear away whatever litter or glitter stands between you and your Maker.

If it helps, make those lofty titles more absurd and bring them down to spiritual size. Doctor their letters so a shaman is a *salmon* swimming upstream in search of a lost frying pan, a healer is a cobbler or *heel fixer* of worn and holey soles, and a teacher is a frustrated *reacher* whose arms fall short of effectively boxing with trickster. Find a plastic fish to soulfully swim against your lost current, a blueberry cobbler to feed your insatiable spiritual snacking tooth, or hold a funny arm extender to be less a pretender and instead a better scratcher of God's back. Engage in less talk and stop checking the clock. Lessen the power search and seek a vast nest perch. Drop the title and go for what's vital. Drop the name and take better aim.

Over the years, we have witnessed people become barely spiritually warmed or receive an arrow prick of n/om and then immediately think they are ready to start healing, teaching, or offering a shamanic ceremony. When nail reception is regarded as eternal possession of the Holy Grail, the nail rusts quickly because the recipient is in a rush to advertise a new title and spiritual offering. Such a hurried pursuer may know on some level that such action is a delusion perpetuated by the mass marketing of notorious spiritual teachers and trickster appealing best-selling authors whose content and delivery are half-baked and wholly fake. And yet they often still persist and lust for spiritual power even when advised not to chase it. A Kalahari Bushman n/om-kxao receives more nails than are easily counted before they are even close to being ready to ably assist another healer. A preacher, priest, rabbi, or Zen roshi takes years of full-time study that involves first assisting other teachers prior to receiving a senior role. The same length of time and amount of dedicated hard work are required to acquire the skills for therapeutic work—years of study, internship, and apprenticeship. The performing arts are equally rigorous. Sacred Ecstatics is as demanding as all these serious professions, and perhaps more so since it is based on reeducating your mind to construct more expansion, retraining your body to better cook and improvisationally perform, and long-term learning in how to creatively alter your everyday. In addition, you must learn how to more effectively receive and better sustain the emotional nail and musical mail of n/om rather than have it freeze, shrink, and fall out of your body as soon as you leave the big room and fancy yourself a big shot who has a hell-per spirit in the pocket or a sham and glam teddy bear held on a leash.

Some folks become addicted to the false promises and trickster mirages of spiritual power, shamanic influence, and spiritual importance that are served up with abandon at New Age workshops. Any recognition or complement that then comes from a peer or teacher results in their trickster mind stealing it for a small room inflation fix, sending them off on another bender. We can tell when students have fallen off the wagon because their expression during a Sacred Ecstatics intensive or session becomes too purposeful, like they are trying too hard to prove they have mastered it all. After a single tactile bounce of n/om or a light body brush with the sacred vibration an incongruent display is exhibited that attempts to show they can perform everything a Bushman healer took a lifetime to develop. Or they may fall back into the habit of constantly recounting trickster stories about presumed magical dreams and "synchronicities" that lack the sweet scent, precious emotion, humbling expansion, speechless heat, altering vibration, changed character, and sacred performance that matter.

Only joining "tricksters anonymous" will enable you to live one day at a time, never trusting yourself to hang around anything that fattens personal spiritual desire. Abstain from whatever tempts you to indulge in a trickster high, and that includes hanging out with peers or standing in front of audiences who encourage and celebrate you in ways that feed your addiction while starving any felt need for wisdom. You will eventually have to trust the leadership of higher power in the old-fashioned way. This is how authentic saints, mystics, shamans, and healers live their lives— they do not trust themselves and hand everything, including public recognition and denigration, over to God. Do the same or be guaranteed that you will be seduced by anything that enables you to posture you are more special, more magical, humbler, or "higher-in-the-archy" than others. The Achilles heel of spirituality is the seduction to steal the thunder and appear as a big deal, and this includes the act of posturing humility, rather than bowing before the big room that alone can heal, reform, and transform.

Only trust feeling the life-changing need for your Creator. Such deeply felt longing for intervention to mend trickster mentation and false representation is what attracts higher power to come near. Honor how the divine wants you to know that no matter the role name, the enacted performance that matters is the same: praying, singing, and dancing while jubilantly trembling with the emotional fire of sacred ecstasy. In other words, forget everything except this highest prescription: "love God with all your heart and with all your soul and with all your might." Consider this prayer experiment: Turn to the left and feel that you have outgrown your trickster shell that is becoming an unbearable hell that makes your ego swell. Know that you can't find the escape hatch on your own. Now pray with C.M. C.,[20] "The Power in whose hands I am may

---

[20] Refer to chapter one for the full testimony of C.M.C.'s experience of sacred ecstasy.

do with me as it will!" Then turn to the right and surrender as C. M. C. did before she was flooded with ineffable joy: "I let go of myself." Release all desire for anything other than handing yourself over to the source and force of creation, the Creator-Destroyer-Resurrector who can only make a house call when your need for higher intervention is most purely felt and sincerely requested.

The sense of lightness and expansion that made the atmosphere around C.M.C. quiver and vibrate only arrives when you stop desiring anything other than enacting the dynamics that expand, heat, and change the room. To be swallowed up in the waves of splendor and glory ineffable requires that you lose yourself in the All-loving where it is more than enough to be filled with the heartfelt songs of love and trust. In the big room everyone within is taught, healed, journeyed, and rendezvoused with mystery. Sacred ecstasy does not leave you inflated with a special name or claims to spiritual fame. It excites with the joy of owning the feeling for a personal, relational rope to God. In your smallness you are able to experience God's all-embracing awe. Allow the rope to pull you into the divine hug of eternal love, the soul of nature, and the all of one endless smile.

Don't Forget Your C.M.C.

It is extraordinary that no one knows the actual name of C.M.C., the Canadian woman whose personal testimony about her life-changing ecstasy is a guiding star for Sacred Ecstatics. Her words ecstatically tower above many of the well-known founders of major world religions—she tapped into the pure sacred vibration and its jubilant elation, without need to recount it through the filter of ideological discourse. We propose that her initials secretly point to what preceded her immersion into a "splendor and glory ineffable"—her antecedent experience and existential condition was *contrarian medicinal contrition.*

As C.M.C. reported to Bucke, prior to her ecstatic awakening she felt like "some creature which had outgrown its shell, and yet could not escape . . . it was a great yearning—for freedom, for larger life—for deeper love." With all of her "strength gone" and "every resource exhausted, nothing remained but *submission*" (Bucke 1969, 324–25). No longer trusting that she could be the captain of her lifeboat, C.M.C. surrendered, submitted, and offered herself to a greater power and let go of herself. This made her soft and tender enough to feel and receive the "infinite love" that "streamed down like holy oil." Her sincere contrition led to being touched by the surrounding magnetism and pulled into the engulfing waves of electric love. Here the C.M.C. of *contrarian medicinal contrition* helps usher in the ultimate healing balm. It is the key to going past outside observing and actually entering the big room sea where C.M.C. sacred ecstasy awaits. The vertical rope hosts a contrarian stretch and the more it is pulled on both ends, the more tension and vibration it creates until it is released to launch another ascent. Like using a slingshot, you pull back the cord, feel its quiver, and release at the right moment so you, the tiny pebble, are thrown into the sky.

The changing dynamics, recipe steps, and four directions of Sacred Ecstatics—along with their construction, engineering, cooking, and performance skills—hold a plethora of contrary opposites from cold to hot, literality to metaphor, sense to nonsense, meaningful word to unrecognizable sound, still trance to moving dance, and so on. Maintaining the difference between any contrary enables a tension to be felt in the cord of relationship holding them together. Quashing one side to allow the other side to rule is what stops the vibration, drains away the n/om, bans the absurd wisdom, locks the mind, binds the body, and kills the spirit. When Brad was given his final examination as a Zulu sangoma in southern Africa he was asked how he deals with good and evil. Had he replied that he wanted to destroy evil so good could forever reign, he would have flunked the test. The answer must avoid an over-emphasis on either side, but instead underscore the importance of tapping into the tension between opposites that is the pulse of creation's life force. Behind change is found an oscillation. If you want to change, then oscillate inside a contrary. Bring on multiple contraries and a multitude of oscillations, all mutually intermingling and amplifying, and you become a mystical wheel rather than a misguided sole on the heel of another trickster deal. Stretch, quiver, and release the arrow! It then becomes a flying wheel, whirling log, spinning quaternary, or windmill that brings the wind of change, the spirit or *spiritus* that breathes life into everything it touches.

When William Blake wrote the words, "without contraries lies no progression," he was addressing practical spiritual engineering. Embrace the fact that you live suspended between the hot and cold, big and small, heaven and earth, flesh and spirit, body and mind, excitation and relaxation, health and sickness, life and death, victory and defeat, and every contrary that defines all the human crossroads. Then resist obliterating one side to give exclusive entitlement and privilege to the other side. Instead surrender to the experiential oscillation, the sacred vibration, and the rocking, swaying body that creates the rub, strike, and spark of earth making friction with heaven.

It is the constant ups and downs and movement all the way around that make the wheel turn, the soul burn, the body heal, and the creative life awaken. Why land on a final answer when the question continues to change? Why settle on one question when the answer forever is altering? Why seriously answer when the small room question is a big room joke? Rather than escape a trembling contrary or try to calm it down, be altered by its alternating vibration and changed by its fully embodied and congruently enacted changing. The line holding a contrary on each end is felt as a rope. Your rope to God holds the oddball below and the odd God above with all the oddly amazing experiences in between. Don't laugh too much at such absurdity, but make sure you giggle enough—hold that unresolved tension at its vibrant sweet spot. Stop fighting to make one side always right, of the light, or full of might. Both join and separate these contradictions and learn to vibrate enough to launch and cook as you travel up and down the rope and back and forth across the performance stage, always in the spin and weave of a wonderfully creative life. Become a well-bred thread of many colors, tones, rhythms, and all the endless smiling qualities that are too numerous to name and understand.

One more thing—the Canadian woman who was "swallowed up" by ecstasy is waiting to be your spiritual mother. Consider her your *Canadian mother change.* Why not carry a Canadian coin in your pocket or purse and from time to time flip it in the air and discover what face it temporarily recommends? Does C.M.C. suggest less head-trips or less telling of your tales? Don't leave home without your Canadian mother change. A *clear mind clarifies* more of C.M.C. as does *cultivating mystery communion* and *conducting more current* on your way to becoming a *consummate master cooker.* The more forms and names of C.M.C. you carry with you, the more you expand, heat, creatively inspire, and change the room until you are in First Creation where the many faces, sides, and contraries of C.M.C. place you on the vast sea amidst the moving tides and rolling waves of sacred ecstasy.

The Ongoing Turning of the Ecstatic Wheel

During a lifetime of spiritual cooking you discover that all ecstatic directions, temperature degrees, experiential domains, and changing performances are not isolated but nested inside each other like Chinese boxes. This is the natural inclusion of First and

Second Creation, neither collapsed into a singular unity nor separated into opposites that are statically and distantly localized. These two faces of Creation are interdependent processes and inseparable dynamics with changing identities, shifting situations, variant threads, alternating currents, simultaneous and sequential steps, proliferating qualities, growing mysteries, and morphing theophanies, all constantly on the move and forever transforming, though our naming of their momentary phases tempts us to think otherwise. In the never-ending oscillations of life you vibrantly journey along the many contrary lines that complement, battle, cancel, re-emerge, pose, juxtapose, turn, encircle, and lead to and away from one another. The whole of your experiential universe is Ouroborean, like the mythical dragon that continuously chases and swallows its own tail. In the circular movement of wholesome ingestion, transformative digestion, and re-emergent progression is found the changing that underlies the endless cycles of creation. Life and death dance on the edge of infinity and sing the songs of divinity. Here the horizontal and vertical planes also morph, bending their lines to form the higher circle that is a deeper form of the utmost straight line. For earth to be as it is in heaven, the latter must encircle the former rather than be held at a distance. Don't think about this mystery for more than a fleeting moment or else risk forgetting you must act in order to circulate the leaven of heaven that makes earthly hearts rise.

Again, the rope to God is the vertical spoke enabling movement between closeness to and distance from the numinous, experienced as being spiritually hot and cold, respectively. When you get too spiritually cold, something inside you announces a request to absurdly doctor your situation. You yearn for the ecstatic elation and mystery elevation that is missing in your life, a sign that it's time for another climb up the vine. This is the gift of suffering and discord — it alerts, pinches, tickles, and orients you to take a journey toward the big room, experience its spiritual cooking, find intimacy with the divine, and be treated by the sound and movement alchemy that converts pain into ecstatic joy. Jewish theologian Martin Buber suggests, "All suffering prepares the soul for vision." D. T. Suzuki amplifies this point further: "The value of human life lies in the fact of suffering, for where there is no suffering . . . there can be no power of attaining spiritual experience . . . Unless we agree to suffer we cannot be free from suffering" (cited in Merton 1957, 94). Once you recognize that ultimate wellbeing lies in the constant movement toward and away from the pole of each direction, you find that it takes all the varieties of experience to form, churn, and turn the changing wheel of life. This complexity is what carries you to the divinity of mystery that most vitally and vibrationally is felt as sacred ecstasy. Guarani elder Tupa Nevangayu describes this remarkably inclusive and transformative co-mingling of suffering and prayer: "The shaman sees what others cannot see. He or she feels the suffering of the world and in one's own life, but deals with this by grabbing the rattle and praying harder each day. Suffering and prayer comprise the way of the shaman" (Keeney 2000, 61-62).

As you turn and return around the four changing directions of the ecstatic circle of life, you are perpetually altered by the way everything is held in one direction and then another as the room ravels and unravels, shrinks and expands, the temperature rises and falls, and the performance exudes and then excludes an extraordinary vitality as it continues to change or stand still onstage. Never forget that the creative activity of your everyday is the ripe fruit harvested from a spiritual ascent. Without entry onto the big room stage of divine mystery's artistry, the art of living creatively falls short. As William Blake put it, "The man who never in his mind and thoughts travel'd to heaven is no artist."

When the atmosphere is spiritually heated, the horizontal plane rises to a higher floor. Here your expressive gifts become most aligned with the divine and you are spiritually and creatively on fire. When you later cool off and hang around too long with a cliché creed and boring deed, the situation begs for the absurd side of the horizontal, earthly rope. Therapeutic intervention now springs forth to doctor and loosen any rigidity of knotted words and convoluted understanding. Deeply felt medicinal absurdity tickles and teases the intellect's dis-ease and its accompanying somatic malaise as the physical movement of laughter, like the shaking of an Etch A Sketch, clears and makes you ready to build the big room again. Honor the serious wisdom of e. e. cummings: "The most wasted of all days is one without laughter." The utmost sacred (rather than frivolous) performance of the deeply absurd also makes the horizontal spoke and earthly floor rise toward heaven. The laughable, flammable antics of a sacred jester, fool, or clown help further raise the spiritual temperature, expand the room, and trigger the sacred vibration, bringing you closer to a higher rationality that is only irrational when observed from a small room. All the contrarian and hungry-for-change hollow ropes—including those that may seem a tinge dopey, goofy, and nutty—help unhinge the dream door, unclog the mystery stream, release the shiver river, and flood the world with the ocean emotion of sacred ecstasy.

Trickster, when wisely employed to prescribe oddly wise and godly hilarious absurdity, enables another genre of ecstatically seasoned enrichment to pour upon a parched and starched, malnourished soul. Paradox, circularity, and the complex juggle of insoluble contraries provide the lubrication that further loosens the collar and releases the holler of a Sacred Ecstatics performance. The non-dumb, crazed, and emblazed wisdom reveals that trickster is also a true face of divinity, one of the sideway views that God uses to erase the small room walls of an overly serious perspective gone flat. The early-twentieth-century artist Filippo Tommaso Marinetti offers this invitation:

> Let's break away from rationality as out of a horrible husk and throw ourselves like pride-spiced fruit into the immense, distorted mouth of the wind! Let's give ourselves up to the unknown, not out of desperation, but to plum the deep pits of the absurd. (Chipp 1968, 285)

There is a time and place for the truth of all things, and this includes trickster coming to turn things upside down and inside out, clearing and expanding the ground for uncommon invention, dream-led healing intervention, creative mystical exploration, and extreme out-of-every-box liberation. There is more complexity to all this movement around the four experiential directions than words can readily survey, purvey, and convey, but the main point is that you must keep changing and transforming to remain as long as possible inside First Creation. You need to discern whether you are going back and forth between cold and hot temperatures, standing inside small or big space, or producing work that is creatively dead or alive, and notice any awful freeze in need of a melt by thawful absurdity. Without all this transformative movement, anything can get stale and worn out—the sacred vibration diminishes, creative flow is blocked, humor disappears, and thoughts become rigidly cold. Life's most exhilarating treasure is found when you move with, rather than resist, the whirling wheel of contrary spokes. You must drape heaven's firmament over hell, infuse creative life into deadbeat routines, deliver heartfelt spiritual heat to melt conceptual ice, and mine serious truth from absurd play. Travel the opposite directions as well: Carry the suffering of hell to heaven, lead the walking dead to the dance of creative life, pour the cool wisdom water on a fire that has run its course, and release the absurd to undo any suffocating clerical collar or philosophical straitjacket. Do so to turn the spinning wheel that weaves a sanctified web, catching those who strayed and lost their way to now be played, prayed, and remade as newfound strands of the holy braid—the rope to God's expansive retreat, heavenly heat, singing heartbeat, and dancing feet.

Being spiritually cooked means leaving the interpreted life behind and becoming a dedicated performer for the gods. Follow divine mystery rather than pursue personal mastery. As Vusamazulu Credo Mutwa advised Brad years ago:

> Human beings were not intended to be sane and intellectual. We were supposed to be wise and made of feelings . . . You are either a green person who lives according to the chaotic rules of the moon and the earth or you are a dry and dead thing that believes that two plus two equals four . . . There are intelligent forces that live through us in strange and illogical ways. If you are a shaman, you must leave yourself alone. Stop judging yourself. You don't know what's happening to you and you don't know what is happening. Furthermore, you must never find out. When something strange happens to you or to a friend or to the world, you want to go and find out why. But in the end, you come back filled with superstition. In searching for answers to the unknowable, human beings ended up in the pool of superstition. In the process of trying to get out of it, they only got deeper into it . . . never question the gods . . . Simply be what you are called to be. There are things in this world which have no explanation, not because there is no explanation, but because our minds are not designed to find out. (Keeney2001, 171-172)

With Credo Mutwa's wisdom in mind, it is time for you to receive the sacred directions cast by the vertical and horizontal axes of Sacred Ecstatics. Go to your formerly harvested sand and use your finger to draw two intersecting lines—a spiritual cross, crossroads, and crossing—on your homemade Kalahari. The center point is where your matchbox now should be placed. Regard the furrows in this sand as marking the vertical and horizontal axes of your ecstatic spiritual life. Now wholeheartedly speak these words as you use the same finger to make the same cross over your heart: "Welcome dearest ropes of the four changing directions." Regard this moment as the ceremonial installation of the spokes of your expanding, heating, and changing wheel for authentic ecstatic spiritual traveling.

After you have been spiritually marked and branded in this way, open the matchbox and take out the string. Rub it along the cross you previously made over your heart. Consider this the installment of your rope to God. Then take the smallest stone and use it to cross your heart again. This indicates your place in the whole scheme of things—a small part that resides on the earthly plane, but truly wants to climb the sky. Now take the object you chose to stand for mystery. Slowly and surely use it to mark the next crossing of your heart, a gesture that invites creativity to awaken and bring the fruit of creation.

Finally, place everything back inside the matchbox, including some of the sand on which it has rested. Hold the matchbox and use it to cross your heart one last time as was repeatedly done before. Regard this as the final sanctification of the four changing directions and their respective crosses, crossroads, and crossings, while realizing that all these tiny objects, as spiritual tools and evocations of mystery, are also incredibly and sweetly absurd. Express thanks for the miraculous contrarian alchemy found in how the smallest of things, along with the least common action, brings you deeper inside the vastness of felt divinity.

Ancestral mystics, shamans, healers, teachers, and saints of all faiths reside inside the big room where they continue to spiritually cook and leave ecstatic tracks for others to follow. Here you find the past, present, and future embodiments of First Creation wisdom that serve as prayer-songs, travel tracks, wisdom tracts, sacred emotion refills, transporting rhythm grooves, wake-up calls, dancing steps, recipe steps, climbing steps, and all other varieties of spiritual cooking. You can even discover what was revealed in the Acts of John, one of the Gnostic texts formerly lost but found in modern times. Jesus is described as joined with his disciples in Gethsemane just prior to being arrested. He asked them to form a circle, holding hands, with himself in the middle, announcing: "I would play on the pipes; dance all of you . . . I am a lamp to thee who seest me. Amen! I am a mirror to thee who understandest me. Amen! I am a door to thee who knockest at me. Amen! I am a way for thee a wayfarer. Amen! Now answer to my dancing! See thyself in me who speak; And seeing what I do, keep silence on my mysteries." This sacred song-and-dance call and its spirited performance protocol provide the ultimate means by which you experience your humanity encircled by divinity.

Later, in the late 1800s, a similar ceremony took place. An historical report sent to the United States War Department stated that Indians and white people were seen dancing together at Walkers Lake, Esmeralda County, Nevada. The government report went on to claim that a man had gathered a large number of Indians and taught them a circular dance. He sang while they danced, and while singing, he shook and trembled all over. Before leaving he said that if they were good to one another, healers would be sent who could heal by touch. This dance became known as the "Ghost Dance" (Mooney 1892–93). Once again song and dance hosted the trembling vibration inspired by sacred emotion, mobilizing ecstatic action that heals as it rejoices in the joyful divine mystery that transforms all human misery.

At least sixty thousand years before Jesus and his disciples danced in Gethsemane—not to mention the more contemporary invocation of the Ghost Dance—the same kind of ecstatic praying, singing, dancing, and vibratory exchange was taking place on Kalahari sand. The mysteries associated with setting your soul on fire and becoming spiritually cooked have reappeared repeatedly throughout human history—at furrowed dance grounds, makeshift ceremonial circles, traveling temples, barely held together praise shacks, cobblestone streets, ecstatically charged living rooms, and the redecorated interiors of awakened hearts. From the early Shakers to the Dance of St. John, which spread throughout Europe in the fourteenth century, the Deerskin and Jumping Dances of the California Yurok, and in many other cultures from the whirling Sufis to rocking rabbis, levitating saints, fence-leaping churchgoers, flying witches, blazin' pagans, wand-waving wizards, fire-walking Hindu and Bantu priests, smoke-puffing medicine handlers, spirit drumming and n/om humming shamans, whistling sangomas, and never shy to die and resurrect magi, all have joined hands to welcome and celebrate the musical, dancing, touching flames of this ecstatic mystery way of spiritual cooking. Its luminous and numinous poly-jubilation of multi-vibration remains alive as long as the original fire burns inside First Creation. With the constant circulation of this eternal return, the mystery of everlasting life is forever reborn.

The passage from a choked life inside a small bottle to the fresh breeze found in the big room is best accompanied by a spiritual temperature transition from cold to hot—the original journey from Second Creation to First Creation. The experiential expansion of the horizontal rope and the spiritual heating of the vertical rope must combine to spur a climb to the upper performance room. These various dynamics and operations are held inside the basic three-step recipe of Sacred Ecstatics. Begin with room expansion and when the fire ignites, leap into it rather than remain on the outside periphery. There remarkable transformation happens at all levels and across all lines. After the burn, make sure you return to the world with a soulful song and dance that helps you better participate in the changing of creation.

Rendering the container of your life vaster, hotter, wiser, funnier, and more creatively multi-dimensional are the same—all metaphors for making conditions favorable for the Creator to act upon your life. Up and down the tones of your vocal chord, dancing in and out of heavenly rhythms, riding across the horizon, and sliding along the temperature gradient, you change as each ending precipitates another transformed beginning. On and on it goes in the circulation of the Creator's vacillating, oscillating, and vibrating conductance of creative existence and divine persistence. The four changing directions, the two intersecting ropes, and the three-steps of the recipe are what simultaneously stage, embody, and evoke the performance of a fire born mystic, shamanic song and dance artist, holy fool jewel, and spiritual wisdom tool. In the transient names with their varying functions, electrical junctions, absurd misdirections, far-reaching teaching classrooms, diverse spiritual climates, and altering creative atmospheres are found the whirling paradoxical contraries that create the wheel of sacred fortune. Here your smallness, errors, misses, and omissions are welcomed and used to recast infinite perfection inside the house of the divine. In the dark, you are able to become a newborn spark of light. In the cold, you are made ready to seek and meet the heat. In mirth you birth vaster wisdom. On earth you are found creating heaven.

> *Dear Lord, we submit our utmost plea for your tender sensitivity, life-changing expansivity, and jubilant festivity. We call upon your hallowed name to alter the room of our minds so we can think right. Touch our hearts so we can feel right. Charge our bodies so we can move right. Set fire to our souls so we can fly right. Help us catch up to the wondrous*

truth that all things take place inside your assuring embrace that forever welcomes and eternally loves.

We are weak, meek, shattered, and faltering — all that you have made us to be so that we may be spiritually transformed and reborn with a quivering thorn and singing song within. Reach down and complete us. Heal our brokenness and lift us from the ground of separation. Render us small, soft, and kind enough to practice unconditional forgiving and unlimited living.

We call upon you, dear Lord, to make us a flame whose aim is to melt away fear and despair. Make our light bright enough to pierce the darkness and show the way home. Sweeten our voice so our words make a joyful noise. Lay your creative passion upon our every day and night. We ask these things because we want to joyfully serve rather than judgementally observe. Send heavenly sunshine into our prayers as we climb up the straight and narrow road to enter your green pasture, greet your higher power, and meet your indescribable glory. We ask these things on behalf of all creation as you bless our participation in your never-ending whimsical parable, mystical musical, and ineffable miracle. Thank you, dear Lord of Lords for your Song of Songs and Dance of Dancing Change that bring us nearer to all that is loving, that is infinite, that is you.

Epilogue

This work took nearly a lifetime to produce. It encompasses the career of Bradford Keeney who has made contributions to the science of cybernetics as applied to human relationship systems, the invention of a formal analysis of change-oriented conversation, the creation of several psychotherapies, a several decades long ethnographic study of diverse healing traditions, and the improvisational performance of music and spoken word, all in the service of hosting and advancing the way of ecstatically charged creative transformation. As important, Brad became recognized in various cultures around the world as an elder holder of traditional wisdom. This was especially true for his relations with ecstatic spiritual traditions including that of the Kalahari n/om-kxaosi, Caribbean shakers, Japanese seiki jutsu practitioners, Brazilian folk healers, Guarani shamans, Balinese balians, and sanctified black church parishioners, among others.

Throughout his career Brad was always creating a larger weave, one that enables a wide range of transformative practice and critical thinking to be joined rather than separated: the mystic, shaman, healer, improvisational performer, creative teacher, mystery preacher, and formal scholar experienced as different sides of the same face. While heralded as a pioneer in many disciplines, Brad's most important work is found in how he helped build a vast context that brings them together on a larger performance stage that invites endless possibilities, including embodied cybernetic performance, creative therapeutics, shaking medicine, shamanic scholarship, syncopated mysticism, spiritual cabaret, and life force theatre, among other rich and complex forms. Within this new territory he wed heartfelt transformational experience with a specification of how to construct a room that can host it and prescribe the action needed to evoke it.

Brad was unable to bring all of this work together without Hillary, whose background in social activism, dance, Zen Buddhism, women's studies, qualitative research, and interdisciplinary scholarship brought a similar diversity and expansive range of experience and practice to the table. She readily recognized the heart of Brad's work and the ways in which it danced across disciplinary fields and experiential domains. More importantly, Hillary received arrows, nails, and spears of n/om, was given full seiki transmissions, and administered powerful holy spirit infusions on her way to becoming thoroughly spiritually cooked. Through her frequent visits to the spiritual classrooms she received her sacred songs, mystical gifts, healing instruments, and teaching tools. Her anointments to give seiki, administer n/om, and captain spiritual journeying place her at the heart of ecstatic spirituality. As a dancer, singer, poet, writer, teacher, scholar, conductor, and director of Sacred Ecstatics she leads the future of this newborn old school way of spiritual cooking, always making room for the changing forms and expression of the ineffable.

We chose to author our book as a relational unity, an inseparable team whose contributions to its production are equal. All ideas expressed here arose in our daily conversations, healing sessions with clients, Sacred Ecstatics intensives, group discussions, and spiritual classroom visitations. We bring relationship to all our work, and that includes the creation of this book. Together we created something unique for the world based on our experiences with the best of ancient and contemporary wisdom traditions — the sacred recipe for setting your soul on fire.

In this spiritual heat you may be mystically taken to the

Kalahari, Caribbean, Japan, the Broadway stage, a Mississippi juke joint, an ancient Persian mosque, and other places where the sacred ecstasy of First Creation is experienced. Until now there has not been a set of terms, conceptual tools, and articulation of performance skills that span different ecstatic traditions, what we specifically call the practical know-how of *spiritual engineering* (see Keeneys 2018). Our work traverses the boundaries of multiple lineages and respects their unique contributions while emphasizing their shared performance dramatology rather than debating their varying interpretations. We offer practical heuristics that help bring forth the experience and embodiment of sacred ecstasy. Here is found the singular rope to God whose alternating forms and shifting names create an ever-expanding gateway and highway to the infinite source and force of never-ending, always-changing creation.

REFERENCES

al-'Arabi, Ibn. 1911. *al-Futuhat al-makkiyya,* volume 1. Cairo: Bulaq.

al-'Arabi, Ibn. 1911. *The Tarjuman al-Ashwaq: A Collection of Mystical Odes.* (Trans. Reynold A. Nicholson). London: Royal Asiatic Society.

Bell, Hesketh J. 1889. *Obeah: Witchcraft in the West Indies.* London: Sampson Low, Marston, Searle & Rivington.

Berger, Peter. 2004. *Questions of Faith.* Malden, Mass.: Blackwell Publishing.

Bucke, Richard Maurice. 1969. *Cosmic Consciousness.* New York: E. P. Dutton (originally published by Innes & Sons, 1901).

Castagne, Jean. 1930. "Magie et Exorcisme Chez les Kazak-Kirghizes et Autres Peoples Turcs Orientaux." *Revue des Etudes Islamiques,* 53–151.

Chipp, Herschel, B., ed. 1968. *Art: A Source Book by Artists and Critics.* Berkeley: University of California Press.

Chittick, William C. 1989. *Sufi Path of Knowledge: Ibn al-Arabi's Metaphysics of Imagination.* Albany: State University of New York Press.

Corbin, Henry. 1969. *Creative Imagination in the Sufism of Ibn Arabi.* Princeton, N. J.: Princeton University Press.

Dalai Lama. 2003. *Destructive Emotions: How Can We Overcome Them?* New York: Bantam Dell.

Eliade, Mircea. 1964. *Shamanism: Archaic Techniques of Ecstasy.* Princeton, N.J.: Princeton University Press.

Ernst, Carl W. and Bruce B. Lawrence. 2002. *Sufi Martyrs of Love: The Chishti Order in South Asia and Beyond.* New York: Palgrave MacMillan.

Foster, Nelson and Jack Shoemaker, eds. 1996. *The Roaring Stream: A New Zen Reader.* Hopewell, N.J: The Ecco Press.

Fox, George. 1952. *The Journal of George Fox.* (Ed. John L. Nickalls). New York: Cambridge University Press.

Geyshick, Ron with Judith Doyle. 1989. *Te Bwe Win.* Toronto: Summerhill Pr. Ltd.

Halifax, Joan. 1988. *Shaman: The Wounded Healer.* New York: Thames and Hudson.

Halifax, Joan. 1991. *Shamanic Voices: A Survey of Visionary Narratives.* New York: Penguin Books.

Herbert, Michael, ed. 1998. *D. H. Lawrence Selected Critical Writings.* New York: Oxford University Press.

Hinson, Glenn. 2000. *Fire in My Bones: Transcendence and the Holy Spirit in African American Gospel.* Philadelphia: University of Pennsylvania Press.

Holm, Gustav. 1911. *Ethnological Sketch of the Angmagsalik Eskimo.* Copenhagen: Reitzel.

Hurston, Zora Neale. 1940. "Ritualistic Expression from the Lips of the Communicants of the Seventh Day Church of God, Beaufort, South Carolina." Library of Congress: Collections of the Manuscript Division.

Hurston, Zora Neale. 1981. *The Sanctified Church.* New York: Turtle Island Foundation.

Hurston, Zora Neale. 2010. *Dust Tracks on a Road.* New York: Harper Perennial.

Jochelson, Waldemar I. 1924–26. "The Yukaghir and the Yukaghirized Tungus." In *Jesup North Pacific Expedition IX*, 2 vols. American Museum of Natural History Memoirs, 13, 2–3.

Johnson, Clifton H. 1969. *God Struck Me Dead: Religious Conversion Experiences and Autobiographies of Ex-Slaves.* Philadelphia: Pilgrim Press.

Karjalainen, K. F. 1921–27. *Die Religion der Jugra-Volker.* Hamina, Finland: Folklore Fellows Communications.

Keeney, Bradford. 1995. *Shaking Out the Sprits*. New York: Station Hill Press.

Keeney, Bradford. 1999a. *Gary Holy Bull: Lakota Yuwipi Man*. Philadelphia: Ringing Rocks Foundation and Leete's Island Press.

Keeney, Bradford. 1999b. *Ikuko Osumi, Sensei: Japanese Master of Seiki Jutsu*. Philadelphia: Ringing Rocks Foundation and Leete's Island Press.

Keeney, Bradford. 1999c. *Kalahari Bushman Healers*. Philadelphia: Ringing Rocks Foundation and Leete's Island Press.

Keeney, Bradford. 2000. *Guarani Shamans of the Rainforest*. Philadelphia: Ringing Rocks Foundation and Leete's Island Press.

Keeney, Bradford. 2001. *Vuzumazulu Credo Mutwa: Zulu High Sanusi*. Philadelphia: Ringing Rocks Foundation and Leete's Island Press.

Keeney, Bradford. 2002. *Shakers of St. Vincent*. Philadelphia: Ringing Rocks Foundation and Leete's Island Press.

Keeney, Bradford. 2003a. *Hands of Faith: Healers of Brazil*. Philadelphia: Ringing Rocks Foundation and Leete's Island Press.

Keeney, Bradford. 2003b. *Ropes to God: The Bushman Spiritual Universe*. Philadelphia: Ringing Rocks Foundation and Leete's Island Press.

Keeney, Bradford. 2004. *Balians: Traditional Healers of Bali*. Philadelphia: Ringing Rocks Foundation and Leete's Island Press.

Keeney, Bradford. 2005. *Bushman Shaman: Awakening the Spirit Through Ecstatic Dance*. Rochester, Vt.: Destiny Books.

Keeney, Bradford. 2007. *Shaking Medicine: The Healing Power of Ecstatic Movement*. Rochester, Vt.: Inner Traditions International.

Keeney, Bradford. 2009. *The Creative Therapist: The Art of Awakening a Session*. New York: Routledge.

Keeney, Hillary and Bradford Keeney. 2012. *Circular Therapeutics: Giving Therapy a Healing Heart*. Phoenix: Zeig, Tucker, & Theisen.

Keeney, Bradford and Hillary Keeney. 2014. *Seiki Jutsu: The Practice of Non-Subtle Energy Medicine*. Rochester, Vt.: Healing Arts Press.

Keeney, Hillary and Bradford Keeney. 2013. *Creative Therapeutic Technique: Skills for the Art of Bringing Forth Change*. Phoenix: Zeig, Tucker, & Theisen.

Keeney, Bradford and Hillary Keeney. 2015. *Way of the Bushman: Spiritual Teachings and Practices of the Kalahari Ju/'hoansi*. Rochester, Vt.: Bear & Company.

Keeney, Hillary and Bradford Keeney. 2019a. "Revisiting the Shaman's Ecstasy: The Intense Emotion that Ignites the Performance of Song and Dance." *Journal of Dance, Movement & Spiritualities*: 5.2.

Keeney, Hillary and Bradford Keeney. 2019b. *The Creative Therapist in Practice*. New York: Routledge.

Keeney, Hillary, Bradford Keeney, and Ronald Chenail. 2015. *Recursive Frame Analysis: A Qualitative Research Method for Mapping Change-Oriented Discourse*. Special e-book publication for *The Qualitative Report*.

Keeneys, The. 2017. *Climbing the Rope to God: Mystical Testimony and Teaching*. Createspace.

Keeneys, The. 2018. *The Spiritual Engineering of Sacred Ecstasy*. Createspace.

Kerr, Hugh T. and John M. Mulder, eds. 1994. *Famous Conversions*. Grand Rapids, Mich.: Wm. B. Eerdmans Publishing.

Kottler, Jeffrey and John Carlson. 2004. *American Shaman: Odyssey of Global Healing Traditions.* New York: Brunner-Routledge.

Krishna, Gopi. 1971. *Kundalini, the Evolutionary Energy in Man.* Boulder: Shambhala.

Krishna, Gopi. 1993. *Living with Kundalini.* Boulder: Shambhala.

Lame Deer, John Fire and Richard Erdoes. 1972. *Lame Deer, Seeker of Visions.* New York: Simon & Schuster.

Lewisohn, Leonard, ed. 2014. *The Philosophy of Ecstasy: Rumi and the Sufi Tradition.* Bloomington, Ind.: World Wisdom, Inc.

Mails, Thomas. 1991. *Fools Crow: Wisdom and Power.* San Francisco: Council Oak Books.

Mails, Thomas and Dallas Chief Eagle. 1979. *Fools Crow.* Lincoln, Neb.: University of Nebraska Press.

Mavor, James W., Jr., and Byron E. Dix. 1987. *Manitou: The Sacred Landscape of New England's Native Civilization.* Rochester, Vt.: Inner Traditions International.

McDaniel, June. 1989. *The Madness of Saints: Ecstatic Religion in Bengal.* Chicago: University of Chicago Press.

McDaniel, June. 2018. *Lost Ecstasy: Its Decline and Transformation in Religion.* Chalm, Switzerland: Palgrave Macmillan.

Merton, Thomas. 1957. *Zen and the Bids of Appetite.* New York: New Directions.

Mooney, James. 1892–93. "The Ghost Dance Religion." In *Fourteenth Annual Report of the Bureau of Ethnology to the Smithsonian Institution.* Washington, D.C.: Government Printing Office.

Neihardt, John G. 2008. *Black Elk Speaks.* Albany: First Excelsior Editions.

Pagani, Samuela. 2019. "The Spiritual Mother of Ibn 'Arabi: Fatima of Seville." *L'Osservatore Romano,* June 1, 2018. http://www.osservatoreromano.va/en/news/spiritual-mother-ibn-arabi.

Rasbihari Lal & Sons. 2005. *Sri Gaudiya Kanthahara: A Necklace of Vaisnava Verse.* Loi Bazar, Vrindaban, Mathura, Uttar Pradesh: India.

Rasmussen, 1921. *Myter og Sagn fra Grønland.* Østgrønlændere, I. Glydenalske, Bogforlag: Kobenhavn.

Saint John of the Cross. 2007. *The Living Flame of Love.* (Trans. David Lewis). New York: Cosimo.

Sieroszewski, Wenceslas. 1896. *Yakuty.* St. Petersburg: Tipografia Glavnogo Upravleniia Udelov.

Sobel, Mechal. 1988. *Trabelin' On.* Princeton, N. J.: Princeton University Press.

Stone, Barton. 1847. *The Biography of Elder Warren Barton Stone Written by Himself with Additions and Reflections.* Cincinnati: J. A. and U. P. James.

Stuernagel, A. E. 1928. "Being Filled with the Spirit: The Melodies of Heaven Overflow in the Soul." *The Latter Rain Evangel* 20, no. 10:8.

Swedenborg, Emanuel. 1743–1744. *Swedenborg's Journal of Dreams.* (Ed. William Ross Woofenden). New York: Swendenborg Foundation, 1977.

Teresa of Avila. 2006. *The Life of Teresa of Avila.* (Trans. David Lewis). New York: Cosimo.

Thurber, James. 1966. *James Thurber: Writings and Drawings.* New York: Literary Classics of the United States.

Tolstoy, Leo. 1899. *My Confession: My Religion: The Gospel in Brief.* New York: Thomas A. Crowell Co.

Tyler, Peter. 2010. *St. John of the Cross*. London: Bloomsbury Academic.

Underhill, Evelyn. 1961. *Mysticism*. New York, E. P. Dutton & Co.

van Biema, David. 23 August 2007. "Mother Teresa's Crisis of Faith," *Time Magazine*. Accessed February 14, 2016. http://time.com/4126238/mother-teresas-crisis-of-faith/.

Weber, Max. 1963. *The Sociology of Religion*. (Trans. Ephraim Fischoff). Boston: Beacon Press.

Weber, Max. 2015. "Politics as Vocation" pp. 129–198, and "Discipline and Charisma" pp. 59–72 in *Weber's Rationalism and Modern Society*. (Trans. and eds. Tony Waters and Dagmar Waters). Basingstoke, U.K.: Palgrave Macmillan.

Work, John Wesley, Sr. 1915. *Folk Song of the American Negro*. Nashville, Tenn.: Fisk University Press.

Yamada, Koun. 2004. *The Gateless Gate: The Classic Book of Zen Koans*. Somerville, Mass.: Wisdom Publications.

Yogananda, Paramahansa. 1938. *Cosmic Chants*. Accessed December 5, 2018. http://www.yogananda-srf.org/Cosmic_Chants.aspx#.XAf1bhNKg8Y.

Yogananda, Paramahansa. 2015. *Autobiography of a Yogi*. CreateSpace Independent Publishing.

Printed in Great Britain
by Amazon